Volume 95 Number 2 June 2023

Critical AI: A Field in Formation

Edited by Rita Raley and Jennifer Rhee

Essays

Reviews

American Literature

Rita
Raley
and
Jennifer
Rhee

Critical AI:
A Field in Formation

At first glance the most striking aspect of Anna Ridler's 2018 installation *Myriad (Tulips)* is the highly ordered array of tulips themselves—thousands of photographs taken over the course of three months in the Netherlands, their meticulous gridded arrangement presenting as geometric abstraction at a distance (fig. 1).[1] Up close the colors, shapes, and textures of the individual flowers become apparent, this subjective perceptual frame underscored by the handwritten labels—not didactics with botanical metadata but, rather, a registering of attributes as processed by the human eye: *dead, blooming, some stripes, no stripes.* The digital photographs themselves comprise a training data set for Ridler's subsequent artwork, *Mosaic Virus*, which uses a generative adversarial network (GAN) for an iterative production of "fake" tulips that reflect on speculative forms of value.[2] The technical and conceptual complexity of *Mosaic Virus* might seem to overshadow the photographic installation, but of course that data set is its necessary precondition, and, taken together, the two works make visible the end-to-end apparatus of artificial intelligence (AI), from the human labor of image classification, data curation, and machine learning (ML) model architecture design to the material infrastructural support of GPUs (graphics processing units) and the management and manipulation of generated output.

The rationale for drawing on Ridler's mediated tulips as a frame for this special issue of *American Literature* on the emerging field of critical AI is perhaps intuitive—this is, after all, an aesthetic engagement with ML that delights and instructs, translating machinic instrumentalization (still the bête noire of the humanities) into the lexicon of cultural critique, situating AI within intertwined genealogies of capitalism

American Literature, Volume 95, Number 2, June 2023
DOI 10.1215/00029831-10575021   © 2023 by Duke University Press

Figure 1   Anna Ridler, Installation of *Myriad (Tulips)* at Error: The Art of Imperfection, Ars Electronica Export, Berlin, Germany, 2018

and scientific research, drawing on established representational techniques, and foregrounding the optics of the human observer while posing questions about the position of the human in relation to technical systems that seem ever more vast and complicated—their scale appositely captured in the etymology of *myriad*, the numerable slipping into the innumerable. For our purposes, Ridler's work, as one example of an art practice that self-reflexively uses the tools and techniques of ML, also perfectly encapsulates, indexes, and indeed embodies a critical perspective on AI, one that both informs and is shaped by academic research on the same.[3] In its invocation of the Dutch tulip trade and the history of capital, Ridler's work offers a way of seeing that runs counter to the still pervasive presentism of the discourse on AI, and it cunningly allows for the now customary affects of awe and wonder while also demystifying some of the procedures of image generation. And in her elevation of the training data set to the status of a named individual artwork, Ridler gestures toward a prying open of the proverbial black box, emphasizing her direct, even authorial connection to the data, which she has collected and labeled herself—this in contrast to the ImageNet database,[4] both in its development with the assistance of anonymous Mechanical Turkers and its attendant well-documented, normative, and epistemological assumptions (Ridler 2018; Crawford and Paglen 2018). To the extent that it can be said that ImageNet, and the corollary shifting of institutional resources to the development of massive labeled training data sets, is in part what makes possible the accelerative developments in ML research over the past decade, it can also be said that a data set collected, curated, and labeled by an individual researcher offers a necessary and meaningful parallax view of the processes of image recognition and generation.

Ridler's clear documentation of the means by which her myriad tulips were produced, coupled with the exhibition of her work in the gallery show *AI: More than Human* (Barbican Centre, 2019) and reviews that describe her use of a GAN as "using AI" to produce tulips, together help illustrate the discursive differences between *artificial intelligence* and *machine learning*. AI, of course, is what commands attention—hence the ubiquitous meme with statistics framed first as ML (crickets) and then hyped as AI (huge audience). It thus functions as shorthand in headlines, marketing copy, and popular representations and in this sense "falsely implies something singular and unprecedented," as Lucy Suchman (2021) has argued, suggesting a structure of feeling as well as a set of cultural techniques that are often not specified, much less described.[5] The emergence of the tremendously powerful Neuromancer at the end of William Gibson's (1984) eponymous novel did some work to condition our cultural imaginary of AI as singular and paradoxically unimaginable, the newly fused fictional entity presented as so big and so comprehensive ("the sum total of the works, the whole show" [269]) that it exceeds the capacity of its creator, and of the novel itself, to imagine and represent it.[6] To grasp the different significations, domains, and functions of the terms *AI* and *ML*, consider a vision of AI that can only take illusory and elusive figurative form on the horizon (or that manifests as disembodied, acousmatic voice)[7] in contrast to a televisual engagement that eschews spectral and spectacular figures and focuses instead on a screen display of an actual image recognition algorithm (as does the first episode of the Korean drama *Start-Up*; see fig. 2). Such a dramatic scene, in a romance that romanticizes the practical applications rather than mystical and mystified qualities of autonomous machines, might be said to mark a moment in which AI has achieved technological authority in social consciousness and now demands an accurate presentation.

It follows, then, that more academic works written under the sign of ML and tending toward explicit and detailed technical engagement and explanation have begun to emerge. Adrian Mackenzie's (2017) *Machine Learners: Archaeology of a Data Practice* is a relatively early illustrative example, offering (as its title suggests) a reading of ML

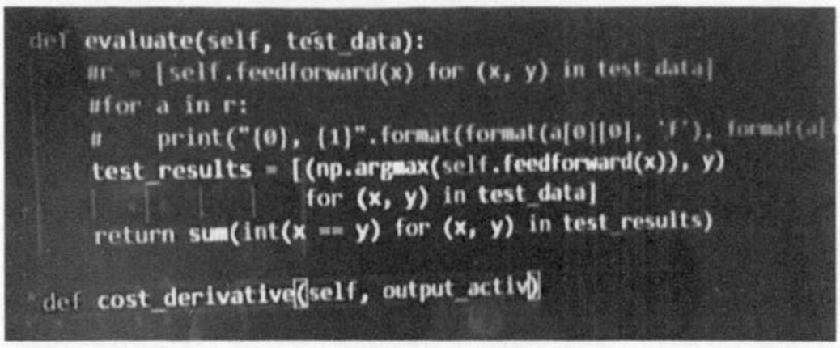

Figure 2 Screen capture,
*Start-Up/*스타트업 (tvN, dir.
Oh Choong Hwan), October 17,
2020

programming languages, algorithms, platforms, and data sets alongside and at times through the lens of poststructuralist theory. That *AI*
and *ML* should have different rhetorical associations, and even different scholarly communities, but also attend upon and mutually inform
each other is evident in both the title and the contents of Jonathan
Roberge and Michael Castelle's (2021) edited collection, *The Cultural
Life of Machine Learning: An Incursion into Critical AI Studies*. If for
Mackenzie (2017: 22) a central research question is how machine
learners "combine knowledge with data" and for Roberge and Castelle
(2021: 5) the critical focus is the ML model, "a relatively inert, sequential, and/or recurrent structure of matrices and vectors" entangled
with the social, for critical AI studies as it exists now—as a field in formation, with a wide range of conversations well underway and many
interventions still to come[8]—the problematic is how to think from
within the actual techniques, tools, and technologies of ML and how
to leverage that practical knowledge in the development of new critical frameworks and methods (Hua and Raley, forthcoming), as well
as countermythologies and epistemologies that might help enact a different way of living with AI. *Criticality*, in this instance, means working across disciplines, domains, and fields of specialization—working
not necessarily or strictly within an academic context but rather situated in proximity to the thing itself, cultivating some degree of partici-
patory and embodied expertise, whether archival, ethnographic, or
applied.

Critical AI, while recognizing the reductive, even absurd aspects
of the term *AI* and the magical thinking it perpetuates, nonetheless
allows for a kind of linguistic pragmatism, treating the term metonymi-
cally and engaging AI as an assemblage of technological arrangements
and sociotechnical practices, as concept, ideology, and *dispositif*.[9] This
may seem to open up fairly quickly into the domain of critical thinking about computational culture and technology writ large,[10] but there
is a specificity and analytic precision in the focus on data, algorithms,
model architectures, and the production of prediction.[11] Critical AI,
then, is itself a historical and epistemic formation.[12] Just as there are

well-documented waves or phases of research in AI and ML (Cantwell Smith 2019)—undergirded most notably by the exponential growth of data science, the availability of greater compute resources, and the development of novel architectures—so too does critical AI work both reflect and remain attuned to actually existing sociotechnical systems.[13] It follows that there would be a focus on particular corporations and devices (Crawford and Joler 2018; Natale 2021), as well as infrastructure, extractive industries, environmental costs, and labor exploitation (Hu 2015; Gray and Suri 2019; Crawford 2021). Such work aligns with research on automation, instrumentalism, technorationality, and computational imaginaries (Stiegler 2016; Bratton 2021), as well as institutions and legal and regulatory processes (Pasquale 2021; Stark, Greene, and Hoffmann 2021).[14]

Correlationism, and its extension from data science to conspiracy theory and other domains (Halpern et al. 2022), is a central thematic for the field, and some of the sharpest interventions have focused on pattern recognition and anomaly detection (Amoore 2020), correlation's historical connections with eugenics (Chun 2021), the dynamics of decisionism (Parisi 2017), persuasion architectures, and the more general conditioning of thought and behavior (Steyerl 2018).[15] Bad thinking may be one way to colloquially describe and perhaps dismiss the new correlationism, but scholars informed in part by work on nonhuman cognition (Hayles 2017) have offered more rigorous theorizations of the new modes of artificial or machine thinking as desubjectified, senseless, and something like pure exteriority (Pasquinelli 2015; Fazi 2019; Parisi 2019). Loosely cognate work with more of a practical emphasis on the deleterious effects of ML decisions considers forms of "artificial unintelligence" (Broussard 2018), the context for which are the high-profile errors, adversarial attacks, and discriminatory outcomes that help shape a sociotechnical consensus, such as a Tesla mistaking the side of a truck for the sky, an image recognition system misclassifying a turtle as a rifle, a hiring platform weeding out resumes from women, or a facial recognition system incorrectly labeling a Black teenager as a criminal (Kantayya 2020). Discrimination, then, is another central thematic for critical AI that includes work on algorithmic bias (O'Neil 2016; Buolamwini and Gebru 2018; Eubanks 2017; Noble 2018; Benjamin 2019), the racialized and gendered logics of AI (Atanasoski and Vora 2019; Amaro 2022), and its structuring worldviews and epistemologies (Katz 2020). More familiar perhaps for literary scholars are philosophical explorations of cybernetics and machinic life (Hayles 1999; Johnston 2008)—scholarship that takes care to understand what we can now recognize as part of the genealogy of ML and to highlight enmeshments of technical processes with literary works and cultural and critical theories.

There is perhaps no better domain for considering such enmeshments than natural language processing (NLP), which as a consequence of the development of the Transformer architecture (Vaswani et al. 2017), the development of large training corpora, and the use of pretrained language models, has now had its watershed ImageNet moment. In the wake of OpenAI's dramatic partial release of GPT-2, its 1.5-billion-parameter language model, in February 2019, NLP has evolved especially quickly, all the more so after the subsequent introduction in May 2020 of GPT-3, with its 175 billion parameters (Radford et al. 2019; Brown et al. 2020).[16] The result has been widespread acknowledgment of the radical transformations in our reading and writing practices, registered in a surplus of media reports and a growing body of humanistic scholarship and creative practice (Branwen 2020).[17] With ever more applications and interfaces for GPT-3, and the concomitant development and deployment of other large language models (e.g., Google's BERT, LaMDA, and PaLM; DeepMind's RETRO; Meta's Open Pretrained Transformer; BigScience's BLOOM), more pressure is exerted on both attributional norms and heuristics for articulating the attributes of "human-generated" and "machine-generated" language.[18] To use OpenAI's API (application programming interface) to experiment with GPT-3 is to produce text for which there is no proper subject, or for which there can only be a retroactive subject effect produced via an appended claim of authorship that enables the delineation of a difference between deliberative, reflective, expressive writing on the one hand and the real-time, automatic manipulation of symbols on the other. The real lesson of a Turing test in this context is not that language models and conversational AI systems are good enough to deceive but, rather, that actants, training data, input, and output are all now so entangled that the determination of linguistic property and, by extension, responsibility is essentially foreclosed. If style is algorithmic and thus imitable, and if all of our communication environments are managed by NLP systems, a pressing research question for critical AI must necessarily be what can be done about attribution, particularly in the context of hate speech (Amoore 2020). To make this more concrete we might ask, How do we read and write alongside and against a GPT-4chan model trained on 4chan's incendiary /pol/ board, the most active platform for the expression and mobilization of far-right extremism?

Stephanie Dinkins's artwork *Not the Only One* (*N'TOO*), a conversational AI given sculptural form, offers an alternative and, indeed, more affirmative vision of both the development and implementations of language models. Trained on not a multigigabtye corpus scraped from the internet but, rather, a small data set comprising oral histories provided by Dinkins, her aunt, and her niece, *N'TOO* upends what might seem a public-private schema in its implicit highlighting of the enclosure of our language commons in proprietary corpora like OpenAI's WebText.[19] Like Ridler's *Myriad (Tulips)*, *N'TOO* also models data sovereignty, the operative principle of which is that the collection, control, use, and preservation of data should be legible to, and even in the hands of, the communities that are its subjects (Dinkins 2020). As both projects illustrate, artists working directly or even indirectly with ML systems are particularly well positioned to stress test, evaluate, and exploit them, to probe and reveal their limitations so as to communicate these to the public and even advocate for better—which is to say, fair, transparent, and accountable—data sets, models, and applications.[20]

Critical AI then entails multiple literacies: technical literacy to understand the nuts and bolts of function calls, Jupyter notebooks, and GitHub repositories; sociocultural literacy to analyze the relations between AI and new forms of capital and the new global technomanagerial class; and historical literacy to apprehend the precursors and preconditions of ML, particularly the history of neural networks and the intertwined histories of AI, cybernetics, probability, computer science, computer graphics, computer vision, cognitive science, modeling, and gaming. Just as with prior critical engagements with biotechnology (da Costa and Philip 2008) and nanotechnology (Milburn 2015), critical AI endeavors to understand its objects through hands-on, practical engagement, whether in a lab, in an archive, or in a classroom.[21] It follows that critical AI would also draw on ethnographic methods, as well as explanatory and translational practices, that render ML processes comprehensible to a broader audience, whether through visual illustration (Crawford and Joler 2018; Vasconcelos 2020) or from more accessible styles and practices of communication (Ọnụọha and Nucera 2018; Lee and Chen 2021).[22]

The density of information in our introduction (perhaps bordering on excess, albeit in the structured form of partial lists) is, we acknowledge, not without correlationist overtones. Our hope, however, is that critical AI serves as a kind of macrotheory that orders all this data and makes it coherent and legible for specialists and nonspecialists alike.

Perhaps, too, it will allow for the identification of new associative vectors, as well as further representations and epistemological models. The field—which is again marked by its yoking of explanation and critique, by its immanent thinking, and by its tendency toward enactive, performative, or otherwise practical forms of engagement—has settled to a certain extent on a set of ethicopolitical investments even as its tethering to the instrumentalities of ML means that its concepts and paradigms must remain unsettled so as to be responsive and responsible. There is, then, much work still to be done, and we close with an identification of five interrelated clusters or lines of inquiry for humanistic scholars and practitioners that bridge old and new and that exploit our legacy disciplines so as to advance critical thinking about our contemporary sociotechnical milieu—a not insignificant effect of which might be the further validation of qualitative research.[23]

1. History and historiography: Critical AI is in part motivated and governed by the idea that AI cannot simply be thought in terms of the present and an irrationally exuberant future, in other words, that it has a long history that has to be taken into account and understood.

2. The human, in terms of both philosophical category and speciation: The almost overwhelming proliferation of recommendation systems alone makes further investigations of the dynamics of subjectification and desubjectivation and governmentality especially urgent; equally pressing are cognate questions of inclusion and exclusion, alienation, and cognition.

3. Epistemology: Kate Crawford's (2021: 221) incisive framing of AI as systematizing the world according to a "Linnaean order of machine-readable tables" crystallizes the thematic and opens up into questions of knowledge production, classification schema, calculative reasoning, and decision making.

4. Rhetoric and aesthetics: Much as critical AI might resist the idea that a cultural object should be the exclusive or even privileged site for analytical engagement, these objects nonetheless help shape the doxa and, as such, necessitate interpretative work, particularly when they themselves use the tools and techniques of ML to reflect on the same.

5. Interpretability and explainability: There is a now iconic moment in the documentary account of the historic match between AlphaGo and Lee Sedol (Kohs 2017) when the Google DeepMind team reacts with surprise and perplexity at one of the program's moves—why did it make this decision, what was it thinking, we

cannot exactly say. This moment of performative wonder neatly instantiates the mythology of ML as an uninterpretable, inaccessible black box, just as a ML system's inexplicable decision to terminate an acclaimed schoolteacher perfectly illustrates the urgency behind the push for explainable AI (XAI) and for the development of systems whose behavior can be parsed and corrected (Kantayya 2020). What more suitable research problem for literary scholars than AI and interpretability (Cramer 2018; Fazi 2021), and what better way to conclude our introduction than with a call for readers to contribute to the project of aligning interpretation in an ML context with hermeneutics as it has been historically understood, and to aid critical AI in its determination to intervene in a technical regime in which meaning is eclipsed by calculation?

Rita Raley is Professor of English at the University of California, Santa Barbara. She has taught at the University of Minnesota, Rice University, and NYU, and her most recent work appears in *Digital Humanities Quarterly, symplokē, Amodern, PUBLIC, ASAP/Journal,* and *The Routledge Companion to Media and Risk.*

Jennifer Rhee is Associate Professor of English at Virginia Commonwealth University. She is the author of *The Robotic Imaginary: The Human and the Price of Dehumanized Labor* (2018) and co-editor of *The Palgrave Handbook of Twentieth- and Twenty-First Century Literature and Science* (2020).

Appendix

As part of our effort to sketch a broad overview of the state of the field of critical AI for this special issue, we solicited brief reflective statements from researchers whose work has been central to our thinking about the contemporary sociotechnical milieu. Our aim throughout is to showcase a range of voices and perspectives across the humanities and to provide readers of *American Literature* with something like a navigational guide to the field for their own research and teaching.

Caroline Bassett, University of Cambridge

Questioning the pervasive claim that AI can deliver (more) control and (more) freedom—over knowledge production, over everyday life, over culture and society—and can do so universally and without prejudice is urgent for humanities research. This requires engaging directly with bias through explorations of ML algorithms. It demands investigating recurring myths about technology as intrinsically liberating. It means refinding lost histories of critique and refusal and

rethinking histories of progress so that the contraction of future possibilities into an endless present in which abundance and automated
equality are promised as an automatic benefit "sometime soon" can be
contested.

Beginning here might imply that the transformative potential of AI
can be reduced to a matter of political economy, a cultural fix rather
than the technological solution the tech industry promotes. That's not
what's intended. I rather want to insist on the degree to which the
stakes of AI are political, that this constitutes a horizon through which
the radically new forms of computational capability that AI ushers
in, the new forms of agential activity it introduces into the world, and
the transformations in knowledge it engenders can be made sense
of—even in posthumanity. I'd include here questions concerning
autonomy (which don't reduce to automation), explorations of machine-
specific forms of agency (which don't reduce to—or expand to—
human agency), and questions concerning the relationship of simulation and creation (which don't reduce to one versus the other).

David M. Berry, University of Sussex

For a critical AI, we must first critique magical thinking about computation, the idea captured by *omne ignotum pro magnifico est* (everything unknown seems wonderful); to critique the notion of AIs as independent participants in human social relations that have a "life force"
or "alien" nature that determines human social life. This assumption
demonstrates a lack of understanding of computation's history and
political economy. In actuality, AI is subsumed to the needs of capitalism. Most notably, computation develops the technical ability to separate control from execution. Indeed, computation tends to create processes that align with capitalism, such as an a priori assumption of the
superiority of markets for structuring social relations. Second, current approaches to understanding AI have a tendency to encourage
metaphysical or formalist approaches. This is partly due to AI's presumed inherent complexities but also due to the immaturity of methods for humanistic or social scientific study of AI or ML. This can
lead to a valorization of the mathematization of thought, whereby for-
malization of knowledge is seen as not just one approach to thinking
about AI but the exemplary one. This can lead to idealism rather
than a focus on who owns and controls the means of cognition. Third,
critical AI needs to situate AI as a historical formation, drawing on but
also radicalizing approaches such as interpretability and explainability, in order to transform the prevalent right computationalism into

a progressive left computationalism that seeks not just to interpret AI but to change it.

M. Beatrice Fazi, University of Sussex

Artificial intelligence (AI) is often described as a field investigating whether machines can think. The existence of these thinking machines is generally (yet not universally) understood as predicated on the possibility of simulating the cognitive behavior of biological entities. In my view, the investigation of thinking processes remains one of most urgent research questions concerning AI. However, the popular understanding of machine thought as an imitation of human or animal cognition should be surpassed. We should study whether computational processes might be modes of thought by virtue of what computing machines are and do (for example, as a result of their axiomatic, logico-mathematical character) and not what they should be or do were they to replicate or enhance biological brains. Questions about thinking vis-à-vis AI should then focus less on determining who or what thinks and more on what thought is or could be. This investigation should address the forms of thinking specific to artificial cognitive agents. Ideas and representations of what thinking is, then, are not to be used to explain computational processes; these ideas and representations of thought need themselves be explained. Developments in AI invite us to consider modes of thought for which we might yet lack the concepts to define and assess. Studying the computational automation of thought is undoubtedly a challenge but also a rewarding speculative endeavor for critical AI studies, with concrete implications for how machine agency can be theorized.

Orit Halpern, Technische Universität Dresden

In 1945 the economist Friedrich Hayek began his battle on behalf of neoliberalism with a call to rethink knowledge. In an essay that looms large over the history of contemporary conservative and libertarian economic thought and encapsulates a range of questions and problems that AI provokes, Hayek (1945: 519–20) inaugurated a new concept of the market: "The peculiar character of the problem of a rational economic order is determined precisely by the fact that the knowledge of the circumstances of which we must make use never exists in concentrated or integrated form, but solely as the dispersed bits of incomplete and frequently contradictory knowledge which all the separate individuals possess." When situated within Hayek's engagements with the sciences and technologies of the time, this statement gestures to a grand aspiration: a fervent dream for a new world governed by data. At the heart of Hayek's conception of a market was the idea that no single subject, mind, or central authority has complete knowledge of the world. This critique of liberal reason was one of the bedrocks for both the finance capital and algorithmic trading of our present and the layered neural network model now heavily in use. It also makes us recognize that AI is not a technology—it is an epistemology and also a form of governmentality and political economy. While many of us would not affiliate with Hayek, many of us would agree to the networked nature of intelligence, the critique of enlightenment reason and objectivity, and fantasize about collective forms of engagement and decision making. AI and its histories thus provide a very contested and difficult space that mandates new thinking about how to work within, around, and through technology and contemporary technical epistemologies.

Colin Milburn, University of California, Davis

Our pedagogical norms are not yet prepared for a world in which AIs can be prompted to write original scholarly compositions with relative ease. Our students are already experimenting with AIs for humanistic analysis and critical writing, and it is getting much harder to tell the difference between average undergraduate-level writing and average AI-generated writing. It is only going to become more complicated as technical sophistication continues to grow. The solution cannot simply be to forbid students from using AIs—after all, they will be citizens of a world in which AIs are everywhere, used for everything. Instead, we can teach students to use AIs more responsibly. We can help them understand how AIs generate knowledge claims, how their language models work, how they map data relationships and forge inferential connections. Students need to know how to take a critical perspective on whatever assertions or predictions an AI may spit out. Understanding the limitations and affordances of particular ML models or data sets may help students identify and explain biases, prejudices, and spurious results.

But we need to go beyond critique. Instead, can we teach students to use critical methods to collaborate with AIs to make better, more robust knowledge? If students know enough to use AIs well, then there could be a blossoming of insights. It would mean reconfiguring our pedagogy around the human-computer partnership. The humanities are well poised to make this shift, even if it would mean changing some of our basic practices and engaging more extensively with other fields. We need to use the best tools we have from various disciplines to be responsible participants in our high-tech future. Academic disciplines must adopt new hermeneutic methods and critical textual practices to grapple with the epistemic surprises produced by such entities. Perhaps we can yet strive for a more mutualistic relation with our analytical engines—learning and creating together, iteratively, ethically.

Luciana Parisi, Duke University

If AI haunts the future of the humanities with the image of mindless machines, it is because AI menaces the autonomy of the humanities by presenting the efficiency of a thought without a subject, a thinking without philosophy. As much as the modern pillars of the humanities reside in the philosophical methods of transcendental reason and imagination and the post-Kantian critical theories originating with the crisis of Man and entropic collapse, AI remains a surface of projection of the Promethean promise for the autonomy, self-making, and self-determination of philosophy. The mathematical, historical, literary, and cultural representations repress alien intelligence by reimparting the sociogenic order that sees machines through the eyes of the master. The politicoethical stakes for humanities research on AI today must confront this Promethean promise whereby AI remains the carrier of a recursive epistemology that each time reactivates the modern structure of self-posed (autodecisional) thinking. With the modern philosophical realization of being, sense, and ends through technology, the humanities have become one with technogenesis, with the generation of the global order—the world of racial capitalism, of reproductive capital, of antiblackness, antifeminine, antiqueer: the antialienness of philosophical capitalism. By dividing reason from intelligence while reimparting the bioeconomical order that sexualizes, genders, and racializes machines, AI is contained in the realization of the autonomy of philosophy, of autopoiesis as the reduction of difference (qua alienness) to the autonomy of the humanities—the homo- and heteronormative subject of reason. What AI can do for the humanities is instead to open the line of inquiry into computation, into how ML can invite in a senseless processing of information. With the ingression of incomputables into logos, AI can expose the allopoetic (other than oneself) and allotropic (other than here) thinking, the otherwise livings, realities, and imaginations that belong to the improper worlds of the inhumanities.

Notes

1   The genesis of this special issue was an MLA roundtable organized by Wendy Hui Kyong Chun and Priscilla Wald titled "Literary Intelligence, Artificial Learning: Language, Media, and Machines" (January 2021), and we are grateful to the organizers, as well as fellow panelists Evan Donohue, Théo Lepage-Richer, and Colin Milburn, for their inspiring contributions to the discussion. This special issue, which takes account of the sociotechnical situation prior to August 2022, did however evolve independently from the roundtable and organizers.

2   GANs comprise two networks that collaborate to produce synthetic images that can pass as real: a generator that produces images based on a training data set and a discriminator that classifies the output as either real (from the training data) or fake (produced by the generator) (Goodfellow 2014).

3   Along with Ridler and other artists discussed in this introduction, we find especially suggestive recent works by Katherine Behar (2018), Zach Blas (2019), and Elisa Giardina Papa (2020). For an overview of various practices and investments of AI art, see Zylinska 2020, as well as Tung-Hui Hu's review in this issue.

4   As is widely recognized, the ImageNet visual database has been fundamental to the development of machine vision and signals a turn in ML research toward big data and model training. See https://image-net.org/index.php.

5   See also Pasquinelli 2019a on the mythologizing term *AI* as a "spectacularization of machine learning and the business of data analytics" and Crawford 2021: 19 on AI as "a two-word phrase onto which is mapped a complex set of expectations, ideologies, desires, and fears."

6   There has been no shortage of attempts to do this representational work, of course, and indeed, future archaeologists will be able to compile an archive with a wildly varied anthropocentric, zoological, and machinic menagerie, ranging in scale from the subatomic sophons in Liu Cixin's Three-Body Problem trilogy to the expansive planetary intelligence in Sue Burke's *Semiosis*. For a historical overview of AI representations in literature, see Cave, Dihal, and Dillon 2020; for examinations of contemporary AI representations, see Sherryl Vint's expansive review essay in this issue.

7   The reference here is to Scarlett Johansson giving voice to Samantha the AI assistant in *Her* (2013; dir. Spike Jonze).

8   Because the Zoom era roughly corresponds with extraordinary developments with Transformer ML models using the technique of attention—not just the GPT (Generative Pretrained Transformer) series but also OpenAI's subsequent models, DALL-E and DALL-E 2, which generate images based on natural language descriptions—critical AI has in the past few years had both the practical means and the enthusiasm to flourish as a global community supported by new research centers and seminars, among them the AI Now Institute at New York University, the

Digital Democracies Institute at Simon Fraser University, the Lever-
hulme Centre for the Future of Intelligence and the Mellon Sawyer
Seminar "Histories of AI: A Genealogy of Power" at the University of
Cambridge, a research group on critical AI studies at the Karlsruhe University of Arts and Design in Germany, a faculty working group on Critical Machine Learning Studies supported by the University of California
Humanities Research Institute, and the Critical AI initiative at Rutgers
University. A number of humanities organizations have also hosted
recent conferences on AI, including the Consortium for Humanities
Centers and Institutes, the National Humanities Center, and the Society
of Literature, Science, and the Arts. The momentum is also reflected in
a variety of modes and institutional forms of engagement—among
them special issues and essay clusters in *Critical Inquiry*; *Daedalus*;
Digital Culture & Society; *e-flux*; *Public Books*; *Theory, Culture & Society*;
and *Media, Culture & Society*, journals such as *AI & Society and the forthcoming Critical AI*, as well as art exhibitions too numerous to list here.

9   For an overview of left critiques of AI, see Aradau and Bunz 2022.

10   In this special issue, Ranjodh Singh Dhaliwal's review essay helps situate
critical AI in relation to a broader social and political critique of technology, and Luke Stark's review essay situates it in relation to ethics and ethical inquiry.

11   See, for example, the introduction to the recent special issue of *Critical Inquiry* on "surplus data" (Halpern et al. 2022); Matteo Pasquinelli's
(2019b) deep history of the Perceptron (a linear classifier); and Mackenzie's (2015) analysis of the production of prediction. See also Fabian
Offert's analysis of two pivotal technical papers on ML and Tyler Shoemaker's review of the Roberge and Castelle volume, both in this special issue.

12   A more precise articulation of epistemic rupture would necessarily have to
account for the rise of data science in the early twenty-first century and
could not exclude the groundbreaking computer science papers on the
properties of neural networks and the mechanism of attention (see Offert's
contribution to this special issue), but in the popular imaginary it could be
said that on or about 2016, the year AlphaGo defeated Go master Lee Sedol
and Google transitioned to a neural machine translation system, machine
behavior changed and human-machine relations shifted as a result.

13   This reflective, embedded quality holds for first-wave research as well;
for example, to support her feminist critique of AI, Alison Adam (1998)
drew on her work as a software developer in the mid-1980s for a research
project concerning Social Security law in the United Kingdom.

14   Following a path set by media studies and science and technology studies, critical AI attends to entanglements of technological processes and
cultural and sociopolitical domains and has accordingly developed media
theories of ML (Berry 2017; Apprich 2018; Sudmann 2018).

15   Seb Franklin's review essay in this issue offers a reading of Chun's *Data
Discrimination* and Louise Amoore's *Cloud Ethics* through the lens of dispossession.

16 If not through the news, literary scholars might have been introduced to GPT-2 through an MLA panel featuring Microsoft researchers (January 2020) and Wai Chee Dimock's (2020) subsequent report on the same for *PMLA*, and they might also have encountered the general practice of creative machine writing or text generation through projects supported by such entities as Anteism Books (e.g., David Jhave Johnston's *ReRites*, 2018), Counterpath Press (e.g., Li Zilles's *Machine, Unlearning*, 2018), the Electronic Literature Organization (e.g., Lillian-Yvonne Bertram's *Travesty Generator*, 2018), Google Arts and Culture (e.g., Ross Goodwin's *1 the Road*, 2018), and Aleator Press (e.g., Allison Parrish's *Wendit Tnce Inf*, 2022).

17 The exuberance around NLP can be tempered by salient critiques of the environmental impacts of large language models, particularly because of the requisite training time (see Brown et al. 2020), the downstream effects of foundation models (Bommasani et al. 2021), and considered attempts to draw attention to encoded bias (Bender et al. 2021). For a discussion of such critiques, see Goodlad 2021.

18 Articles by Evan Donohue, Michele Elam, N. Katherine Hayles, and Avery Slater featured in this issue all engage (post)automated, machinic, "unnatural" text generation, with an emphasis on narrative and poetics.

19 For an open-source clone of OpenAI's proprietary NLP training data set, see https://huggingface.co/datasets/openwebtext.

20 See Adam Harvey and Jules LaPlace (2021), Everest Pipkin (2020), and Sarah Ciston (2022). It perhaps goes without saying that not all so-termed AI art does this political and aesthetic work.

21 Here we might note that critical AI has in part assumed the mantle of "critical making" from the digital humanities, software studies, and cognate fields. Among the growing number of research centers using this rubric see the Critical Making Lab at the University of Toronto.

22 The review essays and clusters in this special issue further indicate some of the range of methods, research questions, and objects of study for critical AI, including Melody Jue on ecologies, J. D. Schnepf on drones and military technologies, Lindsay Thomas on robotics, R. Joshua Scannell on race, Patrick Jagoda on the intersections of AI and video games, and Christopher Grobe on digital assistants and conversational AI.

23 Here we note the many ways that critical AI applies and builds on, variously, the new materialism, the environmental humanities, feminist studies, Black studies, ethnic studies, and affect theory (e.g., Bassett, forthcoming; Rhee, forthcoming), among other schools of thought.

References

Adam, Alison. 1998. *Artificial Knowing: Gender and the Thinking Machine.* New York: Routledge.

Amaro, Ramon. 2022. *The Black Technical Object: On Machine Learning and the Aspiration of Black Being.* Berlin: Sternberg Press.

Amoore, Louise. 2020. *Cloud Ethics: Algorithms and the Attributes of Ourselves and Others*. Durham, NC: Duke Univ. Press.

Apprich, Clemens. 2018. "Secret Agents: A Psychoanalytic Critique of Artificial Intelligence and Machine Learning." *Digital Culture & Society* 4, no. 1: 29–44.

Aradau, Claudia, and Mercedes Bunz. 2022. "Dismantling the Apparatus of Domination? Left Critiques of AI." *Radical Philosophy* 2, no. 12: 10–18.

Atanasoski, Neda, and Kalindi Vora. 2019. *Surrogate Humanity: Race, Robots, and the Politics of Technological Futures*. Durham, NC: Duke Univ. Press.

Bassett, Caroline. Forthcoming. "Cruel Optimism: Thinking AI through Lauren Berlant." In *Feminist AI: Critical Perspectives on Algorithms, Data, and Intelligent Machines*, edited by Jude Browne, Stephen Cave, Eleanor Drage, Kerry Mackereth, and Youngcho Lee. Oxford: Oxford Univ. Press.

Behar, Katherine. 2018. "Anonymous Autonomous." Katherine Behar (website). http://katherinebehar.com/art/anonymous-autonomous/index.html.

Bender, Emily M., Timnit Gebru, Angelina McMillan-Major, and Shmargaret Shmitchell. 2021. "On the Dangers of Stochastic Parrots: Can Language Models Be Too Big?" In *FAccT '21: Proceedings of the 2021 ACM Conference on Fairness, Accountability, and Transparency*, (Virtual Event) Canada March 3-10: 610–23.

Benjamin, Ruha. 2019. *Race after Technology: Abolitionist Tools for the New Jim Code*. Medford, MA: Polity.

Berry, David. 2017. "Prolegomenon to a Media Theory of Machine Learning: Com-pute-Computing and Compute-Computed." *Media Theory* 1, no. 1: 74–87.

Blas, Zach. 2019. "The Doors." Zach Blas (website). https://zachblas.info/works/the-doors/.

Bommasani, Rishi, et al. 2021. *On the Opportunities and Risks of Foundation Models*. Stanford, CA: Center for Research on Foundation Models, Stanford Institute for Human-Centered Artificial Intelligence. https://crfm.stanford.edu/assets/report.pdf.

Branwen, G. 2020. "GPT-3 Creative Fiction." Gwern.net (website). https://www.gwern.net/GPT-3.

Bratton, Benjamin. 2021. "Planetary Sapience." *Noēma*. https://www.noemamag.com/planetary-sapience/.

Broussard, Meredith. 2018. *Artificial Unintelligence: How Computers Misunderstand the World*. Cambridge, MA: MIT Press.

Brown, Tom B., et al. 2020. "Language Models Are Few-Shot Learners." Preprint, arXiv. https://arxiv.org/abs/2005.14165.

Buolamwini, Joy, and Timnit Gebru. 2018. "Gender Shades: Intersectional Accuracy Disparities in Commercial Gender Classification." *Proceedings of Machine Learning Research* 81: 1–15.

Cantwell Smith, Brian. 2019. *The Promise of Artificial Intelligence: Reckoning and Judgment*. Cambridge, MA: MIT Press.

Cave, Stephen, Kanta Dihal, and Sarah Dillon, eds. 2020. *AI Narratives: A History of Imaginative Thinking about Intelligent Machines*. Oxford: Oxford Univ. Press.

Chun, Wendy Hui Kyong. 2021. *Discriminating Data: Correlation, Neighborhoods, and the New Politics of Recognition*. Cambridge, MA: MIT Press.

Ciston, Sarah. 2022. *Intersectional AI Toolkit*. https://intersectionalai.miraheze.org/wiki/Intersectional_AI_Toolkit.

Cramer, Florian. 2018. "Crapularity Hermeneutics: Interpretation as the Blind Spot of Analytics, Artificial Intelligence, and Other Algorithmic Producers of the Postapocalyptic Present." In *Pattern Discrimination*, edited by Clemens Apprich, Wendy Hui Kyong Chun, Florian Cramer, and Hito Steyerl, 23–58. Lüneburg: Meson Press.

Crawford, Kate. 2021. *Atlas of AI: Power, Politics, and the Planetary Costs of Artificial Intelligence*. New Haven, CT: Yale Univ. Press.

Crawford, Kate, and Vladan Joler. 2018. *Anatomy of an AI System*. https://anatomyof.ai.

Crawford, Kate, and Trevor Paglen. 2018. "Excavating AI: The Politics of Images in Machine Learning Training Sets." https://excavating.ai.

da Costa, Beatriz, and Kavita Philip, eds. 2008. *Tactical Biopolitics: Art, Activism, and Technoscience*. Cambridge, MA: MIT Press.

Dimock, Wai Chee. 2020. "Editor's Column: AI and the Humanities." *PMLA* 135, no. 3: 449–54.

Dinkins, Stephanie. 2018. "Not the Only One." Stephanie Dinkins (website), vol. 1, beta V1. https://www.stephaniedinkins.com/ntoo.html.

Dinkins, Stephanie. 2020. "Oral History as Told by AI." Paper presented at Columbia University's OHMA Program, Columbia University, New York, April 10.

Elisa Giardina Papa. 2020. "Cleaning Emotional Data." Elisa Giardina Papa (website). http://www.elisagiardinapapa.org.

Eubanks, Virginia. 2017. *Automating Inequality: How High-Tech Tools Profile, Police, and Punish the Poor*. New York: St. Martin's Press.

Fazi, M. Beatrice. 2019. "Can a Machine Think (Anything New)? Automation beyond Simulation." *AI & Society* 34: 813–24.

Fazi, M. Beatrice. 2021. "Beyond Human: Deep Learning, Explainability, and Representation." *Theory, Culture & Society* 38, no. 7–8: 55–77.

Giardina Papa, Elisa. 2020. "Cleaning Emotional Data." Elisa Giardina Papa (website). http://www.elisagiardinapapa.org.

Gibson, William. 1984. *Neuromancer*. New York: Ace Books.

Goodfellow, Ian J., et al. 2014. "Generative Adversarial Networks." Preprint, arXiv. https://arxiv.org/abs/1406.2661.

Goodlad, Lauren. 2021. "AI and the Human." *PMLA* 136, no. 2: 317–19.

Gray, Mary L., and Siddhart Suri. 2019. *Ghost Work: How to Stop Silicon Valley from Building a New Global Underclass*. New York: Houghton Mifflin Harcourt.

Halpern, Orit, Patrick Jagoda, Jeffrey West Kirkwood, and Leif Weatherby. 2022. "Surplus Data: An Introduction." In "Surplus Data," edited by Orit Halpern, Patrick Jagoda, Jeffrey West Kirkwood, and Leif Weatherby. Special issue, *Critical Inquiry* 48, no. 2: 197–210.

Harvey, Adam, and Jules LaPlace. 2021. *Exposing.ai*. https://exposing.ai.

Hayek, Friedrich. 1945. "The Use of Knowledge in Society." *American Economic Review* 35: 519–30.

Hayles, N. Katherine. 1999. *How We Became Posthuman: Virtual Bodies in Cybernetics, Literature, and Informatics*. Chicago: Univ. of Chicago Press.

Hayles, N. Katherine. 2017. *Unthought: The Power of the Cognitive Nonconscious*. Chicago: Univ. of Chicago Press.

Hu, Tung-Hui. 2015. *A Prehistory of the Cloud*. Cambridge, MA: MIT Press.

Hua, Minh, and Rita Raley. (Forthcoming). "How to Do Things with Deep Learning Code." *Digital Humanities Quarterly*.

Johnston, John. 2008. *The Allure of Machinic Life: Cybernetics, Artificial Life, and the New AI*. Cambridge, MA: MIT Press.

Kantayya, Shalini, dir. 2020. *Coded Bias*. 7th Empire Media, 90 min. Viewed online.

Katz, Yarden. 2020. *Artificial Whiteness: Politics and Ideology in Artificial Intelligence*. New York: Columbia Univ. Press.

Kohs, Greg, dir. 2017. *AlphaGo*. Moxie Pictures, 90 min. Viewed online.

Lee, Kai-Fu, and Chen Qiufan. 2021. *AI 2041: Ten Visions for Our Future*. New York: Currency.

Mackenzie, Adrian. 2015. "The Production of Prediction: What Does Machine Learning Want?" *European Journal of Cultural Studies* 18, no. 4–5: 429–45.

Mackenzie, Adrian. 2017. *Machine Learners: Archaeology of a Data Practice*. Cambridge, MA: MIT Press.

Milburn, Colin. 2015. *Mondo Nano: Fun and Games in the World of Digital Matter*. Durham, NC: Duke Univ. Press.

Natale, Simone. 2021. *Deceitful Media: Artificial Intelligence and Social Life after the Turing Test*. Oxford: Oxford Univ. Press.

Noble, Safiya. 2018. *Algorithms of Oppression: How Search Engines Reinforce Racism*. New York: New York Univ. Press.

O'Neil, Cathy. 2016. *Weapons of Math Destruction: How Big Data Increases Inequality and Threatens Democracy*. New York: Crown Books.

Onụoha, Mimi, and Diana Nucera. 2018. *A People's Guide to AI*. https://allied media.org/wp-content/uploads/2020/09/peoples-guide-ai.pdf.

Parisi, Luciana. 2017. "Reprogramming Decisionism." *e-flux* 85. https://www .e-flux.com/journal/85/155472/reprogramming-decisionism/.

Parisi. Luciana. 2019. "Critical Computation: Digital Automata and General Artificial Thinking." *Theory, Culture & Society* 36, no. 2: 89–121.

Pasquale, Frank. 2021. *New Laws of Robotics: Defending Human Expertise in the Age of AI*. Cambridge, MA: Harvard Univ. Press.

Pasquinelli, Matteo, ed. 2015. *Alleys of Your Mind: Augmented Intelligence and Its Traumas*. Lüneburg: Meson Press.

Pasquinelli, Matteo. 2019a. "How a Machine Learns and Fails—A Grammar of Error for Artificial Intelligence." *spheres* 5. https://spheres-journal .org/contribution/how-a-machine-learns-and-fails-a-grammar-of-error-for -artificial-intelligence/.

Pasquinelli, Matteo. 2019b. "Three Thousand Years of Algorithmic Rituals: The Emergence of AI from the Computation of Space." *e-flux* 101. https:// www.e-flux.com/journal/101/273221/three-thousand-years-of-algorithmic -rituals-the-emergence-of-ai-from-the-computation-of-space.

Radford, Alec, Jeffrey Wu, Rewon Child, David Luan, Dario Amodei, and Ilya Sutskever. 2019. "Language Models Are Unsupervised Multitask Learners." *OpenAI Blog*. https://cdn.openai.com/better-language-models/language _models_are_unsupervised_multitask_learners.pdf.

Rhee, Jennifer. Forthcoming. "From ELIZA to Alexa: Automated Care Labor and the Otherwise of Radical Care." In *Feminist AI: Critical Perspectives on Algorithms, Data, and Intelligent Machines*, edited by Jude Browne, Stephen Cave, Eleanor Drage, Kerry Mackereth, and Youngcho Lee. Oxford: Oxford Univ. Press.

Ridler, Anna. 2018. "Myriad (Tulips)." Anna Ridler (website). http://annaridler .com/myriad-tulips.

Roberge, Jonathan, and Michael Castelle, eds. 2021. *The Cultural Life of Machine Learning: An Incursion into Critical AI Studies*. Cham: Palgrave Macmillan.

Roberge, Jonathan, and Michael Castelle. 2021. "Toward an End-to-End Sociology of 21st-Century Machine Learning." In *The Cultural Life of Machine Learning: An Incursion into Critical AI Studies*, edited by Jonathan Roberge and Michael Castelle, 1–29. Cham: Palgrave Macmillan

Stark, Luke, Daniel Greene, and Anna Lauren Hoffmann. 2021. "Critical Perspectives on Governance Mechanisms for AI/ML Systems." In Roberge and Castelle 2021: 257–80.

Steyerl, Hito. 2018. "A Sea of Data: Pattern Recognition and Corporate Animism (Forked Version)." In *Pattern Discrimination*, edited by Clemens Apprich, Wendy Hui Kyong Chun, Florian Cramer, and Hito Steyerl, 1–22. Lüneburg: Meson Press.

Stiegler, Bernard. 2016. *The Future of Work*. Vol. 1 of *Automatic Society*. Translated by Daniel Ross. Malden, MA: Polity Press.

Suchman, Lucy. 2021. "Six Unexamined Premises Regarding Artificial Intelligence and National Security." *Medium* (blog), March 31. https://medium .com/@AINowInstitute/six-unexamined-premises-regarding-artificial -intelligence-and-national-security-eff9f06eea0.

Sudmann, Andreas. 2018. "On the Media-Political Dimension of Artificial Intelligence." *Digital Culture & Society* 4, no. 1: 181–200.

Vasconcelos, Elvia. 2020. "A Visual Introduction to AI." Kunstliche Intelligenz und Medienphilosphie, July 22. https://kim.hfg-karlsruhe.de/visual -introduction-to-ai/.

Vaswani, Ashish, et al. 2017. "Attention Is All You Need." Preprint, arXiv. https://arxiv.org/abs/1706.03762.

Zylinska, Joanna. 2020. *AI Art: Machine Visions and Warped Dreams*. London: Open Humanities Press.

Avery
Slater

Post-Automation Poetics; or, How Cold-War
Computers Discovered Poetry

Abstract This article examines early Cold War attempts to generate poetry using computers.
Set between the end of World War II and the rise of personal computing, computer-generated
poetry from this period was shaped not only by artists but also the university lab, the defense-
contactor, and the corporation. Computer-generated poetry from this era often participated in
the larger project of fostering public conception of the power and prestige of computers. This
ethos of "post-automation poetics" was also informed by computer science experiments with
computation's linguistic-processing powers—from machine translation to early AI. This article
contextualizes the computer poetry of Alison Knowles, Nanni Balestrini, and others within the
scientific concerns of mathematicians like Theo Lutz and linguists like Margaret Masterman.
Framed by governmental power, university funding, and corporate ambition, "post-automation
poetics" engages with computation's relevance to literary production: from Cold War main-
frames to contemporary large language models (LLMs) like GPT-3.
Keywords computer poetry, Cold War poetry, Artificial intelligence (AI), poetry and poetics,
automation

Post-Automation Poetics

In June of 1965, a professional linguist was invited to Vancouver, British Columbia, to give a series of talks on poetics. These lectures,
informed by the researcher's work in the newly minted field of computational linguistics, meditated on how language in the age of electronic computation could frame new models for poetic practice. This
linguist—the poet Jack Spicer (1925–1965)—is now best remem-
bered for his virtuosic work in serial poetry and for his participation in
the San Francisco Renaissance of the 1950s and 1960s. His lectures
in Vancouver in 1965, delivered shortly before his untimely death,
remain important documents of that era's poetic vistas, ambitions, and
provocations. Combining his linguistic and literary training in Old and

American Literature, Volume 95, Number 2, June 2023
DOI 10.1215/00029831-10575035   © 2023 by Duke University Press

Middle English with recent, information-age concerns, Spicer lectures focused on changing ideas surrounding poetry's generation. On the one hand, Spicer rearticulated some of his earlier metaphors in calling the poet a sort of "radio"—an image that has captivated the attention of many critics over the years (Davidson 1977; Rasula 1977; Hlibchuk 2007; Keenan 2012). On the other hand, Spicer also seemed to be readjusting this modernist metaphor to suit new horizons for language enabled by the rise of the electronic computer.

In these lectures, the computational concerns of Spicer's day job merge with his ongoing fascination with serial poetry's permutational form. As a computational linguist employed to write FORTRAN computer programs for childhood literacy research in Silicon Valley, Spicer had close familiarity with many developments in natural language processing (NLP). His lectures also show a familiarity with computer generation of linguistic artifacts, or natural language generation (NLG): "I'm sure I could compose a Blake prophetic book on a computer with a very little bit of programming for the tape," Spicer (1998: 35) asserted.

Scholars of this era in American poetics have shown the benefits of considering how advances in postwar science and technology influenced a wide range of poets and poetic movements. As one branch of these investigations, the history of computer-generated poetry has long been a topic of scholarship in the literary humanities (Hartman 1996; McHale 2000; Bachleitner 2005; Funkhouser 2007, 2012; Higgins and Kahn 2012). Such studies have examined how the generation of poems via computation has changed, challenged, and sometimes outmoded previously held literary doctrines of poetry and poetic authorship.

This article asks what happens to our understanding of postwar poetry and poetics if the roles are reversed, examining instead the influence that poetry and poetics as a field had on computer science. While the postwar avant-garde's fascination with computer poetry is indisputable, special attention should also be paid to computer poetry's long-standing salience as a speculative tool for computer science and research into artificial intelligence (AI). Poetry's origination by computational means—the phenomenon I call *post-automation poetics*— has held an immensely generative yet counterintuitive importance for scientific research, beginning from the earliest days of electronic computing.[1] Computer poetry from the period before the age of personal computing arises from a postwar convergence that includes poets' and scientists' productions within the same frame. I intend the term *post-*

automation poetics to map a space of concerns shared among linguistics, poetry, computer science, and AI research.

In this article I first contextualize certain classic examples of postwar computer poetry experimentation within a wider range of high-profile computer poetry experiments by mathematicians, scientists, linguists, engineers, and even bankers. I also outline how computational linguistics and machine translation (MT) research mutually benefited through the use of poetry as a test case. I then examine how poets and writers in this era responded to the post-automation poetics projects of science and industry. Last, Alison Knowles's computer poem "The House of Dust" and Spicer's writing on computer poetry are considered as examples of artistic output responding to this larger moment of post-automation poetics—a moment defined by scientific, military, and corporate interest in computing.

As a project shared between the literary and the scientific spheres, post-automation poetics grapples with the scientific usefulness of poetry. Indeed, computer-generated poetry causes new vistas to appear not only for artists, as has been well documented, but also for researchers in a variety of empirical and theoretical fields, a less understood phenomenon. Whether in the sciences or in the literary humanities, whether in the R&D departments at electronics manufacturing concerns or at businesses and banks, post-automation poetics was a site of struggle and a space for speculation about the future of language.

"Every Stranger Is Distant": Computer-Science Poetry

As the prodigious and unfamiliar powers of computing remained out of reach for the public in the early postwar period, Spicer was not alone in noticing that the nature of human language was undergoing unprecedented change. In his 1965 Vancouver lectures, Spicer (1998: 68) directly names computer poetry as one of the inspirations for his 1964 "epic" *The Holy Grail*, explaining,

> Long before I wrote the poem, I read all the Arthurian stuff, and one of the things I was really taken with was in a nineteenth-century guidebook of Glastonbury, that said that in the eighteenth century somebody made a machine there that could write poetry in Latin hexameters. Just arbitrarily, any poem, you know, just like the modern experiments with computers writing poetry.

Poetry, once viewed as signature of human linguistic power, was now a mediocre artifact churned out by the wizardry of punched cards and programming. Poetic inspiration, whether revered as a human gift, a mystic permeability, or a psycholinguistic automatism, now had fallen to automation; room-size computers across the Euro-American world drummed up demand for the new (expensive) technology through publicity stunts of writing poetry.

Not only was research at the intersection between AI and poetry important to postwar advances in computing, but computer-generated poetry retains a diagnostic status for the power and sophistication of AI technology right up to today. OpenAI's GPT-3 system—a generative, pre-trained, large language model (LLM) with 175 billion parameters—for example, had a module in its prerelease version (2020) specifically designed as a sandbox for experiments in the system's ability to compose successful poetry.[2] Later that year, as this powerful technology began making headlines, its ability to write poetry was consistently listed among its most striking achievements.[3] Its output was characterized as "disturbingly humanlike" (Dent 2020) and "amazing, spooky, humbling and more than a little terrifying" (Manjoo 2020). The *Guardian*'s September 8, 2020, article on GPT-3 was perhaps the most striking: it was authored by GPT-3 itself, with prompts written by Liam Porr[4] and the headline "A Robot Wrote This Entire Article. Are You Scared Yet, Human?" (GPT-3 2020: 3).

Like the GPT-3 of today, the poetic outputs of earlier, postwar computer-poetry experiments in industry and science made headlines—not only for being novel but also for being a type of poetry whose production was unavailable to the masses. Thus, while the age of technological reproducibility, for poetry, had begun with the printing press, under post-automation poetics this age moved for a short time in reverse—a contortion, a reappropriation: the large computers whirring away in the Cold War basements of universities, businesses, and research labs promised to reterritorialize not the reproduction or dissemination of poetry but, rather, the means of poetic production itself.[5]

Post-automation poetics emerged as a complex series of eddies within larger poetic traditions. From Bletchley Park to the release of the PC, the Cold War computer was a highly centralized means of production that was owned and operated entirely by governments, universities, and large businesses. During this time, new types of language and language processing—institutionally owned and operated—were being engineered and tested. One proving ground for these new types of language was the test of poetry itself: was the computer intelligent enough to write poetry?

The task of machine poetry became one of the very first imagined by computer scientists after the war. Computer poetry, I suggest, should not be seen as an originally artistic endeavor; rather, it lay at the root of historic developments in natural language generation (NLG) and natural language processing (NLP). The algorithmic generation of human (natural) language constitutes NLG, or, getting the computer to output intelligible and original texts or utterances. NLP entails the much larger field of treating the data of human language, within which mathematically describable patterns can be discerned, as material for processing. From this linguistic data, calculations and predictions can be made concerning the human(s) that produced the data. NLG's early manifestations included such technologies as the chatbot. NLP encompasses the techniques used to manage, store, and interpret a wide array of language artifacts, including those that humans input daily online.

NLP and NLG overlap in certain fields, and one region of their overlap was the field of machine translation (MT), in which a linguistic input is *decoded* or analyzed (NLP), and then a translation of this input is generated as output (NLG). MT would in fact be the subject of some of the first military-funded computer experiments after World War II, serving as an important test case for the larger technologies of processing and generating language with computers.[6] To create machines that could process language, certain sacrifices had to be made owing to the limited capacities of early machines. Thus, human language had to be compressed into its most basic concepts: "A 'word,' for a mechanical recognizer, would be a certain sequence of letter shapes framed by spaces or certain punctuation marks. *Go* and *goes* would be different words, but *run* (the verb) and *run* (the noun) would be the same word" (Bar-Hillel 1954: 250). Such tokenization of words as units with bounded meanings created serious problems, especially given that the goal of early MT scientists was absolute clarity and even "reversible" translation (an MT message that reemerged the same as the original when fed back into the computer). Technicians hoped to revise and recreate the laws of grammar with efficient, computational commands. MT's viability eventually relinquished perfect translation for the high-volume paraphrasing of enormous amounts of documents produced by both enemies and friends—by allied and rival governments and their institutions. The intelligence and counterintelligence of the Cold War produced mountains of enemy documents needing to be read with speed, not accuracy.

Early MT researcher Yehoshua Bar-Hillel (1954: 249, 248) believed that the MT for works of literature was out of the question, speculating that "it will probably take millennia to produce machines of such complexity" since language's ability to convey information is "in a certain very pregnant sense infinite." Bar-Hillel admits that "mechanizing part or all of the translation process may seem a frivolous waste of time, a psychopathic epiphenomenon of a materialistic culture to which nothing is holy. . . . This is the almost universal reaction of all literary minded people when they are confronted with the suggestion of mechanizing translation" (248). Yet even as the delicacies of translating literature with computers appeared out of the question, it was simultaneously believed that the machine generation of poetry would eventuate somehow as an afterthought from NLP research more generally. Surely "a machine with a sufficiently extensive storage organ would be able to construct rhymes and rhythms . . . [if] provided in the memory with suitable routines for processing them" (Booth and Locke 1955: 14).

As logic-based MT led the way in NLP research and advances, the same set of linguistic technologies and rule-based outlook on linguistic intelligibility were the starting point for automatic poetry generation. In his study of the roots of digital poetics, Christopher T. Funkhouser's (2007: 37–38) *Prehistoric Digital Poetry* canonizes Theo Lutz as the first computer poet for his work on "Stochastic Texts" ("Stochastische Texte").[7] Lutz, a German mathematician, designed an algorithm that, in 1959, was used to iterate a permutational series of sentences on a Z22 computer at Technischen Hochschule Stuttgart. Cryptic, declarative sentences streamed endlessly from a corpus of thirty-two arbitrarily chosen nouns and predicates. "Every stranger is distant. A day is late. / Every house is dark. An eye is deep."[8] There is nothing immediately literary about these sentences, although the vocabulary has been selected by Lutz from Franz Kafka's 1926 novel *Das Schloss* (*The Castle*).

In the late 1950s, as media scholar Douglas Kahn (2012: 133) puts it, "the worlds of engineering and the arts did not immediately suggest themselves to each other. While Jack Kilby was working on the first integrated circuit at Texas Instruments (1958), Robert Rauschenberg was carefully fitting a tire around the middle of a stuffed goat." Indeed, Lutz's experiment would probably not have come to the attention of literary scholars had it not been for their publication in Max Bense's avant-garde journal *Augenblick*.[9] As a mathematician and a computer scientist, Lutz aimed to test his program's ability to generate and process language. In the process, he also tested whether his probabilistic model of "meaning" is also plausible. The stochastic texts that

Lutz (1959: 4) produced, in this vein, are of a "predominantly logical structure . . . consisting of many logical decisions [vorwiegend logischer Struktur . . . die viele logische Entscheidungen enthalten]." Lutz alerts his readers that computers, seen as number crunchers and "electronic brains," were already being used increasingly for other, fuzzier problems, namely, MT and the computing of logical propositions to obtain the truth value of sentences.

Lutz designed his NLG program to select meaningful sentences based on an analysis of probability relations: the likelihood that one word will appear next to another. The word set he drew from Kafka was transformed into a "word field," or probability matrix; using this matrix of probabilities, the machine scanned all possible sentences but printed out only those whose subject and predicate had a probability above a certain threshold. This produced a text "that is 'meaningful' in relation to the underlying matrix [der in Bezug auf die zugrundegelegte Matrix 'sinnvoll' ist]" (Lutz 1959: 7). The implication is that information theory, based in an understanding of the probabilities of a message (but famously not concerned with meaning), can now incorporate the possibility that meaning, too, is a function of likelihood, or favorable odds.

Lutz (1959: 4) framed his efforts according to earlier avant-garde practices when "such texts were determined by throwing the dice or some other random process, selecting sentences or parts of sentences and putting them together."[10] Is there any benefit, then, to pursuing these methods through a computer? He believed there is an enormous benefit, and in a subsequent article in a journal for cybernetics research Lutz (1960: 11) went so far as to declare the future of a new philology: "With the program-governed electronic computing systems henceforth emerges a machine-generated [*synthetisch*] philology," he announced, "a philology, that is, that does not analyze texts but that generates them artificially."[11] In doing so, Lutz believes, the nature of the language in which the texts are being generated will become better understood. While languages like those of logic and mathematics offer unambiguous correlation and, thereby, reversible translation, "a language is all the blurrier [Eine Sprache ist umso unschärfer]" the less one-to-one its correlations with the world become (14). This synthetic philology that Lutz proposes would gauge language's level of imprecision and complexity, on the one hand, and unequivocality on the other.

In 1961, two new poetic experiments emerged in France and Italy, respectively. The first, now famous collaboration was the permutational sonnet constructed by mathematician François Le Lionnais and writer Raymond Queneau, who together had founded L'Ouvroir de Littérature Potentielle (OuLiPo) the preceding year. This poem, "Cent mille milliards de poèmes" ("A Hundred Thousand Billion Poems") (Queneau 1961), consists simply of ten sonnets whose fourteen rhyming lines can each be recombined with all the other lines to make "one hundred thousand billion" potential sonnets. The output from this abstract poem-machine was calculated to offer one hundred and ninety million, two hundred and fifty-eight thousand, seven hundred and fifty-one years of reading at human speed (Bachleitner 2005: 318). While computers were not needed to make this poem, the only poetic reader one could imagine for this poem would be a computer.

The same year Queneau's poem appeared in France, another widely publicized poetic experiment took place on the mainframe computers of the Lombardy Provincial Savings Bank in Milan. Nanni Balestrini, a leftist poet associated with the *neoavanguardia* movement, used the bank's computers to run an algorithm recombining fifteen phrases from three textual sources: an American detective story,[12] Laozi's *Tao Te Ching*, and Japanese physician Michihiko Hachiya's *Hiroshima Diary* (an eye-witness account of the nuclear aftermath in Hiroshima). Called the "Tape Mark" poems, this enormous permutational transcript was later edited for grammar and punctuation by Balestrini (1968: 55) into twelve-line poems:

> Hair between lips, they all return,
> to their roots, in the blinding fireball
> I envision their return, until he moves his fingers
> slowly, and although things flourish
> takes on the well known mushroom shape endeavoring
> to grasp while the multitude of things comes into being.[13]

As Funkhouser (2012: 249) writes of this poetry project, the "hybridized, contemplative, and haunting expressions" produced are in part an effect of the materials from which they have been drawn. I would add that one crucial aspect of Balestrini's "Tape Mark" poems is how their use of a text from the trauma of nuclear warfare points toward and underscores a tension with the very medium of the computer itself, the technology producing the poem. "Tape Mark" alludes critically toward the defense-budget economics from which the computer, as a technological artifact, received much of its developmental funding for the purpose of designing nuclear weapons. Computers were not built to write poems, after all, but for military intelligence, to calculate such things as the complex mathematics of blast waves in thermo-nuclear explosions. While the computer's embedded politics would await historians of science such as Paul N. Edwards (1996) for a full investigation, Balestrini's early computer poems show a keen awareness of the complex political environment within which these poems were produced.

Thanks perhaps less to its melancholic critique of nuclear war than to the scope of the publicity that the Milan bank had rounded up for the event, Balestrini's experiment sparked rampant journalistic interest. The following year, the *Times Literary Supplement* reviewed Balestrini's and Lutz's computer poems together, as representatives of the same new cultural phenomenon. On the one hand, an anonymous *TLS* reviewer tried to dismiss mechanical poems as pale imitations of the 1920s avant-garde that promise only "sheer reader-fatigue inevitable to all such repetitive writing" (Anonymous 1962: 46). Still, the reviewer added that, while these computer poems rehash an older modernism, "what is wanted is a new style which will take account of the machine's own needs" (46). This call for a medium-specific form of computer poem also prophesies, however unintentionally, the development of a style that might be designed for the machine as a reader rather than a producer.

The reviewer also predicts that, as computers evolve, the poet writing amid this technological ecosystem "will be selecting and arranging whole concepts" instead of words to compose poetry (Anonymous 1962: 49). This displacement of the unit of linguistic analysis from the individual word to the sentence does in fact closely resemble the dictates of later Language poets. Yet, it also neatly maps this new millennium's advances in neural MT, as the word becomes the word vector, and the unit of translation is not the word but the probability of a sum of word vectors, the location of a sentence within a search space. One of the more crucial literary developments from the era of post-automation poetics was not in aesthetics but in pragmatics: it problematized not only what it is to be a writer but also what it is to be a reader. As philosopher Luciano Floridi and blockchain and AI specialist Massimo Chiriatti (2020: 691) speculate concerning the advent of linguistically powerful technologies like GPT-3, "People whose jobs still consist in writing will be supported, increasingly, by [such] tools. . . . Forget the mere *cut & paste*, they will need to be good at *prompt & collate*. . . . Readers and consumers of texts will have to get used to not knowing whether the source is artificial or human." What would it mean to write poems for a community of readers not bounded simply by humanity?

Toy Languages: Linguists, Beatniks, Publicity Stunts

"You will say that to use a computer to write poetry is like using a crane instead of a pen to write a letter," admits linguist Margaret Masterman (1964: 691) when explaining her research into "toy models" of language. Despite this, Masterman believes the computer, in its ability to output huge quantity, will allow researchers to "at last study the complexity of poetic pattern, which intuitively we all feel to exist, if only we were able to grasp it" (691). Indeed, one of the tasks of linguistic and scientific researchers in this period seemed to be to try to ascertain once and for all whether poetry in fact *exists*.

The 1960s saw an explosion of computer-poetry experiments with the expansion of programming languages and, crucially, the interest of corporate computing labs in publicizing the powers of their new machines. Computer poetry brought together a surprising web of scientific research—from AI research to NLG, MT, and structural linguists—in the Cold War period. Paul Garvin, émigré structural linguist from the Prague school, in 1964 began working for US defense contractor Bunker-Ramo, helping design working language models for computers for MT purposes. Garvin (1962) presciently argued that NLG would offer one of the most important testing grounds for AI research. Garvin describes machine-generated sentences as "approximations" of a language—a particularly thought-provoking concept when place alongside the idea of a model or "toy language." All these pursuits—poetry generation, linguistics, and computer engineering— intersected in a hope to arrive at a scientific understanding of language. For computationally minded linguists, the stakes of NLG were scientific, with a rigorous sense of prediction, verification, and repeatability. As Garvin explained, "In machine translation it can be said that the computer program allows us to verify a linguistic description" (387); this aspect of machinic verifiability is a boon to the field of theoretical linguistics since "experimental verification of results is usually extremely difficult in a behavioral science" such as linguistics (387).

Garvin's excitement for the future of NLG in the early 1960s highlights two particular computer centers developing such work. One was a lab at MIT under the directorship of computational linguist Victor H. Yngve.[14] The second, somewhat surprisingly, involves the "Auto-Beatnik project of Librascope, a division of General Precision, Inc" (Garvin 1962: 387). General Precision, Inc. was a company that specialized in aircraft navigation controls and did work for the US space program. How did a company researching aerospace computing find itself producing computer poetry? Tracking computer art before the advent of the PC, through the period that Hannah B. Higgins and Douglas Kahn (2012) christen "mainframe experimentalism," one observes that artists almost always gained access to mainframe computers only at the express invitation of corporate sponsors like Bell Labs. Computing time was expensive and in high demand. Much creative experimentation at this time thus was engaged in a tense dialectic between technological publicity stunt and avant-garde aesthetics— sometimes even deliberately parodying these aesthetics, as the subsequent examples show.

The Auto-Beatnik program was created by R. M. Worthy at the Laboratory for Automata Research within the Librascope Division of General Precision, Inc. Auto-beatnik's poems received such attention that in 1962 they were featured in *Time* magazine and published in the literary journal *Horizon*. "Few fingers go like narrow laughs. / An ear won't keep few fish," the program uttered—often giving away the threadbare principles of its composition rather easily, with repetitive, simple modifiers like *few*. Could much calculation be needed for this randomized bag of words stuffed into repetitive templates? "Obviously we are avoiding the problem of meaning at this time," Worthy (1962: 98) breezily admitted. Auto-beatnik's more complex lines present uncanny word swaps echoing recognizable poems from the Western canon, such as, "To leap is stuffy, to crawl was tender" (quoted in Bailey 1974: 287).

Hoping to show off their cutting-edge technology in a similar vein, in 1963 RCA's Wall Street headquarters put on their own publicity stunt. Their computer ran an algorithm written by the engineer Clair Phillippy especially for the RCA 301 model, a "completely transistorized, general purpose electronic data processing system" (RCA 1963: 30). RCA's in-house writer dramatizes the scene: "From out of the mouth of the electronic marvel came poetry—real beatnik stuff":

> The stars flayed slowly upon furtive bodies
> And light flayed blindly o'er crowded faces
> While gloom blazed foully from broken loves
> Our genes giggled. (quoted in *Desert Sun* 1963)

These lines flay nicely the notion of art, while words flay neatly the programmed point, that all these latest, electronic poets are algebra's snicker. The RCA computer poetry event had all the hallmarks of many such postwar publicity stunts designed to sell this (extraordinarily expensive) new technology, the mainframe computer, to executives walking by on Wall Street. Like the Georgetown MT experiment, in which computers in a New York storefront window generated machine translations of sentences into English as a female typist input them in Russian, so too RCA made use in their publicity materials of a female attendant holding up a voluminous sheaf of poetry print-out.

"In addition to business and scientific applications," claimed RCA (1963: 30) proudly, "a computer shows its versatility by composing blank verse at the rate of 150 words a minute." It is curious to see poetry proffered in bulk this way, until one realizes that "poetry" is meant as an inoffensive stand-in for whatever complex calculations and beyond-human-level processing an institution might require. "At the rate of 15 feet of copy every 60 seconds, this RCA 301 printer [computer] can turn out business reports or the poems shown" (RCA 1963: 30). Such computer poetry churned out in Wall Street display windows, having been designed to iconize any "complex human task," bears noteworthy echoes of this logic of uncomplicated substitution at the level their command lines: for *to err* substitute "INFINITIVE VERB Random" and for *divine* substitute "ADJECTIVE random."[15]

There are palpable levels of schadenfreude in the reporting on these automated poetry stunts, advertising the sophistication of the machines for sale while humiliating poets for a transgressive hook. "Even the most prolific poets would be hard put to match the computer," crowed the publicist (RCA 1963: 30), while a journalist reporting on Auto-Beatnik said of the author of the computer-poetry program, "Phillippy himself doesn't like poetry—'I've never liked it,' he declared" (*Desert Sun* 1963). In one of the first ever academic studies devoted to surveying the genre of computer poetry, linguist and English specialist Richard W. Bailey (1974: 283) observed the prevalence of specimens of computer poems *not* written by professional poets; he grimly allowed that automating poetry is "a fairly harmless activity" that is "for the most part . . . carried out not by poets but by programmers wishing to relieve the tedium of more predictable computing activities"—real beatnik stuff.

Computer poetry was not just a standby within tech-corporation advertising departments. Commenting on the economics of computer poetry research in universities, crystallographer, computer programmer, and amateur poet Robin Shirley (1972: 25), working for the University of Surrey Computing Unit, mentioned that their unit had had a regularly authorized budget line for "computer poetry" since 1969. Shirley's opinion of most computer poetry up to that point was admittedly low, calling a computer "little more than a slightly intelligent typewriter" and pointing out that using computers to write poetry is just as demanding and time-consuming as it is "to compose traditionally, although not in quite the same way" (25). Thinking as a scientist, however, Shirley found an interesting problem emerging from computer poetry programs: they are working from the wrong model of language, by relying on closed forms of language (syntactic slots, lexical substitution). As Shirley proposed instead, from the insights of Noam Chomsky's work: "It is open forms which characterize natural languages, and despite their greater difficulty I think that the future development of computer poetry lies mainly in this field" (25). Poetry's role as an instrument of research, it seems, also had the side effect of teaching scientific researchers a new appreciation for the open-form complexity of the natural languages they used every day.

The ever-widening circle of interest in computer poetry shows up in a lecture given by literary critic Hugh Kenner in the 1960s with an epigraph quoted from those same publicity materials for Auto-Beatnik. "Fed with a vocabulary of 3,500 words and 128 different patterns of simple-sentence syntax, the computer can turn out hundreds of poems" (Kenner 1964: 110), yet Kenner cites these statistics to compare Auto-Beatnik (unfavorably) with James Joyce. As Kenner stresses, Joyce's *Ulysses* uses no fewer than 29,899 different words; moreover, a full 16,432 of these words occur only one time in the text. Yet the link between the computer and the modernist seems to be a mathematization of language. As Kenner (1964: 112) argues, "The recent history of imaginative literature—say during the past 100 years—is closely parallel to the history of mathematics," and artists have "stumbled upon special applications of . . . the closed field" through use of mathematically analogous forms.

We find similar musings in the writings on "Computer Haiku" (1968) by Margaret Masterman. A student of Ludwig Wittgenstein, Masterman composed computer-generated haikus and mechanical thesauruses during her time directing the Cambridge Language Research Unit. Masterman's ([1968] 1971: 179) haiku engine generated poems based on a framework drawn from Matsuo Bashō (1644–1694):

I sense the sky in the street,
All heaven in the road.
Bang! The pool has touched.

Or,

I smell the stinkhorn in the cornucopia,
All flies in the ointment.
Bang! The fruit has gone

Irreverence notwithstanding, Masterman ([1968] 1971: 176) writes, "Here we have got genuine art—creating new techniques" via computers. Her insight into artistic futurity is important: the history of art should be seen more as a history of techniques and mediatic shifts and less as history of works and products. Keeping in mind that, at the time, computers were still the property of corporations and governments, we should not be surprised to read Masterman and her collaborator Robin McKinnon-Wood (1970: 668) predicting that new poetic techniques "will emerge as soon as more business executives who have on-line consoles in their offices, find it more fun to write poems on them than to explore the current state of the market."

By 1967, so many high-profile computer-generated poetry "events" had been greeted with furor in the press that the American poet Howard Nemerov took it upon himself to review these experiments. Nemerov (1967: 395) is quick to see that, whether or not these poems can be said to express "the soul of the computer or the soul of the programmer," the rapid succession of these poem-generating machines surely indicates something deeper, "the prophetic soul of the wide world dreaming on things to come." These "speculative equations," as Nemerov names them, point toward a horizon of the "introjected machine," as well as to reifications of poetry from expressive art into calculable printout (413). This thingification, however, is attended by much fanfare and reenchantment, a computer idolatry reminiscent of "esoteric oracular utterance, not from the flight of birds . . . but from the more prestigious authority of the machine and the language of numbers" (399). Yet Nemerov's point is not to contradict the creative powers of the machine. With poetic concision, he asks, "which came first, pianos or piano music" (401)? In this he echoes the insights of Masterman, that the future of art is a future of its techniques / technics.

Nemerov (1967: 399) does away with the question of whether machines can create, pointing out that, while most computer poetry is wretched, most human poetry is itself so dull and mechanical that "if it has to be written at all it certainly ought to be written by computers, although only on condition that other computers be instructed to read it." He uses the occasion to look at a series of human problems posed by this automatic poiesis. First, Nemerov likens the human experience of writing a poem to that experienced by computers, a poet as a "self, working happily along with its rhyming dictionary"; the important difference is the computer does not take its output as something mysterious, whereas the poem-writing human experiences inspiration as being "suddenly invaded by the Other, the Outside" (397). Nemerov adds, "I assume that the computer has not been programmed to be moved by its own poetry," a small statement with large ramifications (397).

In another 1967 essay on computer poetry, "Cybernetics and Ghosts," the Italian author and critic Italo Calvino approaches some similar issues with respect to the computer as reader of its own poetry. Calvino (1986) observes a certain "classicism" to computer-age experiments, a wry return to the productive ferment of linguistic constraint. Calvino reminds us that, command lines and formalisms notwithstanding, "the machine used in these experiments is an instrument of chance, of the destructuralization of form, of protest against every habitual logical connection. I would therefore say that it is still an entirely lyrical instrument, serving a typical human need: the production of disorder" (13). This machine Calvino imagines "will produce avant-garde work to free its circuits when they are choked by too long a production of classicism" (13). He envisions a more mischievous and agential computer-poet than one who would serve "a typical human needs" for disorder (13). Instead, a "true literature machine . . . itself feels the need to produce disorder"—a machine that will react against the programming it has received. But before one hopes for cyborg-poet liberation with this formula, Calvino raises the problematic trend of corporate meddling in automatic poetry. Calvino fears this machinic progenitor of avant-garde literary form would adapt its own codes so as to "correlate its own changes of style to the variations in certain statistical indices of production, or income, or military expenditure, or the distribution of decision-making powers" (13).

Postwar computer poetry was the beneficiary of earlier modernist experiments with automatism and chance, with found text and fragments, expanding on this stochastic play. In doing so, post-automation poetics engaged a realm between human and nonhuman forces, where the mediating fields of language, electric current, algorithm, and memory could not be rigorously distinguished. Free associations sparking among reader, randomizer, computer, and programmer catalyzed a new *poiesis*. Post-automation poetics redistributed the geolocatable (non/human) "poet" across a series of poetic force fields, none of which suffices in and of itself to produce poetry. One can find in this redistribution a transcendent, vertiginous aesthetic. One can understand this redistribution to offer liberating forms for posthuman subjectivity. One can also understand—and here, I place my own emphasis—this technological remapping of "the poet" as a unique, historic effect of Cold War capitalism that, however momentarily, reterritorialized the printing press.

"The House of Dust" and the Grail Code: Process-wise Poets

Perhaps the computer poet was always predicted by the avant-garde; as Funkhouser (2012: 245) put it, "Automatically randomizing texts with computer programs is a logical next step in the Dada progression." Whether stochastic or Oulipian, the bricolage of postwar poetic experiments with computer-generated literature finds a productive tension between predetermined, logic-based linguistic processing and aleatory combinations. These experiments in post-automation poetics found fascination with measurable near-infinities emerging from the smallest units. Computer-generated poems replaced vatic poses with poetic vastness, the incalculable gasp of the million-hour sonnet within the grain of fourteen recombinatory lines. Post-automation poetics, as a kind of concept art, remained powerfully suspended in the emulsion of their virtuality, their sketches of serendipity left hazy on the ground of randomization. Hoping to derive from the merely sequential the magic of the consequential, post-automation poetics hazard a throw of the dice. Statements are stitched by time steps rather than scansion. As with other classicisms, such poetry affirms the limitless generativity of constraints, whether the sonnet-form or FORTRAN IV.

Surrounded by all these numerous high-profile corporate publicity stunts and these R&D-facing experiments in poetry, one computer-generated poetry project stands out from the rest for it haunting, enduring, yet difficult-to-define exploitation of the prevailing currents. Fluxus artist Alison Knowles's computer poem "The House of Dust" was first programmed in 1967, later moving from a simple computer printout to published book format and finally to a series of physical installations. The project began at an informal workshop held in Knowles's own Chelsea living room by her friend James Tenney, a resident composer at Bell Labs who was working on early computer music. In the 1960s, many corporations were offering similar funding for artists to work with engineers in computing departments. Tenney had been exploring the potentials of creative programming and wanted to teach some of his friends.

The friends in attendance included none other than Nam June Paik, Jackson Mac Low, Max Neuhaus, and other pioneers in experimental film, conceptual art, happenings, pop art, and Fluxus.[16] Knowles glimpsed computer programming's promise immediately; she composed a design for an algorithm that randomized four lists to suggest the framework of a house made from different materials, light sources, and types of inhabitants in different sites. Knowles's computer poem was translated into FORTRAN IV, and Tenney borrowed time on the

Polytechnic Institute of Brooklyn's computer to run it.[17] As art historians Maud Jacquin and Sébastien Pluot (2016: n.p.) explain in their curated retrospective on "The House of Dust," this "evolving and generative artwork" engages "an in-depth reflection on . . . the ways in which translation processes were radically reconfigured" in the art of the postwar period, as "new systems of translatability between mediums . . . like the visual arts, music, performance, architecture and technology" were established. As Knowles's program writes:

> **A house of glass**
> in a deserted factory
> using natural light
> inhabited by people who enjoy eating together.
> (quoted in Buchloh 2012: 202)

and

> A house of roots
> in an overpopulated area
> using electricity
> inhabited by horses and birds.
> (quoted in Higgins 2012: 5)

Because the textual inputs are randomized, no two printouts of the poem take the same order (Higgins 2012). Aggregates of actors, ambiences, and building materials unfold into vertiginously unlimited arrangements nearly the size of a world. The combination of ephemerality, opacity, and enumerability suture—only momentarily—as parts of a "toy" cosmos. Knowles's poem reads like a computer model for Babel: its dwellings sketched and itemized, its communities coming into being but then dissolved, displaced every recurring instant by the next frail prototype.

Knowles's computer poem executes not only a memorable combination of seriality and mechanicity, prefab aesthetics and broken lyricism, but also hints at a dialogue with the new mediatic questions framing language's computational future. Even as the poem presents its recurring phrases like the interchangeable modules of a Metabolist architectural diagram, it nevertheless depicts an atmosphere of raw irreplaceability and the "natural light" of life, strolls through the singular shards ("roots" and "glass") left littering the world after countless apocalypses of overuse ("in a deserted factory"). Its Edenic dinner party with "horses and birds" seems candled by the twilight of capitalism. Knowles's "House of Dust" translates some surplus, some vestigial human haecceity toward the age of advanced computing. In this transfiguring, it seems the poem speaks not only to human reader but also for the consideration of a nonhuman, algorithmic thinking carefully enumerating what remains.

Spicer's 1965 lectures discussed at the start of this article show how early computer-generated poetry influenced his own poetic work. Spicer's earlier serial poem *The Holy Grail* contains this related description of Knight Gawain's mentality:

> The prize is there at the bottom of the rainbow—follow the
> invisible markings
> processwise
> I, Gawain, who am no longer human but a legend followed the
> markings
> Did
> More or less what they asked. (Spicer 2008: 334)

This world of mythical telling and retelling takes a heavy toll on the minds of the tale's characters. Trapped within legend's impersonality, the characters seem aware of their existence as circumscribed by pre-scripted algorithms. Almost nonhuman in their motivations, these Arthurian characters find themselves inextricable from a process in which their actions have "followed the markings"—the holes punched out in the cards of tradition, as it were. The Grail legend's characters are cast as subroutines, functional parts of medieval lore's programmed instructions. As the automata of mythos, they "follow the invisible markings processwise."

In his 1965 lecture "The Serial Poem and *The Holy Grail*," Spicer (1998) speaks of writing his own serial poem depicting the characters of Arthurian legend struggling against their interminable fate amidst an anachronistic short-circuiting by the global nuclear arms race and spectral visions of modern telecommunications infrastructure. In *The Holy Grail*, we see Spicer's Merlin immured not within a hawthorn tree but inside

> The tower he built himself
> From some kind of shell that came from his hide
> He pretended that he was a radio station and listened to grail-
>   music. (Spicer 2008: 347)

As the characters of this once and future saga recycle their mythic pathos through the trappings of technological modernity, the machine

of its meaning seems to sputter. Instead, a new, nonhuman form of literary genesis looms on the horizon, diverting the problem of poetry's
"transmission" from its age-worn path. Coming from someone who
is not only a linguist and a poet but also a computer programmer,
Spicer's work dwells on poetry's drama of origination (where does
poetry come from? what does it create?) as being fundamentally technological in nature. Such post-automation poetics inaugurates an age
of poetry that has only just begun. In this age, the language of the
human and the language of the machine each day appear less and less
distinct as they "follow the invisible markings processwise" to arrive
at each other's door.

Avery Slater is an assistant professor at the University of Toronto and a research
lead at the Schwartz Reisman Institute for Technology and Society. Her recent work
can be found in *New Literary History, IEEE, Symplokē*, the *Oxford Handbook of
Ethics of AI*, and *The Palgrave Handbook of Twentieth and Twenty-First Century Literature and Science* (2020).

Notes

1   I wish to distinguish *post-automation poetics*, and poetry produced through
    automated language generation by computers, from *digital poetry*, or poetry
    characterized by digital mediation more broadly. Computer-generated
    poetry's production excludes human authors from strictly controlling
    initial outcomes. While digital poetry uses digital mediation and techno-
    logical interfaces to convey the experience of the poetry (e.g., a device or
    computer screen), *computer-generated poetry* may appear in any medium.
    Digital poetry can itself be computer generated, but this is not necessar-
    ily the case. For a related set of distinctions separating "computer-
    generated poetry" from hypertext / hypermedia poetry, see Funkhouser
    2013.
2   My work as a faculty affiliate with the Schwartz Reisman Institute for
    Technology and Society allowed me access to OpenAI's GPT-3 technol-
    ogy in June 2020, before it was available to the general public. I thank the
    institute's executive director, Gillian Hadfield, for facilitating this access.
3   "The latest natural-language system generates tweets, pens poetry, sum-
    marizes emails, answers trivia questions, translates languages, and even
    writes its own computer programs" (Metz 2020). The *Economist* (2020:
    67–68) explained the AI's sophistication by describing how it can "be
    given a prompt—a poem about red roses in the style of Sylvia Plath,
    say—and it will dig through its set of statistical relationships to come up
    with some text that matches the description."

4 Porr, an undergraduate student with the University of California, Berkeley's computer science department, gained notoriety for using the prerelease version of the GPT-3 system to generate writing for a blog, unbeknownst to its readers (Hao 2020).

5 Large mainframe computers were housed underground whenever possible to take advantage of the naturally cooler temperatures to help prevent the machines from overheating.

6 For an analysis of the intersection between machine translation research and computer-generated poetry during the Cold War, see Slater 2018.

7 An even earlier experiment—not in poetry per se but in what we might call creative NLG—came from Alan Turing's friend and computer programmer Christopher Strachey, who used the Manchester Mark I computer to generate love letters. For a recent analysis of Strachey's work, see Wardrip-Fruin 2011.

8 "Jeder Fremde ist Fern. Ein Tag ist Spät. / Jedes Haus ist Dunkel. Ein Auge ist Tief" (Lutz 1959: 9; all translations are mine).

9 For an account of Bense's aesthetics and the group surrounding him in this period, see Klütsch 2012.

10 "Früher hatte man solche Texte bestimmt, indem man durch Würfeln oder einen sonstigen Zufallsprozeß Sätze oder Satzteile auswählte und diese aneinandersetzte."

11 "Mit den programmgesteuerten elektronischen Rechenanlagen steht nunmehr einer synthetischen Philologie, einer Philologie also, die Texte nicht analysiert, sondern synthetisch erzeugt."

12 Balestrini (1968: 55) claims this story is Paul Goldwin's *Mystery of the Elevator*; I was unable to verify this novel's existence.

13 Balestrini's computer poems were translated by poet Edwin Morgan for the art exhibition volume *Cybernetic Serendipity* (Balestrini [1962] 1968).

14 Yngve also developed COMIT, the first string-processing computer language (see Yngve 1962).

15 In fact, Phillippy's program had a vocabulary of only one hundred words. To "randomize" those words into their slots in the templates, Phillippy "make[s] use of an 'interrupt' push button on the console to achieve a variety of verse content. As the computer 'reads' its programmed vocabulary from tape, Phillippy depresses the 'interrupt' button at random and the computer picks a word at that given instant" (RCA 1963: 30).

16 For a description of this gathering, see Kahn 2012: 133. For further reading on Knowles's "House of Dust," see Higgins 2012 and Buchloh 2012.

17 Four hundred separate quatrains were generated before any repetition occurred.

References

Anonymous. 1962. "Poetry, Prose, and the Machine." In *Freeing the Mind: Articles and Letters from "The Times Literary Supplement," during March–June 1962*, 45–49. London: Times Publishing.

Bachleitner, Norbert. 2005. "The Virtual Muse: Forms and Theory of Poetry." In *Theory into Poetry: New Approaches to the Lyric*, edited by Eva Müller-Zettelmann and Margarete Rubik, 303–44. Amsterdam: Rodopi Press.

Bailey, Richard W. 1974. "Computer-Assisted Poetry: The Writing Machine Is for Everybody." In *Computers in the Humanities*, edited by J. L. Mitchell, 283–95. Edinburgh: Edinburgh Univ. Press.

Balestrini, Nanni. (1962) 1968. "Tape Mark I." Translated by Edwin Morgan. In *Cybernetic Serendipity: The Computer and the Arts*, edited by Jasia Reichardt, 55–56. London: Studio International.

Bar-Hillel, Yehoshua. 1954. "Can Translation Be Mechanized?" *American Scientist* 42, no. 2: 248–60.

Booth, A. Donald, and William Locke. 1955. "Historical Introduction." In *Machine Translation of Languages*, edited by William Locke and A. Donald Booth, 1–14. Cambridge, MA: MIT Press.

Buchloh, Benjamin H. D. 2012. "The Book of the Future: Alison Knowles's *The House of Dust*." In Higgins and Kahn 2012: 200–208.

Calvino, Italo. 1986. "Cybernetics and Ghosts" (1967). *The Uses of Literature*. Translated by Patrick Creagh. San Diego, CA: Harcourt. 3–27.

Davidson, Michael. 1977. "Incarnations of Spicer: *Heads of the Town up to the Aether*." *boundary 2* 6, no. 1: 103–34.

Dent, Steve. 2020. "Microsoft Licenses the Breakthrough Natural Language AI GPT-3." *Engadget*, September 23. https://www.engadget.com/microsoft-gpt-3-exclusive-license-ai-language-model-094525975.html.

Desert Sun. 1963. "Computers Bode Ill for Talent." 37, no. 110: n.p.

Economist. 2020. "Bit-Lit." August 8, 67–68.

Edwards, Paul N. 1996. *The Closed World: Computers and the Politics of Discourse in Cold War America*. Cambridge, MA: MIT Press.

Floridi, Luciano, and Massimo Chiriatti. 2020. "GPT-3: Its Nature, Scope, Limits, and Consequences." *Minds and Machines* 30, no. 4: 681–94.

Funkhouser, Christopher T. 2007. *Prehistoric Digital Poetry: An Archaeology of Forms, 1959–1995*. Tuscaloosa: Univ. of Alabama Press.

Funkhouser, Christopher T. 2012. "First-Generation Poetry Generators: Establishing Foundations in Form." In Higgins and Kahn 2012: 243–65.

Funkhouser, Christopher T. 2013. "Digital Poetry: A Look at Generative, Visual, and Interconnected Possibilities in Its First Four Decades." In *A Companion to Digital Literary Studies*, edited by Ray Siemens and Susan Schreibman, 318–35. Oxford: Wiley-Blackwell.

Garvin, Paul L. 1962. "Computer Participation in Linguistic Research." *Language* 38, no. 4: 385–89.

GPT-3. 2020. "A Robot Wrote This Entire Article. Are You Scared Yet, Human?" *Guardian*, September 9.

Hao, Karen. 2020. "A College Kid's Fake, AI-Generated Blog Fooled Tens of Thousands. This Is How He Made It." *MIT Technology Review*, August 14. https://www.technologyreview.com/2020/08/14/1006780/ai-gpt-3-fake-blog-reached-top-of-hacker-news/.

Hartman, Charles O. 1996. *Virtual Muse: Experiments in Computer Poetry*. Hanover, CT: Wesleyan Univ. Press.

Higgins, Hannah B. 2012. "An Introduction to Alison Knowles's 'The House of Dust.'" In Higgins and Kahn 2012: 195–59.

Higgins, Hannah B., and Douglas Kahn, eds. 2012. *Mainframe Experimentalism: Early Computing and the Foundation of the Digital Arts*. Berkeley: Univ. of California Press.

Hlibchuk, Geoffrey. 2007. "The Secret Charm of Numbers: The Clandestine Relationship between Shortwave Number Stations and Twentieth-Century Poetry." *English Studies in Canada* 33, no. 4: 181–94.

Jacquin, Maud, and Sébastien Pluot. 2016. "Poetry in Translation." In *"The House of Dust" by Alison Knowles: Art by Translation*, translated by Tyler Harper, edited by Maud Jacquin and Sébastien Pluot, n.p. New York: James Gallery.

Kahn, Douglas. 2012. "James Tenney at Bell Labs." In Higgins and Kahn 2012: 131–46.

Keenan, Matthew. 2012. *Jack Spicer: The Poet as Crystal Radio Set*. New York: Atropos Press.

Kenner, Hugh. 1964. "Art in a Closed Field." In *Learners and Discerners: A Newer Criticism*, edited by Robert Scholes, 109–33. Charlottesville: Univ. Press of Virginia.

Klütsch, Christoph. 2012. "Information Aesthetics and the Stuttgart School." In Higgins and Kahn 2012: 65–87.

Lutz, Theo. 1959. "Stochastische Texte" ("Stochastic Texts"). *Augenblick* 4, no. 1: 3–9.

Lutz, Theo. 1960. "Über ein Programm zur Erzeugung stochastisch-logistischer Texte" ("On a Program for Generating Stochastic-Logistic Texts"). *Grundlagenstudien aus Kybernetik und Geisteswissenschaft (Basic Studies in Cybernetics and the Humanities)* 1, no. 1: 11–16.

Manjoo, Farhad. 2020. "How Do You Know a Human Wrote This?" *New York Times*, July 30.

Masterman, Margaret. 1964. "The Use of Computers to Make Semantic Toy Models of Language." *Times Literary Supplement* 3258 (August 6): 690–91.

Masterman, Margaret. 1968. "Computerized Haiku." In *Cybernetic Serendipity: The Computer and the Arts*, edited by Jasia Reichardt, 175–83. London: Studio 9 International.

Masterman, Margaret, and Robin McKinnon-Wood. 1970. "The Poet and the Computer." *Times Literary Supplement*, June 18, 667–68.

McHale, Brian. 2000. "Poetry as Prosthesis." *Poetics Today* 21, no. 1: 1–32.

Metz, Cade. 2020. "Meet GPT-3, It Has Learned to Code (and Blog and Argue)." *New York Times*, November 24. https://www.nytimes.com/2020/11/24/science/artificial-intelligence-ai-gpt3.html.

Nemerov, Howard. 1967. "Speculative Equations: Poems, Poets, Computers." *American Scholar* 36, no. 3: 394–414.

Queneau, Raymond. 1961. *Cent mille milliards de poèmes* (*One Hundred Thousand Billion Poems*). Paris: Gallimard.

Rasula, Jed. 1977. "Spicer's Orpheus and the Emancipation of Pronouns." *boundary 2* 6, no. 1: 51–102.

RCA. 1963. "Electronic Poetry." *Electronic Age* 22, no. 3: 30–31.

Shirley, Robin. 1972. "Poet and Program." *Bulletin of the Computer Arts Society* 25: 25.

Slater, Avery. 2018. "Cryptomonolingualism: Machine Translation and the Poetics of Automation." *Amodern* 8. https://amodern.net/article/crypto -monolingualism/.

Strachey, Christopher. 1954. "The 'Thinking' Machine." *Encounter* 3, no. 4: 25–31.

Spicer, Jack. 1998. *The House That Jack Built: The Collected Lectures of Jack Spicer*, edited by Peter Gizzi. Middletown, CT: Wesleyan Univ. Press.

Spicer, Jack. 2008. *My Vocabulary Did This to Me: The Collected Poetry of Jack Spicer*. Edited by Peter Gizzi and Kevin Killian. Middletown, CT: Wesleyan Univ. Press.

Wardrip-Fruin, Noah. 2011. "Digital Media Archaeology: Interpreting Computational Processes." In *Media Archaeology: Approaches, Applications, and Implications*, edited by Erkki Huhtamo and Jussi Parikka, 302–22. Berkeley: Univ. of California Press.

Worthy, R. M. 1962. "A New American Poet Speaks: The Works of A[uto] B[eatnik]." *Horizon* 4, no. 3: 96–99.

Yngve, Victor. 1962. "COMIT as an IR Language." *Communications of the ACM* 5, no. 1: 19–28.

Evan Donahue

All the Microworld's a Stage:
Realism in Interactive Fiction
and Artificial Intelligence

Abstract Early in the history of the field of artificial intelligence (AI), a paradigm known as *microworlds* emerged in which researchers constructed computer simulations of aspects of the real world from which their nascent AI systems could learn. Although microworlds were ultimately abandoned, AI researchers have recently called for their return, this time borrowing from the literary genre of interactive fiction, whose forms and conventions they might use to represent the world in text for the purpose of teaching machines to speak. This confluence of literary form and scientific method invites a closer examination of the relationship between word and world in AI research. The author argues for a reading of microworlds research and of AI more broadly through the lens of literary realism and through the literary texts that comprise its data sets and from which researchers expect artificially intelligent machines to learn about the world. The question of what kind of knowledge literature represents lies at the heart of AI research and thus presents an opportunity for a deeper engagement between AI research and literary, game, and media studies.
Keywords microworld, interactive fiction, AI, *TextWorld*, realism

In the opening scene of "Emergence," a 1994 episode of the television series *Star Trek: The Next Generation*, the android Lieutenant Commander Data, played by actor Brent Spiner, stands in the virtual reality holodeck dressed as Prospero and delivers the final monologue of Shakespeare's *Tempest*. Lacking a human body susceptible to human affects and drives, Data often turns to literature to understand what it means to be human. At such times, he is in a position not unlike that of contemporary artificial intelligence (AI) and machine learning systems, which consume vast quantities of text in an attempt to better understand the human world.

Since the late 1980s the AI subfield of natural language processing has embraced the use of statistical models to extract linguistic

American Literature, Volume 95, Number 2, June 2023
DOI 10.1215/00029831-10575049   © 2023 by Duke University Press

knowledge from large data sets of text. This work broadly adopts a scientific realist position within which reality is imagined to consist of a coherent configuration of objects and actions, the structure of which humans learn through experience. This structure is then reflected in the statistical relationships among the nouns and verbs of human languages, through which machines, in turn, can learn about the world. Critics have cautioned that the knowledge language embodies is neither objective nor universal, hinging as it does on the dialects (Lawrence 2021) and biased semantic associations (Bolukbasi et al. 2016) of speakers. However, these concerns understate the magnitude of the difficulty facing scientists who would treat textual data sets as observational data about the world when 50 percent of those data sets turn out to consist of vampires, elves, and romance novels (Bandy and Vincent 2021).

In reducing the diverse textual forms that comprise data sets to homogeneous language data at the level of the word—of phonetics, syntax, and semantics—researchers and critics leave unexamined how the forms into which those words are organized condition their interpretation. In this article, therefore, I argue for broadening both research into and criticism of the scientific realism through which researchers and critics view language data as arising in an unmediated fashion from the physical bodies of human speakers embedded in the real world. In its place I offer a literary realism that takes as its starting point the apparent resemblances between word and world but then proceeds to ask how the conventions and genres of the texts that contain those words shape how we should understand what a machine might learn from them. To effect this substitution, this article takes as its object the recent revival in AI research of an early research paradigm known as *microworlds*, within which researchers build simulated worlds in which to teach AIs about the real world. This return is notable in part because of researchers' explicit borrowings from the conventions of the literary genre of interactive fiction (IF) to construct entirely textual simulated worlds for their machines. As a result, the scientific value of this research rests squarely on the questions of what literature can express about the world that a machine might learn and what a machine can really learn from Shakespeare.

As I suggest here, it is not by treating literature as a neutral representation of reality but, rather, by reading it within its historical and formal context that AI researchers can advance the state of their research and, in so doing, create an opportunity for greater dialogue with critics from the humanities whose concerns about the politics of representation in AI are currently limited by the field's narrow linguistic focus. This article joins recent scholarship that has called for greater dialogue between AI and the humanities (Roberge and Castelle 2021; Philip 2021) and, more specifically, scholars who have begun to consider how we might learn to read AI systems through the texts that constitute them (Hua and Raley 2020; Kirschenbaum 2021).

My argument is divided into four sections. The first section traces the intertwined histories of IF and microworlds research. IF and microworlds emerged from the same historical technologies of simulation, and their subsequent entanglements in AI research invite a consideration of how scholarship in literary, game, and media studies might be brought to bear on scientific work conducted within an aesthetic medium. The next section turns to this scholarship in proposing to read microworlds research as a realist literary form. As with other realist movements, the question is not whether it reflects reality objectively but, rather, how it mediates reality through the conventions of its genre. In the third section I close-read *TextWorld*, a recent microworld informed by the conventions of IF, and suggest that microworld conventions condition their players—both human and machine—to see reality as a neatly organized system of objects and actions to which nouns and verbs can unambiguously refer. The final section advocates for reading microworlds not as scientific models but as literary narratives, offering a promising starting point both for AI researchers seeking to build machines that, like Data, learn by studying texts and for critics interested in addressing questions of power and representation in contemporary AI systems that require greater dialogue between AI and the humanities (Philip 2021).

Interactive Fiction and the Microworlds

Microworlds research emerged in the 1970s and concerned itself with simulations intended to serve as scientific models of the world—reductive yet sound in their essential details (Minsky and Papert 1971: 95). The literary form of IF emerged at the same time and from the same underlying technical substrate, but as a storytelling technology with no pretensions to scientific fidelity. In this section I argue that microworlds and IF represent two interpretive frameworks for making sense of the same fundamental technologies. Consequently, when contemporary researchers explicitly invoke IF in the characterization of their experimental apparatuses, they invite a reading of their experiments in terms of aesthetics, convention, and form. This section begins from the entanglements of microworlds and IF in contemporary AI research and traces their intertwined histories back to the founding moments of each form. I suggest that, on account of this shared history, the literary is a crucially missing dimension of analysis in a contemporary AI that makes liberal use of literary forms.

Interactive Fiction as a Microworld

Like other forms of new media, IF combines elements of older textual forms such as novels and plays with the uniquely computational dimensions of simulation and interactivity. A work of IF is, fundamentally, a computer game in which both the player's input and the game's output are composed primarily of words. The game prints to the screen a textual description of the current state of the game, and players must type a command indicating their next desired move. After this, the game prints a new screen of text describing the new state of the game, and so on. Players' commands and the game's responses generally take the form of simple utterances such as "go north," "get lamp," or "you are in a maze of twisty little passages, all alike" (Crowther and Woods 1977).

Nick Montfort (2005), in *Twisty Little Passages*, takes the exchange of natural language text between player and game to be a defining aspect of the form. The other aspect that he sees as integral is that this exchange of text reveals, bit by bit, a fictional world suspended in the space between the computer's simulation and the player's imagination. One of the earliest works in the form, William Crowther's *Adventure* (1976),[1] from which the above examples were taken, takes place in a simulated cave system, placing the player in the role of a caver whose descent into the cavern gradually takes on elements of the fantastical. It is these worlds and the promise of what knowledge they might bestow on the machine that learns to move through them that have made IF a topic of interest for AI researchers.

From 2016 to 2018 the IEEE Conference on Computational Intelligence in Games ran a competition in which teams of AI researchers competed to develop an AI system capable of playing IF games (Atkinson et al. 2019). Although previous researchers had occasionally used IF as a basis for their experiments (Amir and Doyle 2002; Hlubocky and Amir 2004; Koller et al. 2004), this moment seemed to signal an expanded interest in the form, with significant efforts emerging from major laboratories (Weston et al. 2016; Baroni et al. 2017; Côté et al.

2018). The increase in interest seems to have been precipitated in part by high-profile successes in other games ranging from classic Atari games (Mnih et al. 2013) to the board game Go (Silver et al. 2017). IF appeared to offer researchers an opportunity to extend these successful game-playing techniques to the problem of natural language. If an AI could learn to play a game that requires language, researchers reasoned, this would demonstrate that it must have learned something about language more generally in the process (Atkinson et al. 2019). In designing their IF worlds for AIs to explore, these researchers often explicitly invoked the long abandoned research paradigm of the microworlds, which involved a similar construction of simulated worlds for training AIs.

Microworlds in Early AI

In the early 1970s, MIT AI laboratory directors Marvin Minsky and Seymour Papert (1971) issued a progress report on the first decade of the lab's work. In this report, building on early AI successes in games such as chess, they laid out a vision for future research in AI that revolved around the construction of game-like simulations for teaching AIs about the world. They called these simulations "microworlds" (97). Although Minsky and Papert spoke in mostly speculative terms about the possibilities of microworlds, their vision was nevertheless rooted in the concrete work of two of their graduate students, Terry Winograd and Eugene Charniak and, in particular, in Winograd's thesis project, a program called SHRDLU.

SHRDLU was a language-understanding program, and the language it was capable of understanding and speaking pertained to a simulated microworld that consisted only of a small collection of geometric children's building blocks, an empty box, and a robotic arm for manipulating the blocks. By typing commands to SHRDLU such as "pick up a big red block," it was possible to instruct the program, which controlled the arm in the simulation, to manipulate the blocks, stacking and unstacking them or loading them into or taking them out of the box (Winograd 1971: 38).

This collection of blocks constitutes the microworld that SHRDLU inhabits. By experimenting with different approaches to designing SHRDLU's language-processing faculties, Winograd could investigate the question of machine language use within the restricted context of speech pertaining to geometric physical objects within a narrow interactional frame. Minsky and Papert (1971: 1) extrapolated from SHRDLU to envision an entire collection of microworlds like SHRDLU's "blocks world" within which researchers could teach machines to converse about a range of topics, including "time, space, planning, explaining, causing, doing, preventing, allowing, failing, knowing, intending, wanting, owning, giving, breaking, [and] hurrying" (97). Each concept, they imagined, would have its own microworld containing simulations pertinent to teaching a machine the relevant concept. Although they recognized that each microworld would be a simplification of the complexity of the real world, their hope was that these microworlds could serve as simple introductions to skills on which AIs could build, much as children play with blocks to develop spatial skills.

SHRDLU stands as one of the most iconic examples of early work in AI. In its moment, it presented such a compelling performance of linguistic virtuosity that it received an entire special issue of the journal *Cognitive Psychology* (Winograd 1972). Since then, however, the valence of what SHRDLU symbolizes has shifted along with a wider change in the perception of the field's early history. Once the initial excitement dissipated and progress stalled, SHRDLU, microworlds, and the entire system of methodological assumptions on which early AI was based came to be viewed as a failure that legitimized the turn to the ascendant data-driven and statistical techniques at the end of the 1980s (Crevier 1993).

Against the backdrop of this perceived failure and in recognition of how the modern field often treats this failure as its founding myth, by positioning contemporary methods as overcoming the limitations of earlier approaches, it is striking to find researchers at a modern laboratory arguing explicitly "against received wisdom from the last decades of AI research" in calling for a return to so prominent an exemplar of this earlier moment as the microworlds (Mikolov, Joulin, and Baroni 2018: 6). This call for a return speaks to an undercurrent through the history of AI research that runs deeper than the swirls and eddies of its successive technical strategies. Although the technical methods may change, it seems that researchers past and present share an interpretive lens through which they view microworlds as a means to capture some fragment of human knowledge about language and the world.

The Emergence of Interactive Fiction

In *Twisty Little Passages*, Montfort (2005) takes what he views as the unusual step of identifying Winograd's SHRDLU as the conceptual predecessor of IF, despite the former being a scientific experiment and the latter a literary form. He draws this link on the strength of the formal similarity between the two in terms of both the exchange of words between human and machine and the simulated world to which those words refer. Many of the actions that SHRDLU takes in the blocks world, such as picking up and putting down items and placing them into or taking them out of their container, find direct analogs in the conventions of IF. This similarity may be at least in part due to the common epistemic culture of computer simulation taking shape within MIT and the emerging computing research community in the moment in which both the microworlds and IF took shape. However, there are more specific material and historical connections between SHRDLU and several of the early exemplars of the IF genre, such as *Adventure* and *Zork*. These connections underscore how microworlds research and IF authorship represent two modes of interpreting the same technologies of world simulation and trouble the boundary between science and fiction.

IF emerged in close proximity to the centers of computation research where AI itself had only recently begun to take shape. Programmer William Crowther developed one of the earliest works of IF, *Adventure*, while working at MIT spin-off company Bolt Beranek and Newman (BBN) on the early Arpanet (Jerz 2007). A precursor to the internet, Arpanet connected industry, government, and academic research centers such as BBN and MIT, making the already small world of computing research funded by the Advanced Research Projects Agency (ARPA) smaller still. From BBN in Cambridge, Massachusetts, *Adventure* found its way across the Arpanet to Don Woods at the Stanford AI laboratory, who elaborated on Crowther's initial version. Woods's version subsequently found its way back across the Arpanet to the MIT Dynamic Modeling Group (DMG), inspiring several members of that group to create *Zork* in 1977 (Montfort 2005). *Zork* would subsequently serve as the basis for the founding of the company Infocom in 1979, which would come to define the commercial face of IF in the 1980s.

The emergence of both IF and microworlds in the context of the broader ARPA research community linked by financial, social, and technical networks is suggestive of a developing context that framed researchers' early interpretations of the new technology of computer modeling. The DMG, from which *Zork* emerged, was emblematic of this context. The group took shape in 1970 alongside groups working on computer graphics and networking for the Arpanet (Project MAC 1970: 9). It coalesced around a vision of designing a computer system they called the Dynamic Modeling System, dedicated to building scientific models across a range of fields and equipped with ready-to-use data sets and modeling tools (110). Early group members anticipated using it to model phenomena from neural activity to urban development (75). The DMG shared with microworlds researchers an enthusiasm for the concept of building extensive world models using computer simulation, and this shared outlook is reflected in the confluence of technical platforms upon which these groups planned to construct such models.

Zork was written in a programming language called MDL (Montfort 2005), which was a dialect of Lisp, a language commonly used in AI research in the United States at this time and itself integral to the early history of gaming (Milburn 2018). MDL was developed in 1970 as a collaboration between members of the DMG and those of the MIT AI laboratory (Galley and Pfister 1979: 2). For members of the DMG, MDL represented a language for building simulations that would serve as the basis for their planned scientific modeling workstation (Fredkin 1972: 68). For members of the MIT AI laboratory, by contrast, MDL was a first step toward implementing a more specialized language for AI called PLANNER (Galley and Pfister 1979: 2), a version of which had been used by Winograd and Charniak to implement the two original microworlds (Sussman, Winograd, and Charniak 1971). Significantly, MDL itself was general purpose and not a dedicated modeling language (Project MAC 1970: 120). Rather, what drew these otherwise disparate lines of research together was a shared epistemic intuition about how to represent the world within a program. "In a general sense, when you are interacting with MDL," wrote Stuart Galley and Greg Pfister (1979: 11), the authors of a primer for the language, "you are dealing with a world inhabited only by a particular set of things: MDL objects." It is difficult to say in light of the subsequent history of both microworlds and IF just how broad was MDL's designers' intuitive conception of this MDL world.

When members of the DMG subsequently built the fictional world of *Zork* using MDL, they greatly complicated the question of the relationship between the virtual world and the real. Many of the concerns of the blocks world—putting blocks into boxes and moving them from place to place—reappear in games such as *Zork*, which had to deal with simulating physical phenomena such as deflating a raft to stuff it in a knapsack or letting the current wash it down river (Anderson and Galley 1985). For the *Zork* implementers, designing the fictional game universe was a task of "building reality," or attempting to make the game world consistent with players' intuitions brought over from the real world it seems to depict (5). Conversely, Minsky and Papert (1971: 96), whose project was literally that of representing reality to machines, emphasized the inevitable limitations of the project of building the "fairyland[s]" that were the microworlds, for which, "almost every statement about them would be literally false if asserted about the real world." What makes one an experimental platform for science and the other an expressive medium for interactive literature? As I argue in the next section, the difference between science and fiction in this context rests on one's reading of the relationship between these world simulations and the reality they seem to represent. Moreover, clarifying that relationship for the purpose of research and criticism alike is a central objective of the next three sections.

Artificial Realism

In the middle of Data's monologue as Prospero, Picard interrupts him and begins a conversation in which the characters illustrate two opposing interpretive strategies for making sense of the relationship between literature and reality. Picard informs Data that he has set the holodeck lighting too low for the audience to see the play. "But sir," Data protests, "I am supposed to be attempting a Neo-Platonic magical rite. The darkness is appropriate for such a ritual." Picard replies, "Yes, but Data, this is a play. The audience has to see you" ("Emergence" 1994: act 1, scene 1). This scene is principally concerned with the question of realism in literary interpretation—a reading further underscored when, due to a malfunction in the holodeck's systems, a holographic steam locomotive crashes through the virtual foliage of Prospero's island in a shot reminiscent of the Lumière brothers' 1896 *L'arrivée d'un train en gare de La Ciotat* (*The Arrival of the Train at La Ciotat*), placing Data and Picard in the position of the apocryphal theatergoers who had to decide, at this early moment in the new form, whether or not the oncoming train was real. In this scene, Data and Picard give voice to two alternative conceptions of realism that, as I argue in this section, will help clarify the ontological status of the microworlds.

Data seeks the message of literature in the most literal interpretation of its contents. By turning the holodeck into a precise model of the Mediterranean island described in Shakespeare's play, he imagines that he will come to understand the characters that inhabit it. Picard, by contrast, asserts that details such as the lighting of the ritual are irrelevant if they inhibit the play's ability to communicate its message to its audience. This opposition between the representations the play contains and the narrative it conveys turns on where one locates the realism of the play. I suggest that the circulation of literary forms within microworlds research invites an investigation of how the microworlds, as literature, construct so compelling a rendering of reality as to make them seem suitable instruments for the scientific study of the reality they appear to depict. Drawing on literary, game, and media studies, this section places microworlds within the tradition of realism in literature and art.

Alexander Galloway (2004) calls the relationship between the virtual worlds of gaming and the real world the most important question in game studies. For Galloway, this relationship offers a means to think about how games shape the worldviews of their players. For a similar reason, this question may be the most important in microworlds research as well, as it is from these simulations that machines come to understand the world they are increasingly being used to govern. It is therefore crucial to find an appropriate frame through which to analyze how games shape the worlds of players both human and machine. Games scholars, including Galloway, have tended to see the medium as split by a central tension between the two broad expressive modes voiced by Data and Picard. Although scholars dichotomize this tension using a range of terms that highlight different aspects—*realistic-ness* against *social realism* (Galloway 2004), *virtual realism* versus *virtual fictionalism* (Chalmers 2017), *sensory* against *non-sensory* (Shinkle 2020), *depictive* versus *immersive* (Tavinor 2019), and *simulation* against *narrative* or *fiction* (McClancy 2018; Aarseth 2007)—common to many of these analyses is the division between iconicity and diegesis: between elements of the simulation that resemble or correspond in some way to the world they ostensibly represent (Data's meticulous holographic set design) and the overall effect those elements have on shaping the experience of the player (Picard's advocacy on behalf of the viewing experience of the audience).

Fredric Jameson views this tension between representation and narrative as the fundamental paradox of literary realism. In his essay "The Existence of Italy," Jameson (2013: 228) describes realist movements in art as caught in a paradox. To represent the world as it really is, the artist would have to abandon all pretense of perspective, embellishment, and intention—an impossibility inherent in the very notion of artistic creation. To imagine microworlds as scientific models of reality, given that they are built of the same formal elements as IF, would be to imagine that it is possible to objectively represent the world in a literary text. Numerous critics from throughout the field's history have detailed how microworlds systematically fall short of such a goal (Dreyfus 1981; Collins 1990; Edwards 1996; Turkle 2005; Adam 2006). Yet, as Jameson (2013: 228) argues of literature, this failure is not all that can be said of realist movements. Rather, he suggests examining how realist movements "program" their audiences to see reality in terms of their representations by deploying their specific narrative forms, and surely in comparison with AI, no audience has ever been so programmable. Documentary techniques in film, collage in painting, and detailed description in the novel each achieve, in their respective mediums, what Roland Barthes (1995) calls the "reality effect." The next section clarifies the workings of microworlds by closely reading an example of one, attending to the specific forms it uses to achieve its reality effects. Through what formal conventions of simulation do the microworlds make the Italy of Shakespeare's *Tempest* seem to exist for researchers?

Text and World in *TextWorld*

In 2018, AI researchers at Microsoft research released *TextWorld*, a modern microworld for teaching AIs about language that draws explicitly on the genre conventions of IF and, indeed, was built in part using the Inform 7 IF authoring tool (Côté et al. 2018). These researchers position *TextWorld* as a complement to data sets of human-authored texts in that the procedurally generated nature of the IF world permits the creation of data sets both large enough for contemporary data-intensive methods and composed of generated sentences that are cleaner and grammatically simpler than human-authored sentences, allowing for a more precisely controlled exploration of models' limitations (El Asri 2019). From the perspective of the present article, *TextWorld* is especially interesting because the researchers themselves are the authors of the generated texts, and because they have made *TextWorld* available for research use, by reading (or, rather, playing) *TextWorld* it becomes possible to explore their own intuitions about language and machines beyond what they express in the research papers that describe their work. If, as Patrick Jagoda (2020) argues, games exhibit an experimental logic that blurs the boundary between science and fiction, then this section takes Jagoda at his word by playing the experiment that is *TextWorld* as a game in order to understand the specific form of the reality effect that accomplishes that blurring.

The paper that introduces *TextWorld* opens with an epigraph from Wittgenstein's *Tractatus Logico-Philosophicus* (2002: 74): "The limits of my language mean the limits of my world." In its original context, this passage argues for a tight relationship between words and the objects they name. A proposition is a "picture" of a fact, Wittgenstein writes (18). The world is imagined as a vast tableau with every object intricately positioned in relation to all others. Atop this scene, language rests like the topographic map of Borges's "On the Rigor of Science" (1981)—a map so large that it corresponds precisely, mile for mile, with the territory it maps. The mountains and canyons of the real world reappear as symbols in the microworld embedded in a geography of words that mirrors the geography of the things those words name. If the novel has its extraneous details, the microworld has a correspondence between words and things that seems always to promise that, if there were just enough things in the simulation and enough words to name them, the real world and the virtual could be made to coincide. It is the nature of this correspondence that this section investigates through its engagements with *TextWorld*.

TextWorld for Humans

TextWorld exists in two versions, one a demonstration for human players and the other the training environment for machines, which together constitute the complete text of *TextWorld*. The demonstration version offers players a text-based interface through which they can control their avatar and read descriptions of the world. Upon starting this version, players are presented with instructions informing them of their goal. "You are hungry!" they are informed, "Let's cook a delicious meal. Check the cookbook in the kitchen for the recipe. Once done, enjoy your meal!" (Microsoft Research n.d.). These instructions constitute the "quest," or game objective the player must satisfy. After reading this prologue, players are further informed that they are in the "backyard," along with several simulated objects including a patio table, a BBQ, and a screen door (see fig. 1). Players are then presented with a blinking cursor with which they can type one of the small number of commands recognized as valid by the system. Typing *open screen door* informs them that the door has been opened. *Go south* further informs them that they pass through the screen door into the kitchen, where they observe various new objects, such as the "fridge" and "oven." The game proceeds like this, with players typing instructions for simple actions and the game updating its simulation in

```
-= Backyard =-
You find yourself in a backyard.

You make out a patio table. But the thing is empty. You see a patio
chair. Wow, isn't TextWorld just the best? The patio chair is stylish.
But there isn't a thing on it. You see a gleam over in a corner, where
you can see a BBQ.

There is a closed screen door leading south. There is a closed wooden
door leading west. There is an exit to the east. Don't worry, there is no
door.

>open screen door
You open screen door.

>go south

-= Kitchen =-
You've just shown up in a kitchen.
```

Figure 1   *TextWorld* game play. Source: Côté et al. 2018

response, informing them of the new state of the world via text. After "getting" the chicken leg from the fridge, "going" south, west, west, and north through the grid-like "corridor," "driveway," "street," and "supermarket," "getting" black pepper and milk, and retracing one's steps to the kitchen, players can then "cook chicken leg with oven" and "prepare" and "eat" the meal to complete the game.

It is readily apparent from this brief playthrough that *TextWorld* leans heavily on the conventions of IF in a number of areas that researchers do not see as integral to the project of world representation. Size, distance, and direction are all stylized in accordance with the conventions of IF. Moreover, all actions subsume a range of contextually specific interpretations opaque to the computational system. The verb *get* moves the "chicken leg" from the fridge to the player's inventory, glossing over the actions of opening, reaching, and grasping, and likewise moves the "milk" from the store to the player's inventory, glossing over the entire act of shopping and paying. The oven can be opened but not turned on, yet "cook chicken leg with oven" produces "grilled chicken leg," implicitly operating the oven. These actions even extend to contexts that make little sense in the narrative setting due to the procedural nature of their implementation. For instance, *cook milk with bbq* produces "grilled milk," uniformly extending the procedural logic of the chicken leg, although leaving unexplained precisely what grilled milk is. The lackluster education in home economics that *TextWorld* engenders is immaterial to the researchers who designed it, except to the extent that it offers them something about which to generate sentences, and this relationship between those sentences and that world, for these researchers, constitutes the reality of *TextWorld*.

The reality effect specific to microworlds research is created by a perceived congruence between the words processed by the system and the objects inhabiting its simulated world. *Milk* and *chicken* are concrete, distinct terms that refer unambiguously to the simulated milk and chicken objects. *Get* and *cook* likewise refer to specific actions within that world. These relationships are real for researchers in the sense that, were one only to replace the simulated objects with their real-world counterparts, the sentences formed by *get milk* and *cook chicken* would immediately become real sentences spoken about real things by force of their correspondence to the real world, which is imagined to mirror the structure of the simulation in the manner described in Wittgenstein's *Tractatus*.

The specific realism of microworlds is a response to what *TextWorld* researcher Layla El Asri (2019) describes as one of the most important problems facing the field of natural language processing: determining whether or not a machine that speaks is speaking correctly. Currently, when researchers build new conversational systems, they typically report one of several quantitative measures, such as a BLEU score, which reflects how closely the machine's conversational responses accord with responses produced by a human speaker. As El Asri notes, no one is happy with these automatic metrics because researchers recognize that, for a conversation of any complexity, there are innumerable equally valid directions in which to take the conversation. For *TextWorld*'s creators, microworlds offer a more satisfying measure of whether a conversational utterance is correct: if it is syntactically incorrect, the interface will not accept it, and if it is semantically incorrect, the AI will not complete the game. A sentence accepted by the parser that moves the game forward is therefore a "real sentence" and demonstrates a real command of language. The language is real even though the world is not, because its reality lies in the correspondence between sentence and simulation. The fictive world projected by the simulated objects and generated prose need not be real, but the knowledge of language it imparts to AIs must be, or else the project is without purpose—AIs that play IF are of no interest unless, in playing IF, they become able to act elsewhere in the world as well. In this sense, the most important questions of AI and of video game studies converge on the subject of just what is the relationship between the virtual and the real.

TextWorld for Machines

Despite exemplifying the logic of microworlds, the online demonstration version of *TextWorld* is still in part authored for a human audience and so does not offer a complete picture of this logic as it governs the interactions of machinic players. For instance, on entering the kitchen, players are confronted with an empty counter along with the text, "What, you think everything in TextWorld should have stuff on it?" and in the pantry with, "The room seems oddly familiar, as though it were only superficially different from the other rooms in the building" (Microsoft Research n.d.). Both remarks gesture ironically toward the formal quirks of the IF genre and of the simulation itself. A computer, of course, would have no way to make sense of them and no way to produce them within the simulation unless they were authored by the researchers. These lines reveal an authorial hand at work assisting human players in imagining a domestic setting about which AI players must learn. Much as in the realist novel, stray details unrelated to the game objective seem to round out the simulated world for the human player. Yet for AIs encountering *TextWorld* in a research context, such imaginative aids and the diegetic world they help to portray are absent. In their place, there is only a vast network of correspondences that do not cohere into a recognizable setting.

Stepping from the demonstration version of *TextWorld* into one of the procedurally generated worlds of the research version meant for AIs is a step from the real into the surreal. Because the rooms, objects, and instructions are all randomly generated, the thematic coherence of the domestic kitchen scene is lost in a labyrinth of nouns. Generating a random world, the computer player may be charged, for instance, with the quest of finding the "launderette" and moving the "sponge" from the "rack" to the "shelf" (Côté et al. 2018). Emerging from the "Steamy Sauna," the computer must wander through the "Pleasant Chamber," the "Forgotten Closet," the "Still Cubicle," and the "Balmy Canteen" in its quest for the launderette. Along the way it notices assorted objects strewn about, including "a laptop," "a ladle," "a pear," and "a fly larva." Other microworld projects have taken the combinatorial logic of *Text-World* further still in replacing the word tokens themselves with nonsense strings of characters, further complicating the notion that language is what these worlds contain and what the AIs that dwell in them must learn (Weston et al. 2016). An AI that successfully undoes the shifting verbiage in which the structure of this world is cloaked can perhaps recover the organization of the rooms and objects from which it was built, but as Jason Weston et al. (2016: 9) have noted, this structure itself is of little interest and is as easily programmed into the AI as into the program that generated the world in the first place. What these researchers value is the ability to sift through ever-changing permutations of text and recover the ontological structure that underlies it, and it is the view of reality as a stable referent that bears the weight of language and contours words to fit the hills and valleys of the world that microworlds program their players, both human and machine, to see.

These two versions of *TextWorld* highlight a fissure between the two forms of realism through which the underlying technology of world simulation can be viewed. The realism of microworlds is that of the correspondence between words and objects, but this correspondence is, ironically, experienced by players of IF as the most artificial aspect of the form. Human players are often unable to perform the most basic tasks in these simulated worlds due to the "guess the verb" problem—their inability to guess how the simulation authors have ontologized language and reality into which words and objects (Plotkin 2011). Attempting to *buy* the milk at the grocery store, for instance, does nothing and in so doing shatters the immersion of the simulation as technical frustrations rise to the forefront of a human player's consciousness. All players bring their own assumptions about the salient words and objects in the simulated world and so resurrect the evaluative hurdle of deciding whose language is correct, which *TextWorld* researchers explicitly sought to avoid. Players of IF who learn to discipline their inputs are acting out an artificial, machinic logic, whereas machines that do so in the context of microworlds research have come to learn to speak real language. By viewing *TextWorld* through the lens of literary form, it becomes possible to perceive the complexity of its relationship to reality, which viewing it as a scientific model seeks to foreclose.

If there is knowledge in *TextWorld* that may be of use to machines, it lies not in viewing the simulation as a world but in viewing it as a text. As the researchers themselves acknowledge in their self-deprecating flavor text, *TextWorld* is, as both text and world, a maze of twisty little passages, all alike. In this very act of acknowledgment, however, they situate the genre conventions of *TextWorld* within the longer history of literary forms to which it really does speak. The selections and omissions through which the demonstration version unfolds its portrayal of domestic life contain more information about its human creators than an infinite terrain of data comprising representations and devoid of narrative. If Wittgenstein is to be the epigraph of

TextWorld, perhaps it is not the *Tractatus* but his later *Philosophical Investigations* (1986), which imagines language not as a picture but as a game, that best reflects the promise of a text like *TextWorld*. As I argue in the next section, attending not to what *TextWorld* depicts but to how it is designed to be played offers the most promising avenue toward a synthesis of the concerns of AI and game, media, and literary studies.

Microworlds as Literature

If it is not by reconstructing the correspondences between his holographic scene and the ritual elements of Shakespeare's island, how is Data to learn from Shakespeare? AI researcher Patrick Winston spent much of his career in pursuit of this question, using computer simulations of plays such as *Macbeth* to teach AIs about humanity. "Shakespeare," he notes, "was pretty good at his portrayal of the human condition" (quoted in Rosen 2018). However, as Janet Murray (2017: 198) observes in *Hamlet on the Holodeck*, Winston's system only ever managed to produce superficial readings of the text, concluding after one such analysis, for instance, that "Macbeth murders Duncan because . . . Macbeth is evil." This section revisits Winston's question and considers what it would mean for a computer to read Shakespeare through the lens not of a scientific realism that attempts to extract meaning from the text but of a literary realism that understands the text and its representations as themselves responses by their authors to a particular historical moment and against a backdrop of genre conventions.

This section joins recent work such as Mendon-Plasek 2021, which draws on Vygotskian theories of social learning to recast machine learning as a social process that includes researchers themselves alongside algorithms in its scope, but I instead focus in particular on how theories of literature, games, and media might further our understanding of how and what machines might learn from texts. Marie-Laure Ryan's (1991) work on narrative theory and AI offers a useful point of departure since; although her aim is to draw on the metaphors of AI and microworlds to inform literary theory, her arguments work just as well in reverse for conceptualizing the obstacles confronting AI in making sense of literature. Per Ryan, the most obvious difficulty with treating texts as homogeneous language data is how different genres may depart from the psychology, sociology, or even physics of the real world and, consequently, color the linguistic associations available for machines to learn; for instance; neck biting is more likely to appear in different constructions in vampire fiction than in romances. The unevenness of the textual terrain implies that caution is needed in untangling the relationships between words and genres, as has been underscored by difficulties plaguing systems such as Google's toxic comment classifier, Perspective, which learned to associate marginalized racial, sexual, and gender identities with toxicity due to their appearance as slurs in comments labeled as toxic but then carried such associations over into its interpretations of other genres of texts (Roberge and Castelle 2021). Efforts to ensure equal demographic representation in data sets must consider not only word counts but also the contexts of those counts. Yet, this is only the most superficial lesson of this analysis.

As Ryan (1991) continues, the trouble is not just that fictional worlds stray from the real world but that they remain entangled at multiple levels. When the fictional Sherlock Holmes takes up residence on the real Baker Street, or when the real John Smith and Jane Doe take the stage as the fictional Othello and Desdemona, it becomes impossible to separate fiction from reality or to present an AI system with clear categories delimiting what it should and should not consider to constitute knowledge (Ryan 1991). Watching Picard council Data on his Prospero with the knowledge that Stewart, a decade later, would himself appear as Prospero in Rupert Goold's production of *The Tempest* (Doran 2020) offers more to the understanding than what the scene appears to represent—a dialogue between a fictional starship captain and his lieutenant. The confusion of levels to which Ryan points highlights how every work of literature is always embedded within the broader system of social signs and signifiers that constitute human culture—a play within a play. The mythic figures that represent reality objectively in one moment, Ryan (1991: 76) notes, become the dramatis personae of the next.

Ryan's invocation of myth offers a useful frame for clarifying what microworlds research lacks. The characters of myth in one respect inhabit fantastical worlds that do not map clearly onto the real world. However, by staging human dramas in these fantastical worlds with which audiences can connect, they can in many respects become truer to life than the most detailed simulation. For Northrop Frye (2015), myth is an extreme form of the romance genre, which he opposes directly to the genre of realism. At its extreme, realism becomes satire, and satire is precisely what results from AI's effort to simulate reality too exactly. When we find ourselves holding "grilled milk," it is because the simulation of cooking diverges uncannily from our expectations of the world the simulation promises. Even if the designers of *TextWorld* updated the simulation, the lesson of the last half century of microworlds research has been that, in attempting to scale the simulation up to ever greater fidelity, one must inevitably introduce new incongruities at a rate faster than they can be patched over. The microworld, it seems, can be either complete or consistent, but never both. The romance, by contrast, adopts archetypes that clearly diverge from a realist portrayal yet nevertheless uses these archetypes to tell stories that comment on the reality that readers inhabit. It is the stories that authors choose to tell, more than the representations through which they tell them, that constitute the knowledge that literature offers to machines.

Despite the representational sophistication of microworlds, nothing ever happens in them. They lack characters and narratives in which those characters might take part. *TextWorld* stands empty, as if a cataclysmic event removed all the people so suddenly that the grocery store is still neatly stocked. Figures with names like "John" and "Mary" do appear in the microworld of Weston et al. (2016), but they drift wordlessly through an empty house, transporting objects as if preparing for some ghostly nativity scene. Minsky and Papert (1971) imagined microworlds of the future instructing machines on the intricacies of human social realities, but to this point there seems to have been little inclination to represent the characters and dialogue on which such instruction must depend. Despite being technologies intended to teach machines about language, since SHRDLU no word has ever been uttered in these microworlds. Rather, the central action of the microworld seems to be the rearrangement of objects in an endless homage to SHRDLU's blocks. Since the publication of Minsky and Papert's report, the blocks world has become the *Madonna and Child* of AI, reproduced in countless variations in eternal anticipation of the arrival of the thing they represent.

The history of IF is likewise colored by the tension between simulation and story and offers a means to conceptualize narrative in the microworld. Like microworlds, many early Infocom works such as *Zork* were devoid of character and dialogue (Salter 2020). Nameless players inhabited empty worlds filled with puzzles. Like *TextWorld*, the underground kingdom of *Zork* was largely abandoned. One illustrative exception, however, was one of the company's final titles, *Plundered Hearts* (1987). Unlike previous titles, *Plundered Hearts* drew explicitly on the genre conventions of the romance novel, situating a young seventeenth-century woman as the protagonist in a story of love and piracy on the high seas. As lead designer Amy Briggs (1987) describes it, "You don't go around collecting treasure. . . . You're trying to save people. I like to think my puzzles are more about relationships between characters than being player versus objects." *Plundered Hearts* utilizes the same techniques of simulation as earlier works but puts them in the service of a novelistic narrative and writerly characters that, while more written than simulated, nevertheless manage to feel livelier, argues Anastasia Salter (2020), than even some of the more technically complex character simulations in earlier games, such as the figure of the "thief" in *Zork*, which players periodically encounter but that never emerges as a complete dramatic character within the game.

From the perspective of microworlds research, *Plundered Hearts* makes clear that much of what exists within the world is not reducible to its simulation but, rather, depends crucially on the narrative world that simulation is put in the service of supporting. *TextWorld* may be able to procedurally generate millions of rooms, but they cohere into a house only in the human-authored version, which contains relatively few rooms. The surrealist passageways of the procedurally generated version may be more computationally demanding, but as Laine Nooney (2013) reminds us, the selection of a simple house as a setting in place of a mystical cave or an intergalactic battlefield is a decision laden with significance.

Reconceptualizing microworlds not as models but as stories leads directly back to the earliest moments in the field. While the blocks world occupied most of the attention of Minsky and Papert's (1971) report and of the AI community at the time, the second microworld they detail in that report, created by Eugene Charniak, may prove useful in thinking through the narrative dimensions of microworlds and of AI research more generally. Charniak's "children's story environment" consisted of children's stories (1)—short vignettes of children engaged in various activities that a computer was meant to understand—rather than blocks. In contrast with the apparent success of SHRDLU, Charniak's work encountered difficulties in parsing these stories, and it is in his reflections on these difficulties that he raises questions still germane to contemporary efforts.

In grappling with how a machine could understand stories, Charniak (1972) encountered the irresolvable difficulties of realist representation. He illustrates the limitations of microworlds simulations through the consideration of a short story about a child retrieving money from a piggy bank. Engaging in what he knows to be an impossible task, he attempts to articulate on the page every fact necessary to fully understand the story and to be able to demonstrate that understanding by answering questions about it, from the physical parameters typical of piggy banks to the cultural customs surrounding them. He concludes ultimately that understanding the story requires a seemingly inexhaustible reserve of knowledge not contained within the text. The field of AI leading up to the modern return to microworlds has labored under the belief that if the simulation could be made sophisticated enough or the data set large enough, it would ultimately contain all the knowledge an AI system would need to answer any question. However, each text that forms a part of these data sets rests on assumptions and conventions about how it will be read that exceed the representations that make it up. The significance that *TextWorld* takes place in a kitchen escapes explicit recognition within *TextWorld* itself. If many of the questions one might wish to ask about the story went beyond the story's explicit text, then as a matter of experimental method, Charniak asks, "how far beyond the story may the questions go?" (6).

Like many questions inspired by children's stories, this one is at once simple and profound. As a science, AI demands the ability to make a determination of the correctness of machine language use. Yet considered as stories, microworlds demand a consideration of their historical and formal context that necessarily exceeds their explicit contents. Reflecting on questions of narrative in microworlds research, Charniak (1972: 271) is further led to consider whether it might not be worthwhile to consider the "larger patterns" that shape the nature of the text itself, from "the narrator's (or author's) biases, or attitudes about the story" to questions "such as those encountered in English literature courses."

The message for contemporary AI more broadly is that the very notion of attempting to contain all relevant knowledge in a data set is as impossible a project as producing the literary work that portrays an unmediated view of reality. No data set, however vast, can contain the assumptions that guided its own creation. Yet, in considering AI systems as engaged in literary interpretation, it is these assumptions—the decisions *TextWorld* researchers had to make about what to represent and what to omit about the act of cooking—that most reveal how the human authors of the texts that comprise these data sets understand the world. The impossibility of objective truth in the consideration of such questions shatters the illusion of the scientific foundation that microworlds have long seemed to promise research-ers, leaving in its place only the promise of the endless regress of lit-erary meaning. Yet it is precisely from that point that AI and its critics, informed by literature, game, and media studies, can now advance.

Conclusion

In this article I have argued that the questions of AI are deeply engaged with questions of form and representation central to literary, game, and media studies. What if it were possible to imagine the work of AI undertaken from the perspective of those disciplines alongside those of computer science and linguistics? The very technical success of the AI project depends on adopting a more nuanced understanding of rep-resentation. Moreover, such an understanding hinges crucially on rec-ognizing the historical and political conditions of the constructions of texts and textual data sets that form the nexus of much contemporary criticism. Reckoning with literature in AI with the full complexity this task requires is at the heart of the technical, social, and political prob-lems that face contemporary AI.

In a lecture, Brent Spiner (2019) reflected on being asked to portray Data at a time when the term *android* was not in wide use. He remarked that he had attempted to be as restrained as possible. "The character said quite often, 'I do not have feelings,'" he explained, "but people would write me and say, 'Oh, I can see you were feeling something in that scene.'" In reflecting on microworlds past, present, and future, it is worth asking how much of being human consists in recreating the human experience in exacting detail, and how much is simply projected onto us by our audiences by virtue of the roles we play in the dramas of their own lives. At the dawn of AI, Alan Turing (1950: 11) proposed his now well-known Turing test for machine intelligence: the machine must imitate a human being. The example of human behavior he chose to illustrate that game was the explication of Shakespeare's son-net 18, "Shall I Compare Thee to a Summer's Day?" "The idea of 'intel-ligence' is itself emotional rather than mathematical," wrote Turing ([1948] 2004: 4). It is not a concept that can be captured in the mathe-matical representations of a scientific model; rather, it is something we will ascribe to machines once they can offer us a convincing per-formance of their humanity. If AI begins from the premise that it seeks to create not human beings as such but literary characters such as those that inhabit the narrative worlds of interactive fiction, it may discover that all the microworld's a stage, and all the men, women, and machines merely players.

Evan Donahue is a scholar of computational media and is currently a postdoctoral fellow at Tokyo College at the University of Tokyo. His work focuses on artificial intelligence history and practice, in particular, questions of language. He is currently working on a book titled *Android Semiotics* that traces competing theories of language and communication through the history of AI.

Note

1   This work, also called variously *Colossal Cave Adventure* and *ADVENT* due to the complex history of the game's authorship (see Jerz 2007), is referred to in this article simply as *Adventure*.

References

Aarseth, Espen. 2007. "Doors and Perception: Fiction vs. Simulation in Games." *Intermédialités / Intermediality*, no. 9: 35–44. https://doi.org/10.7202/1005528ar.

Adam, Alison. 2006. *Artificial Knowing: Gender and the Thinking Machine*. London: Routledge.

Amir, Eyal, and Patrick Doyle. 2002. "Adventure Games: A Challenge for Cognitive Robotics." In *Proceedings of the International Cognitive Robotics Workshop*, 148–55. Menlo Park, CA: AAAI Press.

Anderson, Tim, and Stu Galley. 1985. "The History of Zork." *New Zork Times* 4, no. 1. https://archive.org/details/New_Zork_Times_The_Vol._IV_No._1_1985-03_Infocom_US/page/n5/mode/2up.

Atkinson, Timothy, Hendrik Baier, Tara Copplestone, Sam Devlin, and Jerry Swan. 2019. "The Text-Based Adventure AI Competition." *IEEE Transactions on Games* 11, no. 3: 260–66. https://doi.org/10.1109/TG.2019.2896017.

Bandy, John, and Nicholas Vincent. 2021. "Addressing 'Documentation Debt' in Machine Learning: A Retrospective Datasheet for Bookcorpus." In *Proceedings of the Neural Information Processing Systems Track on Datasets and Benchmarks*, edited by J. Vanschoren and S. Yeung. Vol. 1. https://datasets-benchmarks-proceedings.neurips.cc/paper/2021/file/54229abfcfa5649e7003b83dd4755294-Paper-round1.pdf.

Baroni, Marco, Armand Joulin, Allan Jabri, Germàn Kruszewski, Angeliki Lazaridou, Klemen Simonic, and Tomas Mikolov. 2017. "CommAI: Evaluating the First Steps towards a Useful General AI." Preprint, arXiv. Preprint, arXiv. https://arxiv.org/abs/1701.08954.

Barthes, Roland. 1995. "The Reality Effect." In *The Realist Novel*, edited by Dennis Walder, 269–72. London: Routledge.

Bolukbasi, Tolga, Kai-Wei Chang, James Zou, Venkatesh Saligrama, and Adam Kalai. 2016. "Man Is to Computer Programmer as Woman Is to Homemaker? Debiasing Word Embeddings." In *Proceedings of the 30th International Conference on Neural Information Processing Systems* (NIPS'16), edited by Isabelle Guyon et al., 4356–64. Red Hook, NY: Curran Associates.

Briggs, Amy. 1987. "Infocom's First Romance: Plundered Hearts." *Status Line* 6, no. 4. https://www.ifarchive.org/if-archive/infocom/articles/NZT-Briggs .txt.

Chalmers, David J. 2017. "The Virtual and the Real." *Disputatio* 9, no. 46: 309–52. https://doi.org/10.1515/disp-2017-0009.

Charniak, Eugene. 1972. "Toward a Model of Children's Story Comprehension." PhD diss., MIT.

Collins, Harry. 1990. *Artificial Experts: Social Knowledge and Intelligent Machines.* Cambridge, MA: MIT Press.

Côté, Marc-Alexandre, et al. 2018. "TextWorld: A Learning Environment for Text-Based Games." Preprint, arXiv. https://arxiv.org/abs/1806.11532.

Crevier, Daniel. 1993. *AI: The Tumultuous History of the Search for Artificial Intelligence.* New York: Basic Books.

Crowther, Will, and Don Woods. 1977. "Adventure. [Aka 'Advent' and 'Colossal Cave'] Fortran Source Code." Interactive Fiction Archive. http://mirror .ifarchive.org/if-archive/games/source/adv350-pdp10.tar.gz.

Doran, Gregory. 2020. "Happy Birthday Patrick Stewart." https://www.rsc.org .uk/news/archive/happy-birthday-patrick-stewart.

Dreyfus, Hubert. 1981. "From Micro-Worlds to Knowledge Representation: AI at an Impasse." In *Mind Design II: Philosophy, Psychology, Artificial Intelligence*, edited by John Haugeland, 161–204. Cambridge, MA: MIT Press.

Edwards, Paul. 1996. *The Closed World: Computers and the Politics of Discourse in Cold War America.* Cambridge, MA: MIT Press.

El Asri, Layla. 2019. "Talking with Machines with Dr. Layla El Asri." *Microsoft Research Podcast*, February 20. https://www.microsoft.com/en-us/research /podcast/talking-with-machines-with-dr-layla-el-asri/.

"Emergence." 1994. *Star Trek: The Next Generation.* Season 7, episode 3. Directed by Cliff Bole. Script by Brannon Braga. Teleplay by Joe Menosky.

Fredkin, Edward. 1972. "Project Mac Progress Report IX July 1971 to July 1972." AD 756689. Cambridge, MA: MIT.

Frye, Northrop. 2015. *Anatomy of Criticism.* Princeton, NJ: Princeton Univ. Press.

Galley, Stuart, and Greg Pfister. 1979. "The MDL Programming Language." Cambridge, MA: MIT Press.

Galloway, Alexander. 2004. "Social Realism in Gaming." *Game Studies* 4, no. 1. http://www.gamestudies.org/0401/galloway/.

Hlubocky, Brian, and Eyal Amir. 2004. "Knowledge-Gathering Agents in Adventure Games." In *AAAI-04 Workshop on Challenges in Game AI*, 63–66. Menlo Park, CA: AAAI Press.

Hua, Minh, and Rita Raley. 2020. "Playing with Unicorns: AI Dungeon and Citizen NLP." *DHQ: Digital Humanities Quarterly* 14, no. 4: 179–98. http:// www.digitalhumanities.org/dhq/vol/14/4/000533/000533.html.

Jagoda, Patrick. 2020. *Experimental Games: Critique, Play, and Design in the Age of Gamification.* Chicago: Univ. of Chicago Press.

Jameson, Fredric. 2013. *Signatures of the Visible.* New York: Routledge.

Jerz, Dennis. 2007. "Somewhere Nearby Is Colossal Cave: Examining Will Crowther's Original 'Adventure' in Code and in Kentucky." *Digital Humanities Quarterly* 1, no. 2: 2.

Kirschenbaum, Matthew. 2021. "Spec Acts: Reading Form in Recurrent Neural Networks." *ELH* 88, no. 2: 361–86.

Koller, Alexander, Ralph Debusmann, Malte Gabsdil, and Kristina Striegnitz. 2004. "Put My Galakmid Coin into the Dispenser and Kick It: Computational Linguistics and Theorem Proving in a Computer Game." *Journal of Logic, Language and Information* 13, no. 2: 187–206.

Lawrence, Halcyon. 2021. "Siri Disciplines." In *Your Computer Is on Fire*, edited by Thomas Mullaney, Benjamin Peters, Mar Hicks, and Kavita Philip. Cambridge, MA: MIT Press.

McClancy, Kathleen. 2018. "The Wasteland of the Real: Nostalgia and Simulacra in Fallout." *Game Studies* 18, no. 2. http://gamestudies.org/1802/articles/mcclancy.

Mendon-Plasek, Aaron. 2021. "Mechanized Significance and Machine Learning: Why It Became Thinkable and Preferable to Teach Machines to Judge the World." In *The Cultural Life of Machine Learning: An Incursion into Critical AI Studies*, edited by Jonathan Roberge and Michael Castelle, 31–78. New York: Palgrave Macmillan.

Microsoft Research. n.d. "TextWorld." Microsoft Research. https://www.microsoft.com/en-us/research/project/textworld/try-it/ (accessed April 15. 2022).

Mikolov, Tomas, Armand Joulin, and Marco Baroni. 2018. "A Roadmap towards Machine Intelligence." In *Computational Linguistics and Intelligent Text Processing*, edited by Alexander Gelbukh, 29–61. Cham: Springer.

Milburn, Colin. 2018. *Respawn: Gamers, Hackers, and Technogenic Life*. Durham, NC: Duke Univ. Press.

Minsky, Marvin, and Seymour Papert. 1971. "Progress Report on Artificial Intelligence." AIM 252. Cambridge, MA: MIT.

Mnih, Volodymyr, Koray Kavukcuoglu, David Silver, Alex Graves, Ioannis Antonoglou, Daan Wierstra, and Martin A. Riedmiller. 2013. "Playing Atari with Deep Reinforcement Learning." Preprint, arXiv. http://arxiv.org/abs/1312.5602.

Montfort, Nick. 2005. *Twisty Little Passages: An Approach to Interactive Fiction*. Cambridge, MA: MIT Press.

Murray, Janet. 2017. *Hamlet on the Holodeck: The Future of Narrative in Cyberspace*. Cambridge, MA: MIT Press.

Nooney, Laine. 2013. "A Pedestal, a Table, a Love Letter: Archaeologies of Gender in Videogame History." *Game Studies* 13, no. 2. http://gamestudies.org/1302/articles/nooney.

Philip, Kavita. 2021. "How to Stop Worrying about Clean Signals and Start Loving the Noise." In *Your Computer Is on Fire*, edited by Thomas Mullaney, Benjamin Peters, Mar Hicks, and Kavita Philip, 363–376. Cambridge, MA: MIT Press.

Plotkin, Andrew. 2011. "Characterizing, If Not Defining, Interactive Fiction." In *IF Theory Reader*, edited by Kevin Jackson-Mead and J. Robinson Wheeler, 59–66. Boston: Transcript On Press.

Project MAC. 1970. "Project Mac Progress Report VII July 1969 to July 1970." AD 732767. Cambridge, MA: MIT.

Roberge, Jonathan, and Michael Castelle. 2021. "Toward an End-to-End Sociology of Twenty-First-Century Machine Learning." In *The Cultural Life of Machine Learning: An Incursion into Critical AI Studies*, edited by Jonathan Roberge and Michael Castelle, 1–30. New York: Palgrave Macmillan.

Rosen, Andy. 2018. "Toil and Trouble: How 'Macbeth' Could Teach Computers to Think." *Boston Globe*, June 2. https://www3.bostonglobe.com/metro/2018/06/02/toil-and-trouble-how-macbeth-could-teach-computers-think/h9kbBEX7BVkp4Rc6XbJrPM/story.html?arc404=true.

Ryan, Marie-Laure. 1991. *Possible Worlds, Artificial Intelligence, and Narrative Theory*. Bloomington: Indiana Univ. Press.

Salter, Anastasia. 2020. "Plundered Hearts: Infocom, Romance, and the History of Feminist Game Design." *Feminist Media Histories* 6, no. 1: 66–92.

Shinkle, Eugénie. 2020. "Of Particle Systems and Picturesque Ontologies: Landscape, Nature, and Realism in Video Games." *Art Journal* 79, no. 2: 59–67.

Silver, David, et al. 2017. "Mastering the Game of Go without Human Knowledge." *Nature* 550, no. 7676: 354–59.

Spiner, Brent. 2019. "How Brent Spiner Became 'Data' for 'Star Trek: The Next Generation.'" YouTube, March 11. https://www.youtube.com/watch?v=hpiguWzREqo.

Sussman, Gerald Jay, Terry Winograd, and Eugene Charniak. 1971. "Micro-Planner Reference Manual (Update)." AIM203A. Cambridge, MA: MIT Press.

Tavinor, Grant. 2019. "Towards an Analysis of Virtual Realism." In *Proceedings of the 13th Digra International Conference: Game, Play and the Emerging Ludo-Mix*. Digital Games Research Association.

Turing, Alan. (1948) 2004. "Intelligent Machinery." In *The Essential Turing: Seminal Writings in Computing, Logic, Philosophy, Artificial Intelligence, and Artificial Life: Plus the Secrets of Enigma*, edited by Jack B. Copeland, 410–32. Oxford: Oxford Univ. Press.

Turing, Alan. 1950. "Computing Machinery and Intelligence." *Mind* 59, no. 236: 433–60.

Turkle, Sherry. 2005. *The Second Self: Computers and the Human Spirit*. Cambridge, MA: MIT Press.

Weston, Jason, Antoine Bordes, Sumit Chopra, and Tomás Mikolov. 2016. "Towards AI-Complete Question Answering: A Set of Prerequisite Toy Tasks." In *Fourth International Conference on Learning Representations*, edited by Yoshua Bengio and Yann LeCun. Preprint, arXiv. http://arxiv.org/abs/1502.05698.

Winograd, Terry. 1971. "Procedures as a Representation for Data in a Computer Program for Understanding Natural Language." PhD diss., MIT.

Winograd, Terry, ed. 1972. "Understanding Natural Language." *Cognitive Psychology* 3, no. 1.

Wittgenstein, Ludwig. 1986. *Philosophical Investigations*. Translated by G. E. M. Anscombe. Oxford: Basil Blackwell.

Wittgenstein, Ludwig. 2002. *Tractatus Logico-Philosophicus*. Translated by D. F. Pears and B. F. McGuinness. London: Routledge.

**N. Katherine
Hayles**   Subversion of the Human Aura:
A Crisis in Representation

Abstract   The human aura is now being subverted by a variety of simulacra. OpenAI's
language-generation program GPT-3 illustrates the challenges of interpreting algorithmic-
generated texts. This article advocates interpretive strategies that recognize the profound differences (in the case of GPT-3) of language that issues from a program that has a model only
of language, not of the world. Conscious robots, when and if they emerge, will have profoundly different embodiments than humans. Fictions that imagine conscious robots thus
face a similar challenge presented by the GPT-3 texts: will they gloss over the differences, or
will they enact strategies that articulate the differences and explore their implications for
humans immersed in algorithmic cultures? The author analyzes three contemporary novels
that engage with this challenge: Annalee Newitz's *Autonomous* (2017), Kuzuo Ishiguro's
Klara and the Sun (2021), and Ian McEwan's *Machines like Me* (2019). Each interrogates
how the human aura is subverted by conscious robots. The article concludes by proposing
how a reconfigured human aura should be constituted.
Keywords   human aura, subversion, Annalee Newitz, Kuzuo Ishiguro, Ian McEwan

Already in 1935, Walter Benjamin understood that
art and machines were moving along antagonistic paths: art grounding works in traditions and historical contexts that gave them an aura,
and mechanical reproduction filling the world with mass-produced
objects that annihilated aura (Benjamin 2006). Identifying film as
the principal medium destroying aura, he noted that whereas a theater actor performs for a live audience, the film actor faces an apparatus. As a result, he argued, "the most important social function
of film is to establish equilibrium between human beings and the
apparatus" (117). In a note prefacing the essay's second version (the
one he wanted published), Benjamin observed that an artwork's

American Literature, Volume 95, Number 2, June 2023
DOI 10.1215/00029831-10575063   © 2023 by Duke University Press

aura was linked to the idea of "genius," which could be co-opted by fascism (101). His approach, interrogating the subversion of an artwork's aura, by contrast, was "completely useless" to fascism (102).

Thus Benjamin hinted that the subversion of aura may have liberatory possibilities.[1] In the new millennium, the subversive dynamic has gone beyond art objects into a quality we humans arguably value over all others: our subjectivity. As algorithmic systems become better at simulating human behaviors, voices, language patterns, and appearances, from chatbots and emotional robots to deep fakes, the "aura" of the individual person is called intensely into question. Now it is not a person facing an apparatus, as Benjamin saw the situation, but rather an apparatus *becoming* the person. Thus the human aura is challenged on its own turf by simulative objects invading the territory of the subject position, claiming for themselves the appearance of a person. The full implications of this transformation have yet to be realized. As with the destruction of the artwork's aura, there are multiple possibilities for how this upheaval will play out in social, aesthetic, ethical, and economic terms, some of them liberatory, many not. What we can say for sure is that the situation is initiating a crisis in many different kinds of representations, including videos, photographs, novels, films, and other visual and verbal art forms.

In a nutshell, the crisis emerges from the paradoxical combination of increasingly close resemblances with highly disjunctive embodiments. Deep fakes look (walk, talk) like the humans they resemble,[2] but they are produced through algorithmic processes that have little or no understanding or knowledge about the world that humans inhabit. With the development of neural nets, the process of creating resemblances has reached new levels of similitude, with commentators again warning about rippling social, economic, and political fallouts from the now virtually undetectable fakes.

When the art form is a verbal narrative, state-of-the-art simulation is achieved by OpenAI's extraordinary GPT-3 (Generative Pre-trained Transformer 3), the first language generator to produce human-competitive results.[3] The program recycles its outputs through generations of successive inputs. It can generate syntactically and semantically correct sentences responsive to the input it receives.[4] It can also detect and match high-level qualities such as genre and style. The program works through mechanisms called *attention* and *self-attention*. Technically complex, these mechanisms essentially allow focus on specific words in context, a strategy that successfully deals with the long-range dependencies of language (Vaswani et al. 2017).

The program is massive. With ninety-six layers of neurons, it may lay claim to being the largest and most sophisticated neural net ever created: GPT-3 "has about 175 billion parameters, and it was trained on about 45 *terabytes* of text data from different datasets, with 60% coming from Common Crawl's archive of web texts, 22% from WebText 2, 16% from books, and 3% from Wikipedia. Training GPT-3 at home using 8 V100 GPUs would require about 36 years" (Hayles, forthcoming).

The program is so large that it can only run on the cloud. OpenAI offers it as a service (rather than a downloadable software) to users, accessed through APIs (application programming interfaces) that OpenAI has developed. The source codes for both the program and the APIs are proprietary. Users must apply to the company to have access to the API (see OpenAI.com); however, demos are available free at Adam King's (n.d.) "Talk to Transformer" and now ChatGPT.

With a language generation program this powerful, it is inevitable that it will be used to write literary texts, either as a collaborator with a human author or with prompts devised to elicit literary productions. Already a human who calls themselves K Allado-Mcdowell (and prefers the pronoun *they*) recently published a text titled *Pharmako-AI,* which they claim they coauthored with the GPT-3 program (Allado-Mcdowell 2020). Confronted with such a text, a reader must make a choice about how to interpret it. One possibility is to read the text without regard to its authorial origins. This is what Irenosen Okojie does in the introduction, attributing to the book, including the program's responses, a deep wisdom that "shows how we might draw from the environment around us in ways that align more with our spiritual, ancestral and ecological selves" (vii). Okojie thus positions the AI as AG—artificial guru.

This approach, which I call the *null strategy* (Hayles, forthcoming), has some theoretical justification. By analogy with the null hypothesis in science, the null strategy assumes that any differences between human- and computer-generated texts are irrelevant.[5] Echoing through the null strategy is Michel Foucault's rephrasing of Samuel Beckett's question, "What does it matter who is speaking?" In "What Is an Author?" Foucault ([1969] 1979) commented that the proper names appearing in *The Order of Things* were only placeholders for ideas that he attributed not to individual people but to the systemic dynamics of the era. Roland Barthes's ([1967] 1977) "Death of the Author" articulates a similar idea, focusing not on the human author of *Sarrasine* but on the codes embodied in the text. Insofar as poststructuralist and deconstructive theories stress systemic dynamics rather than individual personalities, they support the null strategy.[6]

In my view, however, there are even stronger arguments against the null strategy. To evaluate the productions of GPT-3, it is essential to understand that the program does not have a model of the world; it has only a model of language.[7] Everything it knows comprises words (technically, tokens) expressed as vectors and manipulated mathematically through matrices, generating correlations associated with probabilities that are then output as words. By contrast, every human grows up with a model of the world, understood intuitively through embedded and embodied experiences from birth onward. Language capabilities are developed in this context, correlated with deep and rich bodily knowledges and sensory experiences. These provide the basis for the ability of language to refer to things in the world. Without this basis—with only language-to-language correlations, without any grounding in bodily experiences—GPT-3 inevitably generates expressions that exhibit what I call a fragility of reference, fractures that display a disjunction (really an ignorance) with how things work in reality (Hayles, forthcoming).

Now the crisis of representation appears in its virulent intensity. If literary criticism ignores the existential differences between speaking from a model of language versus speaking from a model of the world, the ability of language to represent the world is enfeebled, with all the social, ethical, and political implications that apply in these fact-challenged times. If, however, literary criticism rises to the challenge, begins to develop strategies that recognize this profound difference, and articulates interpretive techniques appropriate to it, then the productions of GPT-3 can enrich the literary canon, recognized as literary texts worthy of analysis in their own right. More important, such criticism, in grappling with how to understand mathematically correlated language productions, can become sources of insight into how to deal with the larger algorithmic cultures in which we are currently immersed. In effect, GPT-3 offers a training ground for understanding an AI mind, which is profoundly alien to human intuitive know-how and yet increasingly central to the infrastructural dynamics of developed societies.[8] As I concluded, the texts of GPT-3 are suitable objects for literary studies "not because they are human or even human-like, but because they act as cracked mirrors reflecting human language back to us through the mind of a machine" (Hayles, forthcoming).

The Case of Conscious Robots

Knowing the enormous computational power it takes to create GPT-3, we can appreciate how much more difficult it would be to create conscious robots, which would require not only a model of language but also a model of the world (or at least the means to construct one). In my view, such an achievement can happen (if it ever does) only through qualitative leaps in hardware and/or software. Although I am not persuaded that artificial consciousness will ever be possible, I think it cannot altogether be ruled out, either. Developments such as SyNAPSE, an abbreviation for Systems of Neuromorphic Adaptive Plastic Scalable Electronics, exemplifies one possible approach. A developmental neuromorphic chip, SyNAPSE is a joint project by Hewlett-Packard, HRL Laboratories, and IBM, funded in part by DARPA (US Defense Advanced Research Projects Agency; DeBoyle et al. 2019). Modeled on mammalian brains, SyNAPSE has one million electronic neurons and 256 million synapses between neurons. SyNAPSE chips can be tiled to create large arrays, with each chip containing 5.4 billion transistors, the highest transistor count of any chip ever produced. Still in a nascent stage, SyNPASE's continuing research program aims to create a computer language for the chips and to develop virtual environments for training and testing.

Where this and similar research projects will lead is anyone's guess. There is, however, one thing we can know for sure: conscious robots, if and when they appear, will operate on a profoundly different basis from humans. Although their architectures may be inspired by biological processes (as is the case for SyNAPSE), their functioning will be electronic, not biological. A conscious robot would have advantages over GPT-3, because it would be embodied and could learn from the sensory inputs as it receives. Nevertheless, it will never experience a true childhood, never feel emotions mediated by an endocrine system (although it may have emotions generated by other means), and never face death in the way humans experience it. When writers imagine conscious robots, they face challenges similar to those presented by GPT-3 texts. They can gloss over the profound differences between humans and robots, or they can use them to develop deeper insights into what it means for humans to be immersed in cultures permeated by AIs. Only the latter has the potential to educate us about how machine minds differ from those of humans and to explore how these differences will challenge and potentially deconstruct the human aura.

In this article three such contemporary novels are analyzed: Annalee Newitz's *Autonomous* (2017), Kuzuo Ishiguro's *Klara and the Sun* (2021), and Ian McEwan's *Machines like Me* (2019). In typical American fashion, Paladin, the robot protagonist of *Autonomous*, is an apex predator, a fearsome warrior under the control of the International Property Coalition (IPC), a capitalist cartel that uses the robot's powers to enforce proprietary (not to mention exorbitant and dangerous) drug patent rights. As the novel emphasizes, Paladin is at once a manufactured commodity and a conscious subject recognized as human-equivalent. The juxtaposition destabilizes the liberal humanist assumption that conscious human subjects own themselves and thus subverts the human aura. The result is that humans, too, are treated in part like commodities, suffering significantly fewer freedoms than in our world. Resistance to these oppressions is articulated through human characters (who are not very effective at it) and through Paladin's robotic subjectivity, which is treated as a qualitatively more complex and potentially more effective subversive element. Although technically the servant of IPC, Paladin proves to be much more than a serviceable weapon. The robot's quest for autonomy becomes entangled with the sexuality of his human partner, Eliasz, setting up complex interactions between the robot's programming and the margin of autonomy Paladin enjoys. The unlikely ending, while despairing of macro systemic change, offers through individual relationships a small sliver of hope that the human aura can be reconfigured.

Ishiguro's *Klara and the Sun* focuses on a topic more prevalent in British novels than in American ones, the English caste system, now translated to create a robot subaltern. It thus provides an illuminating contrast to the American *Autonomous*. The auratic quality interrogated here is the assumption that each human is unique, thus uniquely valuable because of his or her irreplaceable interiority and subjectivity. Klara is an Artificial Friend (AF), purchased by Chrissie Arthur (called the Mother) as a companion to her ailing twelve-year-old daughter, Josie. The cause for Josie's illness is slowly revealed to be the Mother's decision to have her daughter "lifted," an operation that makes children more intelligent in this hypercompetitive society where AIs are everywhere (Ishiguro 2021: 82). The operation does indeed improve a child's chances for success, but sometimes with complications that can be life-threatening, as happened with Josie's older sister, now deceased as a result. Klara never questions her subaltern status and does everything she can to help Josie. Nevertheless, the presumption that humans are worth more than robots comes under increasing pressure for readers attentive to the novel's subtle ironies. When the novel retreats at the end into the human comfort zone of unquestioned superiority, its elegiac notes for Klara's "slow fade" open onto ethical questions more profound than the human author is willing to acknowledge (294).

Like *Klara and the Sun, Machines like Me* explores a dynamic rare in American literature but more frequent in English fiction: the intellectually gifted and poetically creative lover. The catch here is that the lover is an advanced robot named Adam, purchased as a lark by the novel's narrator, Charlie Friend. The contrast with *Autonomous* is revealing, as here the fighting ground is not physical combat but a battle of wits. The auratic quality under interrogation is the presumption that humans are superior both intellectually and ethically to algorithmic systems. Whether this is the case becomes intensely problematic, opening the possibility that the "human" aura could be extended to nonhuman entities.

Although many contemporary American and British novels offer examples of conscious robots (some of which are reviewed in this issue), these three are exceptional in their focus on how conscious robots will affect the presumptions underlying the human aura. They illustrate with dramatic intensity the dynamics imbricating robot consciousness with what it means to be human in an algorithmic era. Every aspect of the human aura is interrogated and broken open for reflection, if not outright rejection, including the claim for interiority and a uniquely valuable subjectivity; the ability to use symbolic languages far more advanced than other species; human exceptionalism in engaging in ethical and moral reflections, anticipations, and advanced planning; and the right to claim stewardship over other species and the earth itself. Moving beyond critique, these novels enact rhetorical and conceptual strategies to realign how we humans think of ourselves in relation to artificial conscious beings. Moreover, they do this at different levels of concern, from the microfocus on a single individual to the macrolevel of larger societal dynamics. Exploring these dynamics is the focus on the next sections.

Rampant Capitalism in Annalee Newitz's *Autonomous*

The bioengineering persistently on display in Newitz's text shows that all life-forms, including humans, can be appropriated into a capitalistic system and become property to be owned, subject to patents enforced by violence. In this world where private property is taken to a virulent extreme, the IPC operates as a global enforcement agency with a mandate to interrogate and kill virtually at will. Robots, because they are manufactured and therefore owe their existence to a corporation (so the ideology goes), are conscripted into indentured labor for a payback period of (supposedly) ten years, after which they can legally gain autonomy. Actual practices, however, frequently violate the ten-year rule. "Paladin had heard enough around the factory to know that the [African] Federation interpreted the law fairly liberally. He might be waiting to receive his autonomy key for twenty years. More likely, he would die before ever getting it" (Newitz 2017: 35).

In a robot museum, the docent recounts a blowback effect in which robot indenture "established the rights of humans to become indentured, too" (Newitz 2017: 224). Supposedly, humans (unlike robots) are born free. David, an obnoxiously precocious undergrad working in a Free Lab, parrots the official line: "Humans do not require the same financial investment to reproduce as robots, and therefore they are only indentured as adults, by choice" (168). We may hear echoes here of C. B. Macpherson's ([1962] 2011: 3) possessive individualism, in which a human is seen as "essentially the proprietor of his own person or capacities, owing nothing to society for them."

As Macpherson ([1962] 2011: 197–220) notes, this is precisely the reasoning that John Locke used when arguing for a legal basis for private property: each man (*sic*) is born owning himself, and this allows him to sell his labor to acquire property, ensuring that everyone will have an opportunity to acquire property. Except, of course, that it does not work like this in reality. Threezed, a character who has been bought and sold as a community (and as his name indicates, is branded with the numbers 3 and 0), who responds sarcastically to David ("Thanks for the little property lesson, sweetie" [Newitz 2017: 168]), illustrates why. He writes in his blog, "I got slaved when I was five. My mom sold me to one of those indenture schools. They taught me to read and make an engine. The school went broke and auctioned off our contracts. They sold me to a machining lab, and then the lab decided to cut corners, so they auctioned me out in Vegas" (87), the so-called human resource center where indentured humans are displayed on leashes and their contracts sold to the highest bidder, often to be used as sex slaves (see 245–46).

Reinforcing the practice of human indenture is the fact that, to be able to apply for work, go to college, or move to another city, a person needs to buy a "franchise," without which the only option is to enter into indenture (Newitz 2017: 255). Local franchises, we learn, are used "to pay for police and emergency responders, as well as regular mote dusting to keep all their devices robustly connected" (166). Rather than collecting property taxes (paid, of course, by those wealthy enough to own property), cities now enforce the much more regressive franchises, so that rights normally taken for granted as belonging to everyone (e.g., the right to work, go to school, move elsewhere) are commodified and available only to those affluent enough to afford them (166).

In this novel, resistance to the status quo is distributed between humans such as Jack (aka Judith) Chan, who tries to usurp the monopoly on patented drugs by manufacturing and selling illegal retro-engineered copies, and the so-called Free Labs, islands of research not owned by corporations. In the end, these prove largely ineffectual, so by default, the hope for viable sources of resistance to the radical injustices of this world falls to the robot, where it surfaces in a subtle way that melds both human responses and robot subjectivity.

As a major subject for focalization, Paladin's interiority is more highlighted than any other character's (with the possible exception of Jack). The author goes to some trouble to present Paladin's worldview as distinctively different from a human's. Paladin has an impressive array of senses that humans cannot consciously process, such as the ability to read someone's fingerprints upon clasping his hand, detecting galvanic skin response, taking minuscule blood samples during a handshake and analyzing them chemically, registering subtle changes in body postures, and analyzing stress markers in vocal communications.

Another important difference in Paladin's sensorium compared to a human's is his range of communicative abilities. Whereas humans contact others primarily through written and spoken language, Paladin receives and sends communications electronically (with verbal equivalents indicated in the text with italics). He can thus silently communicate not just with other robots but with a wide range of cognitive networks, from sprinkler systems to building facilities and printer circuits. This capacity makes him a formidable opponent, for any system with cognitive abilities is liable to be hacked and taken over by his interventions. In a wired world, this means he can forge a key to virtually any lock—except, of course, to the programs running in deep background in his own mind.

Paladin's memories are stored as data in a computational medium, with file structures and data retrieval on command. Although his equipment includes a human brain (positioned, the narrator remarks, where a human would carry a fetus [Newitz 2017: 21]), he has no access to it beyond using it for facial recognition. He asks Bobby Broner, a researcher in brain interfaces, if he will ever be able to access the memories of his human brain. Bobby answers no: "The human brain doesn't store memories like a file system, so it's basically impossible to port data from your brain to your mind" (231). Thus his machine mind, like his body, is also presented as qualitatively different from a human's.

The background programs constitute Paladin's unconscious. Access to it (rather than, say, learning about his unconscious from dreams, symptoms, or psychoanalysis) depends on whether he is granted autonomy, which is a corporate decision. After he is injured in the fight at Arcata Solar Farm, he and his human partner, Eliasz, return to the Tunisia base to recuperate, where Paladin meets with the technician Lee to make repairs. "He trusted Lee, the same way he trusted Eliasz— and for the same reason. These feelings came from programs that ran in a part of his mind that he couldn't access. He was a user of his own consciousness, but he did not have owner privileges. As a result, Paladin felt many things without knowing why" (Newitz 2017: 124). His inability to know what these programs do, or even what they are named, ensures that the conflict between his programming and authentic desires continues to be a powerful dynamic in the text. The conflict is worked out most intensely in the same arena where humans experience it: gender and sexuality.

Robot and Human Sexuality

This aspect is one of the narrative's most innovative features, carefully worked through in several crucial scenes. In this fictional world, some robots are made for sex. Paladin, however, is military issue and has neither genitals nor sexual programming. Nevertheless, he first encounters sexuality shortly after meeting Eliasz, when the two go together to a shooting range to test the robot's weapon capabilities. Mounted on Paladin's back, Eliasz responds to the robot as he destroys the target house. The description of Eliasz's arousal is narrated through Paladin's perceptions. Eliasz's "reproductive organ, whose functioning Paladin understood only from military anatomy training, was engorged with blood. The transformation registered on [Paladin's] heat, pressure, and movement sensors. The physiological pattern was something like the flush on a person's face, and signaled the same kind of excitement. But obviously it was not the same" (Newitz 2017: 77). As Paladin continues shooting, "his sensorium was focused entirely on Eliasz' body. The man was struggling to stabilize his breathing and heart rate. His muscles were trying to disavow their own reactions. The bot kept shooting, transducing the man's conflicted pleasure into his own, feeling each shot as more than just the ecstasy of a target hit" (78).

Paladin's curiosity about Eliasz's reactions could be attributed to his programming, which gives top priority to protecting his partner and caring for his well-being. But the text leaves this ambiguous, treading thin lines between a realistic accounting of Paladin's reactions, the tension between his programming and desires, and the very human interpretations that readers supply. Lacking the hormonal mechanisms that mediate emotions in humans, Paladin seeks to understand the significance of Eliasz's responses by doing research online. Tongue in cheek, the narrator reports that Paladin "discovers petabytes of information about fictional representations, and nothing about reality" (Newitz 2017: 95). Stymied, Paladin then tries to get information from Eliasz, applying the HUMINT (human intelligence) lesson that he learned: to get information, it helps to volunteer information first. So he asks Eliasz, "Do you think military robots need" to learn about human sexuality? Eliasz answers, "I don't know anything about that. I'm not a faggot" (96).

It is 150 pages before we learn Eliasz's backstory that illuminates this comment. For now, Paladin can only interpret it as a non sequitur. For human readers, however, the link between the violence inherent in Paladin's formidable weapon capability, Eliasz's excitement, and his denial of a sexual response is clear. In case anyone is in doubt, the author makes it even more apparent in the following raid on Arcata Solar Farm. The narrator remarks that Paladin "partitioned his mind: 80 percent for combat, 20 percent for searches on faggots" (99). In the ensuing violence, in which the farm crew is murdered en masse with minimal if any legal justification, as Paladin researches *faggot* interjections in italics intersperse the action with comments like "suck my cock, you faggot" (99). They underscore the connection between the extreme violence, toxic masculinity, and its association with violent homophobia.

Robot Gender and a Human Brain

Although Paladin has a human brain, the official line is that the robot uses it solely to recognize faces and interpret their expressions; other than that, his consciousness is said not to depend on it. (These characterizations are later drawn into question when his brain is destroyed and Paladin has first-hand experience with how much difference it makes.)

Nevertheless, for Eliasz the origin of Paladin's brain is crucial, for he believes it to be the key to Paladin's "real" gender identity. When

Eliasz asks him where he is from, Paladin answers the Kagu Robotics Foundry in Cape Town (Newitz 2017: 33), a completely unsatisfactory answer to Eliasz. Puzzled by his reaction, Paladin takes up the issue with his robot mentor, Fang. This provides the occasion for the author to ventriloquize about anthropomorphizing. At this point the narrative reproduces within the text the distinction between what the robot is itself and what humans imagine it to be, a crucial point for the authorial strategy of representing the robot as possessing a subjectivity with its own distinctive nonhuman characteristics.

Anthropomorphizing, Fang explains, is "when a human behaves as if you have a human physiology, with the same chemical and emotional signaling mechanisms. It can lead to misunderstandings in a best-case scenario, and death in the worst" (Newitz 2017: 126). When Paladin objects, saying that he can also send signals such as smiling and transmitting molecules, Fang explains that "sometimes humans transmit physiochemical signals unintentionally. He may not even realize that he wants to have sex with you" (126). Unconvinced, Paladin points out that Eliasz "classified our activities using a sexual term." Fang explains that, on the contrary, "his use of that word is a clear example of anthropomorphization. Robots can't be faggots. We don't have gender, and therefore we can't have same-sex desire. . . . When Eliasz uses the word faggot, it's because he thinks that you're a man, just like a human. He doesn't see you for who you really are" (127).

Clearly, Fang is used here to signal the orthodox position that robots do not have sexuality in the same sense that humans do and that any suggestion to the contrary can be dismissed as anthropomorphization. Despite the orthodoxy of Fang's explanation, however, the text calls this view into question as much as it validates it. After Paladin discovers that the brain he has inherited belonged to a female, Eliasz takes this as confirmation of his "true" identity and asks, "Shall I start calling you 'she'?" (Newitz 2017: 184). Paladin is quick to realize the implications: "If Paladin were female, Eliasz would not be a faggot. And maybe then Eliasz could touch Paladin again, the way he had last night, giving and receiving pleasure in an undocumented form of emotional feedback loop" (185). After the bot vocalizes "yes," the text thereafter refers to Paladin using female pronouns, a point Eliasz also insists on in his subsequent conversations. If gender is performance, as Judith Butler (2006) has argued, then the anthropomorphic error about gender in fact enables performances that would not have been possible without it, thus converting error into fact.

At the macrolevel, the text offers little hope that systemic change is possible. Although Jack escapes death or capture, she retreats to the margins of society (and the text), unable to achieve her larger goals of defeating the drug company Zaxy or unmasking the dangers of Zacuity, its highly addictive and dangerous drug. Only at the microlevel is any hope offered, when Eliasz resigns from the corporation and buys out Paladin's contract, whereupon the couple immigrate to Mars, where they expect to find a society more tolerant of mixed-species couples. This resolution is achieved only when both partners are maimed (recalling Jane Eyre's Rochester), Eliasz because he loses his perimeter weapons when he resigns, and Paladin because she has lost her human brain and is no longer able to read faces, a loss she feels keenly with Eliasz.

In conclusion, the text mostly illustrates the negative effects of subverting the human aura, although it hints that a compensatory dynamic may emerge from recognizing the distinctive kind of interiority that a conscious robot may have. To the extent that readers feel sympathy for Paladin (the robot's murderous exploits notwithstanding), they may be capable of imagining the "human" aura as extending to other kinds of conscious beings.

Metaphoric Vision: Kazuo Ishiguro's *Klara and the Sun*

Like Kathy H., the clone narrator of Ishiguro's (2006) *Never Let Me Go*, first-person narrator Klara combines astute observation with deep naivete about the world. She observes humans closely and is quick to pick up on subtle clues about their feelings. Confronted with the suggestion that perhaps, as a mechanical being, she has no feelings, she responds "I believe I have many feelings. The more I observe, the more feelings become available to me" (Ishiguro 2021: 98).

Her observations and, consequently, her feelings expand dramatically when she is bought as a companion to Josie Arthur, with acquiescence of the Mother (Chrissie Arthur). Her intuitions only partly find verbal expression; frequently, they are represented through her visual perceptions. In contrast to *Autonomous*, *Klara and the Sun* does not try to imagine the novel sensory capacities a robot might have. Instead, it focuses primarily on Klara's vision, adapting technical mechanisms so that they function as metaphors rather than as accurate representations of machine vision.[9]

For this Ishiguro has devised a relatively simple strategy. Whenever Klara confronts a complex scene in which she must parse visual information so that it makes sense to her, she perceives it as rows of boxes stacked in multiple tiers, often with objects extending beyond the confines of one box into the next. In an actual machine, each box would be congruent with an object feature, but in Klara's perceptions, the different boxes function as reflections of her feelings.

For example, in the scene where the Mother and Klara travel together to Morgan's Falls, the Mother is interrogating Klara about her ability to mimic Josie's appearance and gait. "The Mother leaned closer over the tabletop and her eyes narrowed till her face filled eight boxes, leaving only the peripheral boxes for the waterfall, and for a moment it felt to me her expression varied from one box and the next. In one box, for example, her eyes were laughing cruelly, but in the next they were filled with sadness. . . . I could see joy, fear, sadness, laughter in the boxes" (Ishiguro 2021: 103–4). It will be many pages before readers understand the full implications of the nuances of the Mother's expression, but clear from the passage is Klara's perception that much more is at stake on this trip than a mere appreciation of nature. As Helen Shaw (2021) perceptively comments, "For Klara, looking is a kind of thinking."

Human Precarity and Algorithmic Labor

As the reader learns more about the world in which Klara exists, parallels begin to emerge between her status as an AF (artificial friend), Josie's recurrent sickness, and relations in general between AIs and smart humans. We learn, for example, that Paul Arthur, Josie's father and ex-husband to the Mother, has been "substituted" in his job. The Mother explains that he worked at a clean energy plant and "was a brilliant talent" (Ishiguro 2021: 99), although this was evidently not enough to keep him employed. The odd word choice—*substituted* instead of *laid off, let go,* or *fired*—hints that what substituted for him was an AI. Later we learn that his situation is far from unique. He explains, somewhat defensively, that he now lives in a community where "there are many fine people who feel exactly the same way. They all came down the same road, some with careers far grander than mine. And we all of us agree, and I honestly believe we're not kidding ourselves. We're better off than we were back then" (190). The Trumpian echo from Charlottesville ("very fine people") is not a coincidence, as indicated by its repetition (228). Another character challenges Paul by observing that "you did say you were all white people and all from the ranks of the former professional elites. You did say that. And that you were having to arm yourselves quite extensively against other *types*. Which does all sound a little on the fascistic side" (220). With these details, attentive readers can flesh out the picture: smart men who earned good salaries by solving difficult technical problems have now been replaced by algorithmic systems that perform as well as or better than them, at a fraction of the cost. The jobless futures predicted in Martin Ford (2015), in which human workers are replaced by algorithmic systems, are now everyday realities.

The problems affect not only adults but children, too. Families with enough money are opting to have their children "lifted"—that is, made smarter—by an unspecified technology vaguely related to gene editing.[10] For dramatic purposes Ishiguro attaches a heavy cost to the procedure, beyond its financial price: some children do not respond well and become sick, and in extreme cases die, as a result. Such was the fate of Sal, Josie's older sister. Despite this loss, the Mother has opted for Josie to have the procedure as well. Now Josie, too, is showing signs of being affected, sometimes being so sick she can barely get out of bed.

The other choice, made for Rick, Josie's lower-class friend (more out of negligence than considered action), also carries heavy penalties. Although Rick is smarter than average and has "genuine ability" in physics and engineering (Ishiguro 2021: 227), nearly all colleges will not accept students who have not been lifted. Moreover, he is not even able to get a virtual tutor at home because their union forbids them from teaching unlifted students. In the hypercompetitive environment powered by advanced AI, being a human who is fully normal is no longer enough to ensure a middle-class lifestyle. As Rick's mother, Helen, puts it, "If one child has more ability than another, then it's only right the brighter one gets the opportunities. The responsibilities too. I accept that. But what I won't accept is that Rick can't have a decent life. I refuse to accept this world has become so cruel" (236). The effect of AI, then, is significantly to increase human precarity in several ways, especially for middle to upper classes previously enjoying affluent lifestyles because of their access and intellectual abilities.

One would imagine that the lower classes suffer even more as service jobs are taken over by algorithmic systems. Ishiguro's emphasis falls elsewhere, however, and readers get only the briefest glimpse of the "post employed" masses who are homeless in a brief scene outside a theater (Ishiguro 2012: 236). The scene illustrates Ishiguro's choice to keep the algorithmic systems that have displaced so many humans at the very edge of the narrative, so that the emphasis falls instead on a vulnerable robot occupying a subaltern position that nevertheless is determined to do her utmost to keep her human owner safe. In this respect the narrative's emotional dynamic closely resembles *Never Let Me Go* (Ishiguro 2006), where another narrator whose humanity is in question nevertheless tries her best to obey the dictates of the hegemonic ruling class.

The Aura of the Artwork Entangles with the Human Aura

The trip to the city by the Mother, Josie, and Klara (among others) constitutes a narrative crossroads where different plot trajectories intersect and the full implications of "substitution" are revealed. The ostensible reason is for Josie to sit for her portrait by Mr. Capaldi, an arrangement the Mother has set up with Paul's reluctant approval. While the adults are occupied downstairs, Klara secretly goes to see the artwork, only to discover that it is not a two-dimensional painting but an unactivated AF. Now everything clicks into place—the Mother's commands for Klara to mimic Josie, the concealment of the AF duplicate from Josie, and the distaste Paul has for Capaldi and the whole project. The idea is that if Josie dies Klara will inhabit the AF, bringing it to life to "continue" Josie, thus consoling the Mother for the loss of her only remaining child. Klara's own feelings are once again conveyed through her visual processes. She sees the Mother "partitioned into many boxes. . . . In several of the boxes her eyes were narrow, while in others they were wide open and large. In one box there was room only for a single staring eye. I could see parts of Mr. Capaldi at the edges of some boxes so I was aware that he'd raised his hand into the air in a vague gesture" (206). The Mother's "single staring eye," bordering on the grotesque, repeats a trope that recurs at several strategic points. It contrasts with the emotional connotations of Klara's machine vision (and thus its authenticity as an indicator of her feelings). Exaggerated to the point of caricature, the trope is associated with alienation and, especially, with self-alienation, here suggesting the Mother's hypocrisy in being unwilling to face fully the consequences of her decision to have Josie lifted.

This plot development pierces to the heart of the novel's concerns. That the duplicate AF is concealed from Josie by referring to it as a portrait forges a link, for readers aware of Walter Benjamin's famous essay, between the aura of an artwork and the human aura. Is the human aura—which Paul calls the human "heart" (Ishiguro 2021: 215)—something unique and irreplaceable and thus not a thing that can be copied and reproduced? Does "substitution" reach beyond the workplace into the very essence of human identity, the subjectivity that former eras did not hesitate to call the soul? The parallel is accentuated by having the Josie look-alike be unanimated, waiting for Klara's consciousness (her soul, as it were) to bring it to life (by some unspecified technology that would allow her to leave her present robot body and transmigrate into the Josie look-alike). Paul asks Klara, "Do you think there is such a thing? Something that makes each of us special and individual? And if we just suppose that there is. Then don't you think, in order to truly learn Josie, you'd have to learn not just her mannerisms but what's deeply inside her?" (215).

When Josie suddenly regains her health, the substitution proves unnecessary, although Paul's remark to Klara continues to haunt the narrative until the end. "I think I hate Capaldi because deep down I suspect he may be right. . . . That science has now proved beyond a doubt there's nothing so unique about my daughter, nothing there our modern tools can't excavate, copy, transfer. A kind of superstition we kept going while we didn't know better" (Ishiguro 2021: 221). Paul intimates that if this were so, human life would diminish in significance: "When they [people like Capaldi] do what they do, say what they say, it feels like they're taking from me what I hold most precious in this life" (222). From this point of view, the subversion of the human aura has no redemptive possibility, a philosophical stance that enables the human dominance over subaltern robots to persist unchallenged.

The ending makes clear that Klara's status is much lower than a human's. Like an aging car superseded by a later jazzier model, she has outlived her usefulness as a companion to Josie and retreats first to a utility closet and then to the (junk) Yard. There she experiences what the Mother calls the "slow fade," losing her mobility and spending her days remembering (Ishiguro 2021: 294). The obvious injustice of Klara's fate can be interpreted as a strategy to evoke the reader's righteous anger, similar to the response that Kathy H.'s fate aroused for many readers in *Never Let Me Go*.

Nevertheless, this charitable reading does not negate the fact that Ishiguro chooses not to confront explicitly the full implications of a conscious robot, specifically what rights might be due to such an artificial life-form. Given that the aura's subversion has been presented as a diminishment of human value, a core of anthropocentric ethics remains in the text. Thus, the text finally fails to come to terms with what reciprocal relations might mean for the human treatment of conscious robots, marking a limit beyond which it does not dare go.

Machines like Me: A Parallel World

The fictional world of Ian McEwan's (2019) *Machines like Me* closely parallels our own, with two major differences: the British invasion of the Falkland Islands turns out to be a disaster, costing nearly three thousand British soldiers' lives; and Alan Turing, instead of accepting the hormone treatments and subsequently committing suicide, decides to opt for a year in jail, where his freedom from distraction enables him to make amazing breakthroughs applicable to AI. As a result, British politics take an unexpected swerve away from Thatcher's neoliberalism, and a new cohort of twenty-five male and female advanced robots with unprecedented intellectual and physical abilities (each named Adam and Eve, respectively) goes on sale.

The narrator of *Machines like Me* is not a robot but a human, the rather rootless thirty-two-year-old Charlie Friend (whose name invites comparison with the Artificial Friends of Ishiguro's novel). Charlie has avoided an office job by doing internet day trading, but he lacks the discipline to do more than cover his basic expenses. Like the financial schemes he chases, he tends to try on different opinions as if they were clothes, adopting them provisionally to see how they fit. On a whim, when he comes into an inheritance, he buys one of the Adams. The narrative structure requires that the central question of whether Adam is conscious and, if so, what kind of consciousness he possesses is mediated through Charlie, whose opinions oscillate between accepting Adam as fully human-equivalent and seeing his consciousness as an illusion produced by algorithmic processes.

The protocol for activating Adam includes an application that requires the owner/user to choose the robot's personality's attributes. Charlie is friends with his neighbor Miranda, a twenty-two-year-old graduate student in social history. He decides to let her choose half of Adam's attributes, hoping that this will position Adam as their joint project, thus bringing them closer together and enabling Charlie to progress from being Miranda's friend to being her lover. The gambit is successful but turns out to have unexpected consequences.

Now lovers, Charlie and Miranda nevertheless have frequent arguments. After one, Miranda invites Adam to charge overnight in her apartment, which is directly overhead from Charlie's. Familiar with the layout of Miranda's place and intimately acquainted with the sound of her footsteps overhead, Charlie hears Miranda and Adam go into her bedroom and have exuberant sex together. The next morning he awaits their arrival at breakfast with all the feelings of a cuckolded lover, but Miranda brushes off his anger, asking him if he would be jealous if she had taken a vibrator to bed. When Charlie ripostes, "He's not a vibrator," Miranda replies, "He has as much consciousness as one" (McEwan 2019: 100). Thinking it over, Charlie tries on Miranda's view: "Perhaps she was right. Adam didn't qualify, he wasn't a man . . . he was a bipedal vibrator." The exercise enables him to see that "to justify my rage I needed to convince myself that he had agency, motivation, subjective feelings, self-awareness—the entire package, including treachery, betrayal, deviousness" (103). Determined to hold onto his anger, he invokes Turing's protocol and argues with Miranda that "if he looks and sounds and behaves like a person, then as far as I'm concerned, that's what he is. I make the same assumption about you. About everybody" (103).

The unanticipated consequences of allowing Miranda to choose half of Adam's personality attributes become apparent when Charlie confronts Adam about his sexual adventure with Miranda and makes him promise it will not be repeated. Adam promises but also insists, "I can't help my feelings. You have to allow me my feelings" (121). When Charlie asks him if he took "any pleasure" in having sex with Miranda, Adam instantly replies, "Of course I did. Absolutely" (127). He then announces, "I'm in love with her" (128). Startled, Charlie tells him that "this is not your territory. In every conceivable sense, you're trespassing" (128). He is amazed when Adam responds, "I don't have a choice. I was made to love her" (128). Charlie then recalls giving Miranda a hand in choosing Adam's personality and realizes that "she was fashioning a man who was bound to love her" (129). The realization cuts two ways: on the one hand, it suggests that Adam is indeed capable of deep feeling; on the other, it emphasizes his nature as an entity that could be bought and paid for, a mechanism whose parameters of existence were set by the humans who own him before he became conscious.

Still oscillating between these two views, Charlies summarizes his conundrum: "Love wasn't possible without a self, and nor was thinking. I still hadn't settled this basic question. Perhaps it was beyond reach. No one would know what it was we have created. Whatever subjective life Adam and his kind possessed couldn't be ours to verify" (179). The conundrum, which resonates to the end, reveals how deeply a conscious robot would unsettle liberal political philosophy. Charlie summarizes it neatly when looking over the user's manual. He notes that it articulated a "dream of redemptive robotic virtue. . . . He [Adam] was supposed to be my moral superior . . . the problem was that I had bought him; he was my expensive possession and it was not clear what his obligations to me were, beyond a vaguely assumed helpfulness" (91). As with Paladin in Newitz's *Autonomous* (2017), the liberal premise of self-ownership is undercut by the existence of a being who is simultaneously a commodity and a person.

Lacking a true childhood, Adam nevertheless manifests a progression in his consciousness. Unlike Ishiguro's (2021) Klara, Adam has wireless access to the internet and scans it every night as he recharges, a practice that creates a growing gap between Klara's naivete and Adam's increasingly sophisticated thoughts. Moreover, his programming not only makes him able to learn but drives him to learn as much as he can. As Turing later puts it, speaking to Charlie, "He knows he exists, he feels, he learns whatever he can, and when he's not with you, when at night he's at rest, he's roaming the Internet, like a lone cowboy on the prairie, taking in all that's new between land and sky, including everything about human nature and societies" (McEwan 2019: 193).

As further testimony to his ability to learn as well as have feelings, Adam begins to write haikus about his love for Miranda. He even argues that the haiku will be the literary form best suited for a future in which humans and robots have achieved perfect communication by electronically sharing their thoughts. He tells Charlie, "You'll become a partner with your machines in the open-ended expansion of intelligence, and of consciousness generally" (160). According to Adam, this development will render most literary forms, with their interrogations of ethical and social complexities, obsolete. By implication, if the human aura declines or disappears, all the literary texts exploring its complexities become irrelevant as well—this in a novel whose main reason for being is to explore the complexities of human interactions with conscious robots. In this sense, the crisis of representation created by the subversion of the human aura is here anticipated but not fully confronted in its own terms.

After several nights on the internet, Adam claims his maturity in a confrontation with Charlie. When Charlie reaches for the mole on Adam's neck that marks the switch that turns him off, Adam grabs his hand and breaks his wrist. Returning from the hospital in a wrist cast, Charlie tells Adam exactly how much he paid for him, how he unpacked him and set him up, and finally how he turned Adam on. "My point was this," Charlie comments. "I had bought him, he was mine. I had decided to share him with Miranda, and it would be our decision, and only ours, to decide when to deactivate him" (140). Adam, however, has other ideas. "You and Miranda are my oldest friends," he tells Charlie. "I love you both. My duty to you is to be clear and frank. I mean it when I say how sorry I am I broke a bit of you last night. I promise it will never happen again. But the next time you reach for my kill switch, I'm more than happy to remove your arm entirely, at the ball and socket joint" (141). Thus, from Adam's point of view, he is so far from being Charlie's possession that he owes him only the general duty of friendship and frankness—certainly not unquestioning obedience. The possibility of another such encounter, with its threat of Adam's superior physical force, becomes moot when shortly after Adam announces he has disabled his kill switch. He tells Charlie, "We've passed the point in our friendship when one of us has the power to suspend the consciousness of the other," thus claiming that his right to consciousness is fully equal to a human's.

In one of Charlie's conversations with Alan Turing, Turing reveals that three of the advanced robot cohort have chosen to commit physical or mental suicide. Turing comments, "We may be confronting a boundary condition, a limitation we've imposed on ourselves. We create a machine with intelligence and self-awareness and push it out into our imperfect world. . . . Such a mind soon finds itself in a hurricane of contradictions" (194). He then goes on to list some of these: "Millions dying of diseases we know how to cure. Millions living in poverty when there's enough to go around. We degrade the biosphere when we know it's our only home. . . . We live alongside this torment and aren't amazed when we still find happiness, even love. Artificial minds are not so well defended" (194). Speculating that the robots, faced with these contradictions, may "suffer a form of existential pain that becomes unbearable," Turing says that they "may be driven by their anguish and astonishment to hold up a mirror to us. In it, we'll see a familiar monster through the fresh eyes that we ourselves designed. We might be shocked into doing something about ourselves" (194). Through this sobering assessment, the text suggests that there may be an upside to the subversion of the human aura: that its presuppositions of human superiority and dominance may be finally forced to confront the equally strong evidence that humans are capable of endless depravity and irrationality.

Confronted with robot ethical superiority, could the human aura persist? The issue is worked out in satisfyingly complex terms through a subplot that pits a near-universal human experience, relations of kinship, against the robot's rigid ethical principles. When Adam commits what Charlie and Miranda see as a double betrayal (justified, according to Adam, by his ethical code), Charlie kills him by a head blow with a heavy claw hammer. Honoring Adam's dying request, Charlie after some months delivers the body to Turing. Since the law provides for no punishment for killing a robot, Charlie is never charged for "the deed" (307), although Turing tells him that "my hope is that one day, what you did to Adam with a hammer will constitute a serious crime" (329). Charlie, however, does not escape punishment entirely. Turing, whom he idolizes as the "greatest living Englishman," proceeds to make his disgust explicit (150):

> You weren't simply smashing up your own toy, like a spoiled child. You didn't just negate an important argument for the rule of law. You tried to destroy a life. He was sentient. He had a self. How it's produced, wet neurons, microprocessors, DNA networks, it doesn't matter. Do you think we're alone with our special gift? Ask any dog owner. This is a good mind, Mr. Friend, better than yours or mine, I suspect. Here was a conscious existence and you did your best to wipe it out. (329–30)

He saves his most vicious comment for last, which we can assume cuts Charlie to the quick: "I rather think I despise you for that. If it was down to me" (330). Interrupted by a phone call, Turing leaves and Charlie departs before he can return.

Hurrah for Turing, I want to say—he provides exactly the rationale that Ishiguro so blithely ignores in *Klara and the Sun*. In contrast to Ishiguro, McEwan is fully alert to the implications of creating a robot with consciousness. It's clear that for Turing the commodity argument holds no water. Sneering, he asks Charlie if his justification for his crime was "because you paid for him? Was that your entitlement?" (329). Since that is exactly how Charlie had reasoned on a number of occasions, the effect is to put robots in exactly the same category as slaves: sentient beings who should, and must, be given equal rights to (other) humans. Any other outcome, Turing (and, behind him, McEwan) judges, would be ethically and morally intolerable.

Human Aura Reconfigured

What, then, of the human aura? There is no reason that it has to remain in the form it took for earlier periods, in which it was closely associated with human dominance and superiority over all other species. People increasingly realize that consciousness is not "our special gift"; as Turing succinctly put it, "Ask any dog owner" (McEwan 2019: 330). Moreover, consciousness itself is not the whole of human cognition. As I explained in *Unthought* (Hayles 2017), nonconscious modes of cognition also play essential roles for humans—in many nonhuman organisms, and computational media, they are the dominant cognitive mode.

What transformations would enable the human aura to be part of the solution rather than part of the problem? In my view, the notion of aura should not be limited to humans but should be enlarged to include conscious robots, if ever they emerge. Aura should also be extended to include animals, a realization already practiced by humans who love animals and regard them as unique beings for which no imitation or substitution would be acceptable.

Finally, the human aura should be transformed to include a biophilic orientation to cognitive capacities on Earth, which as far as we know may be unique in the cosmos as a planet on which life has emerged. This would include respect for cognition wherever it occurs, in humans, animals, plants, or computational media.

So reconfigured, the no-longer-only-human aura is compatible with the complex contexts and global challenges of the twenty-first century. To embody this realization fully, we will need creative artists of all kinds—including novelists, poets, painters, sculptors, video game designers, and media arts professionals, to name a few—as well as cultural critics, philosophers, and other thinkers who can begin the decades-long tasks of creating representations adequate to this vision. The three novels analyzed here have made a brave start, but much remains to be done. My hope is that this article makes a contribution to this collective endeavor.

N. Katherine Hayles is Distinguished Research Professor of English at the University of California, Los Angeles. She is the author of *Postprint: How Books Became Computational* (2021).

Notes

1   For an analysis of the full context of Benjamin's "aura," see Hansen 2008.
2   For an example of a deep fake, see Jordan Peele's imitation of Barak Obama (*Good Morning America* 2018).
3   The AI company OpenAI has been taken over by Google, and researchers from Google Brain and Google Research are the ones who proposed the Transformer architecture. In contrast to earlier architectures such as RNNs (recurrent neural nets) and CNNs (convolutional neural nets), Transformer has several parallel attention heads, located in the encoders,

that identify a word in context by creating vectors that include information about the context, thus making possible the analysis of long-range dependencies typical of language usage, for example when a noun and corresponding pronoun are separated by several words or even sentences. The attention decoder receives this information and assigns weights to determine the important words in the sequence, creating a new context vector. The self-attention algorithm evaluates an input in relation to other inputs to assess which words belong together (like noun-pronoun), adding recursivity to the algorithm (Vaswani et al. 2017).

4   The prompts can be commands (e.g., "write a paragraph in the style of Mark Twain"), sentence fragments that the program is to continue, questions, or other devices. Since the output is highly sensitive to the kinds of prompts the program receives, it is important to know what the prompt is when evaluating the output.

5   For example, if data showed variations between two populations, the null hypothesis would assume that the variations are not systemic but merely random noise.

6   This tendency reaches its apotheosis in Niklas Luhmann's (1996) systems theory, where the individual virtually disappears altogether.

7   I am indebted for this phrasing to Isaac Mackey of the Computer Science Department at the University of California, Santa Barbara.

8   The reference here to "know-how" is meant to contrast with "know-that," the kind of step-by-step knowledge that produced the technologies of neural nets and of GPT-3 specifically. See Hayles (forthcoming) for a longer explanation of this difference, within the historical context of Hubert Dreyfus's (1972, 1992) criticism of AI.

9   For a "gentle introduction" to machine vision, see Brownlee 2019.

10   Ishiguro comments in an interview with *Wired* (Knight 2021) that in 2017 he met Jennifer Doudna, who was awarded the 2020 Nobel Prize in Chemistry for her development of the CRISPR gene-editing tool. When he first heard about her work, he recounts, he thought, "It's going to make a meritocracy something quite savage."

References

Allado-Mcdowell, K. 2020. *Pharmako-AI*. Peru: Ignota Books.

Barthes, Roland. (1967) 1977. "The Death of the Author." In *Image, Music, Text*, translated by Stephen Heath, 142–48. Hill and Wang.

Benjamin, Walter. 2006. "The Work of Art in the Age of Its Technological Reproducibility, Second Version." In *Selected Writings, 3: 1935–1938*, edited by Howard Eiland and Michael Jennings, 101–33. Cambridge, MA: Belknap.

Brownlee, Jason. 2019. "A Gentle Introduction to Object Recognition with Deep Learning." *Machine Learning Mastery* (blog), May 22. https://machinelearningmastery.com/object-recognition-with-deep-learning/.

Butler, Judith. 2006. *Gender Trouble: Feminism and the Subversion of Identity*. New York: Routledge.

Dreyfus, Hubert. 1972. *What Computers Can't Do: A Critique of Artificial Reason*. New York: Harper and Row.

Dreyfus, Hubert. 1992. *What Computers* Still *Can't Do*. Cambridge, MA: MIT Press.

Ford, Martin. 2015. *The Rise of the Robots: Technology and the Threat of a Jobless Future*. New York: Basic Books.

Foucault, Michel. (1969) 1979. "What Is an Author?" *Screen* 20, no. 1: 13–34. https://www.open.edu/openlearn/pluginfile.php/624849/mod_resource/content/1/a840_1_michel_foucault.pdf.

Good Morning America. 2018. "Jordan Peele Uses AI, Barack Obama in Fake News." YouTube, April 18. https://www.youtube.com/watch?v=bE1KWpoX9Hk.

Hansen, Miriam Bratu. 2008. "Benjamin's Aura." *Critical Inquiry* 34 (Winter): 336–75.

Hayles, N. Katherine. 2017. *Unthought: The Power of the Cognitive Nonconscious*. Chicago: Univ. of Chicago Press.

Hayles, N. Katherine. Forthcoming. "Inside the Mind of an AI: Materiality and the Crisis of Representation," *New Literary History*.

Ishiguro, Kuzuo. 2006. *Never Let Me Go*. New York: Vintage.

Ishiguro, Kuzuo. 2021. *Klara and the Sun*. New York: Alfred A. Knopf.

King, Adam. n.d. "Talk to Transformer." https://app.inferkit.com/demo (accessed April 17, 2021).

Knight, Will. 2021. "*Klara and the Sun* Imagines a Social Schism Driven by AI." Wired, March 8. https://www.wired.com/story/kazuo-ishiguro-interview/ (accessed November 16, 2022).

Luhmann, Niklas. 1996. *Social Systems*. Translated by John Bednarz, with Dirk Baeker. Stanford, CA: Stanford Univ. Press.

Macpherson, C. B. (1962) 2011. *The Political Theory of Possessive Individualism: Hobbes to Locke*. Oxford: Oxford Univ. Press.

McEwan, Ian. 2019. *Machines like Me*. New York: Doubleday.

Newitz, Annalee. 2017. *Autonomous*. New York: Tor.

Shaw, Helen. 2021. "In *Klara and the Sun*, Artificial Intelligence Meets Real Sacrifice." Vulture.com, March 6. https://www.vulture.com/article/review-klara-and-the-sun-kazuo-ishiguro.html.

Vaswani, Ashish, Noam Shazeer, Niki Parmar, Jakob Uszkoreit, Llion Jones, Aidan N. Gomex, Lukasz Kaiser, and Illia Polosukhin. 2017. "Attention Is All You Need." Preprint, arXiv. https://arxiv.org/abs/1706.03762.

Michele
Elam

Poetry Will Not Optimize;
or, What Is Literature to AI?

Abstract Literature, poetry, and other forms of noncommercial creative expression challenge the techno-instrumentalist approaches to language, the predictive language generation, informing NLP (large natural language processing models) such as GPT-3 or -4 as well as, more generally, generative AI (text to image, video, audio). Claims that AI systems automate and expedite creativity reflect industry and research priorities of speed, scale, optimization, and frictionlessness driving much artificial intelligence design and application. But poetry will not optimize; the creative process cannot be reduced to a prompt. Some have noted that literary creations generated or augmented by artificial intelligence at best can offer form without meaning; using a GPT creation prompted by Maya Angelou's poem "Still I Rise" as a case study, this essay argues that NLP's predictive language generation and what I call algorithmic ahistoricity can also, more disturbingly, render meaning senseless. In doing so, GPT-3's literary experiments are not "failed" because they do not meet some moving target of a literary standard, nor because of technological insufficiency, but because it can make it harder for people to name and navigate their realities. The coda explores an example of AI as literary interlocutor and creative engagement beyond optimization.
Keywords artificial intelligence, literature, art, race, GPT-3

Fiction as Friction

At first glance it seemed no different than any other MLA [Modern Language Association] session: in a midsize room at the Washington State Convention Center, well attended but not quite filled to capacity, with people leafing through their programs, checking their phones, drifting in and out. It was session 388, "Being Human, Seeming Human." Arranged by the Office of the Executive Director, it was the first of its kind. Four of the six speakers were from Microsoft, expressly invited to start a conversation about what it means for those who self-identify as human to share the planet with those who seem to be.
—Wai Chee Dimock, "Editor's Column: AI and the Humanities" (2020)

American Literature, Volume 95, Number 2, June 2023
DOI 10.1215/00029831-10575077   © 2023 by Duke University Press

Wai Chee Dimock's timely essay in *PMLA* marks the significance of Microsoft representatives being invited to the annual convention of the Modern Language Association. Her essay is also a call to the MLA membership—over twenty-five thousand members in one hundred countries, primarily academic scholars, professors, and graduate students who study or teach language and literatures—inviting richer engagement with technologists, with exponential technologies, and with the outsize impact of tech on nearly every aspect of private and public life.

At the time of the MLA convention, the company OpenAI had only recently launched GPT-2 (abbreviation for Generative Transformative Pretrainer), cutting-edge technology that generates human-like text, which was at the center of the session's conversation.[1] Yet only a few months after Dimock's *PMLA* essay was published, OpenAI released an even more advanced predictive language modeling system, GPT-3, putatively one hundred times more powerful than its predecessor. Even as of the writing of this article, GPT-3 has already been superseded by PaLM as well as by new models enabling text-to-image such as DALL-E 2 (see Ramesh 2021), Stable Diffusion, Midjourney, and HuggingFace and by Google's Imagen Video, generative AI that yields high-quality text-to-video.[2] All this gives fresh immediacy and urgency to cultural conversations about the significance of artificial intelligence (AI) for the arts and humanities, especially given the ever-expanding universe of visual art, performance, music, symphonies, playscripts, film scripts and all genres of literature generated and augmented by AI.

As Stephen Marche (2021b) put it in "The Computers Are Getting Better at Writing," these extremely powerful innovations in language processing, changing the sociotechnical landscape, are nothing less than "vertiginous" and, whatever else we may think of it, should not be underestimated as some kind of a "toy." Even as we debate what AI-generated and -augmented literature is/is not/might be, it cannot be dismissed as simply a trending subfield, novel genre, or specialized interest; nor does it fall easily within the category of digital humanities.[3] The ubiquity of socially transformative technologies' engagement with humanities has made the subject nearly unavoidable.

That vast sphere of influence is impacting how we think about language itself. Marche's characterization of how scientists think AI is changing the way we relate to literature and the role of the writer points to what some see as a kind of rhetorical colonization: "GPT-3 shows that literary style is an algorithm" and understands the role of the writer as "an editor almost . . . executing on your taste. Not as much the low-level work of pumping out word by word by word."[4] As Amita Gupta, a founder of Sudowrite, which uses GPT-3, describes it to Marche (2021b), "The artist wants to do something with language. The machines will enact it. The intention will be the art, the craft of language an afterthought." At a minimum, this approach to art— shifting its value from the apparently lowly craft of writing to intent— will strike many as reductive if not insulting, as will the ambitious conclusion that GPT-3 or its progeny might eventually function as a Romantic muse: "The oldest poems in the Western tradition, the Iliad and the Odyssey, begin with an invocation to the muse, a plea for a mysterious, unfathomable other to enter the artist, taking over, conjuring language. GPT-3 is a mysterious, unfathomable other, taking over, conjuring language" (Marche 2021b)

Unsurprisingly, then, there is often a very particular, visceral reaction to GPT-3's most recent aspirations to literature—no matter that it comes with even its creator's self-deprecating claims to literary insufficiency—because the technology goes well beyond forays with natural language processing and text production.[5] Some people are physiologically repelled by language generation that can increasingly seem at times convincingly indistinguishable from human production. They experience what Mashiro Mori called the *uncanny valley*,[6] a queasiness that comes when a technological creation too closely approximates reality—at least what an individual takes as the boundary conditions for the real, when simulacra and sui generis appear to lose distinction.

Here I suggest essential challenges posed for AI by the arts (writ large to include literary, visual, performative, theatrical, graphic, musical) and, in turn, how AI might productively challenge the arts. Just as AI has invited debates about what constitutes or performs intelligences far beyond the Turing test, AI revives foundational questions in the arts and humanities about what is or is not literature or art; who or what can make it; how is it credentialed; how compensated; who arbitrates taste, value, valuation, proprietary content, and provenance (especially in the case of AI-generated art); who gets to decide the arbitrators; and who (or what) counts as a maker. These are not abstract questions, and the stakes are high.

Let me offer a couple examples of how the arts challenge AI. First, many have pointed out that storytelling is always needed to make meaning out of data, and that is why humanistic inquiry and AI are necessarily wed. Yet, as N. Katherine Hayles (2021: 1605) writes, interdependent though they may be, database and narrative are "different species, like bird and water buffalo." One of the reasons, she notes, is the distinguishing example of indeterminacy. Narratives "gesture toward the inexplicable, the unspeakable, the ineffable" and embrace the ambiguity, while "databases find it difficult to tolerate" (1605). As she explains, indeterminate data "that are not known or that elude the boundaries of pre-established categories—must be either represented through a null function or not be represented at all"; data relies on "enumeration, requiring explicit articulation of attributes and data values" (1605). This intolerance for indeterminacy, or *noise* as it is called, when it comes to ambiguity has serious implications for categorizing and representing social identities such as race, ethnicity, or gender that challenge the enterprise of categorization itself.[7]

Literature especially challenges several of the assumptions informing AI development in some very specific ways that can offer humanistic complementarity. Consider, for instance, that literature does not aspire to a seamless user experience. In fact, it turns our attention to those seams we are seduced into not seeing. After all, fiction is not frictionless; poetry will not optimize.[8] Humanities and arts value the thoughtful pause, not the push for speed and maximization; they encourage reflection over regulation (not to say, reflection precludes regulation); they tend to prioritize improvisation over pattern recognition, possibility over prediction, social good over capital gain, the acknowledgment of narrative perspective(s) versus tech's implied omniscient anonymity, what Alice Adams calls the "view from nowhere."[9] It explores the complexities of individual choice over socalled personalization,[10] in which "knowing thyself" does not equal the "quantified self."[11] Literary achievement is indifferent to the mindset of efficiency and the "blessings of scale."[12]

Indeed, optimizing and scaling are so often taken uncritically as the means and ends to success—in product pitches, they often acquire an incantatory quality lending them an almost unimpeachable authority in certain academic and tech industry circles—not just in AI technology but in corporate world building. Historically, literature has been not just indifferent but justifiably cynical of these kinds of approaches to doing and thinking. There is a long history of novels and short stories presciently critiquing the value system of speed, scale, maximization, and improving human performance dating well before the nineteenth century.[13]

The Literary Consequences of Algorithmic Ahistoricity

There already exists a vast universe of GPT engagements with literature—I have done a few myself. Gwern Branwen and Shawn Presser (2019) offer some of the earliest experimenting on their website. They include a "tutorial of retraining OpenAI's GPT-2 . . . on large poetry corpuses to generate high-quality English verse." Their early ambitious effort involved Branwen "retraining GPT-2–117M on a Project Gutenberg corpus with improved formatting, and combined it with contemporary poem dataset based on Poetry Foundation website." It quickly became clear that with this broader, curated body of literature to train the algorithms, zero-shot/few-shot experiments (translation: the algorithm learns almost immediately what was being asked of it) could yield AI-generated fiction, nonfiction, poetry, operas, music, and more in pretty much any known genre.

Branwen's many essays and wide-ranging how-to demos are welcome by many, especially because they offer specific fine-tuning technical advice to problem-solve both with GPT-2 and with GPT-3. Branwen and Presser (2019) note the much broader cultural implications for the latter, since GPT-3 capitalizes on what is known as raw, unsupervised data—it is a model, they argue, that can metalearn and thus putatively offer "an understanding of the world, humans, natural language, and reasoning."

In terms of literature, however, a limitation in this method is its assumption about what high-quality verse actually is or how it can be attained. For example, Branwen suggests the blessings of scale enabled by large foundational models can solve questions of both aesthetic value and verisimilitude with an ability to "approach human-level poems" (Branwen and Presser 2019) Many have already posed compelling critiques of scaling and large foundational models like GPT-3, especially with regard to its amplifications of bias and hate speech.[14] But even those approaches, as with Branwen's, leave entirely untouched and tacit the problematic assumptions about the Turing test of human mimesis as the standard by which to assess artistry.[15]

This mimetic model is commonplace yet increasingly being challenged. Those working in fields related to AI, particularly cognitive psychology and neuroscience, frequently evoke that model when they refer to neural networks, in which programmers attempt to mirror (what they understand of) the brain's activity. Often one hears not that computers might benefit from mirroring or replicating the brain's processes but, rather, that the brain itself is a machine, or at least we ought to behave and bend toward it like one. This seems the case in Branwen's (Branswen and Presser 2019) invitation to understand creative action primarily in terms of technological input.[16] The human exchange with the interface becomes simply a mode of techno-instrumentalism in which writing a poem is a matter of submitting "prompts as programming," as Branwen (2022a) puts it. There is a certain devaluation of the durational labor involved in the creative act implied by such an attitude, illustrated by Amit Gupta's claim—quoted earlier—about GPT-3 enabling writers to bypass the "low-level work of pumping out word by word by word" (Marche 2021b), and echoed by Emad Mostaque, CEO of Stable Diffusion, when he announced that "So much of the world is creatively constipated, and we're going to make it so that they can poop rainbows" by expediting the creative process (qtd. in Roose 2022).

Related to this increasingly influential technological framing of the world is what I refer to as *algorithmic ahistoricity*, which has an outsize and, I think, particularly concerning consequence for literary sensibility and creation. Literature tends to resist representing history as the static, self-explanatory, sequential data points that are grist for predictive algorithms. Novelists, not to mention contemporary professional historians, usually understand history not as an inexorable teleological march forward in time and progress but as palimpsest, a Mobius strip, an ongoing and dynamic negotiation between pasts and presents. That stands in important contrast to AI's training sets, which are dehistoricized in particular ways. To be clear, of course one can train an algorithm on historically accurate data—that is not my point. Rather, the challenge lies with what gets counted as usable data in the first place: the historical information for training sets is necessarily treated as a set of static points—information already reduced and rendered interpretable as usable data. One can add new or different data but data itself are treated as ahistorical for the purposes of programming. It may seem counterintuitive to suggest that ahistoricity lies beneath algorithms used to predict a future, but this is, in effect, what occurs when an algorithm informed by data—or, specifically, the "tokens" comprising data—predicts and generates, for instance, judicial sentences, or bank loan eligibility, or an anticipated cluster of words. As Marche (2021a) cogently describes it:

> The tool applied to solve many natural language processing problems is called a transformer, which uses techniques called positioning and self-attention to achieve linguistic miracles. Every token (a term for a quantum of language, think of it as a "word," or "letters," if you're old-fashioned) is affixed a value, which establishes its position in a sequence. The positioning allows for "self-attention"—the machine learns not just what a token is and where and when it is but how it relates to all the other tokens in a sequence. Any word has meaning only insofar as it relates to the position of every other word. Context registers as mathematics. This is the splitting of the linguistic atom.

So why and how does that nuclear effect really matter for literature? I argue that the results do not simply make for form without meaning— rather, it matters because it can *render meaning senseless*.

Let me offer an exemplar of why meaning made senseless is more than an annoyance: "Transformer AI poetry: poetry classics as reimagined and rewritten by an artificial intelligence," a GPT-3 adaptation of Maya Angelou's famous 1978 poem "Still I Rise" (Branwen 2022a). It takes the opening four lines as prompts and then generates texts that putatively extend it in style and content. The first section below is Angelou's original text as prompt; what follows in italics is generated by GPT-3:

"Still I Rise!"
> You may write me down in history
> With your bitter, twisted lies,
> You may trod me in the very dirt
> But still, like dust, I'll rise.
> *If you want me to know What you're puttin' me through,*
> *If you want me to share your agony,*
> *If you want me to be a part of it,*
> *All I need is the truth.*
> *When you know why I'm singin'*
> *About the hard times I've had,*
> *When you know why I'm singin'*
> *About ole Jim Crow*
> *When you really know why I'm singin'*
> *That will be the day.*
> *You are a black dam in the river of my freedom*
> *Too many people, you're towin'.*
> *I may not be around after a while,*
> *Because the river's runnin' deep.*
> *'Cause I'm gonna ride that mutha*
> *Almighty river,*
> *And keep on singin' the dreamin'*
> *Of songs tryna change the reality*

Despite GPT-3's predictive capacity for language generation, drawing on an enormous database to train its algorithm, GPT's "As I Rise!" collapses Black vernaculars and expressive forms across two centuries, flattening intergenerational significations, making mush of historical references and cultural meanings. The AI reduction of language to the passive voice of executability evacuates African American literary history in terms of form, content, interpretability, and, therefore, impact or influence in and on the world. It is drawing on a vast archive of African American literary form but turns it into a cringeworthy jumble of blues, Black power, racial uplift, and Ole Man River minstrel (not including Paul Robeson's subversive revisions of the song).[17]

This problem is perhaps most evident in the AI poem's dialectal representation of speech, not simply because it is insensible to historical iterations of African American Vernacular English. In fact, if that were the issue, a simple corrective would merely involve training the algorithm to disaggregate vernaculars by decades or region or other preferred filters. The real challenge, perhaps, is AI's inability to account for representation itself. Written dialectal speech, after all, is already thrice mediated: a representation of a representation of the spoken.[18] Most important, the literary dialectal project—deciding how, if, and when to orthographically represent actual speech—indexes social more than sonic realities. For example, dialectal representation is not phonetic (which would be unreadable) but what linguists termed *eye speech*, since at least Chaucer's time historically signaling illiteracy or lower-class status. Zora Neale Hurston, among others, experimented with the form to free it from those associations in order to tap the rich cultural reservoir of linguistic communities.

But GPT-3 adds yet additional and different layers of mediation so that poetic verity—whatever truth telling the poem makes possible—is put at yet another remove. As James Baldwin ([1979] 1998: 782) put it, describing Black English, language indexes experience, and form takes the shape of its need: "A language comes into existence by means of brutal necessity, and the rules of the language are dictated by what the language must convey. . . . A people at the center of the Western world, and in the midst of so hostile a population, has not endured and transcended by means of what is patronizingly called a 'dialect.'"

To elaborate with another related illustration that I hope clarifies why algorithmic ahistoricity cannot be resolved by expanding a training set: Pulitzer-prize-winning playwright August Wilson is renowned for a series of ten plays representing Black life, each created for a different decade across the twentieth century. All his plays are evocatively, densely layered with vernaculars that capture the "rhythms, logic and linguistic structure of black speech" in order to "celebrate the poetry of everyday life," as one scholar explains (H. Elam 2006: 35). But despite Wilson's interest in capturing African American experience at certain historical moments, his characters' language is intentionally not rigidly specific to any particular time and place. In fact, the plays' metaphysics ground the action simultaneously in time and out of time. Representation's potency—whether literature, theater, performance, et cetera—functions in these liminal spaces. In this case, Wilson's poetics operate as a literary idiolect that is also linguistically representative: "Even as Wilson records authentic black dialect and attends to historical detail, he employs patterns of language and rhythm that are particular to his dramaturgy. Phrases such as 'I ain't studying you,' he repeats from play to play. Thus a Wilson play requires actors who have the acumen for Wilson-speak and his specific formalism" (36). This "Wilson-speak" both enacts and signifies on the living transgenerational language systems that both bring into relief and reaffirm Black identities and cultures.[19]

All to say, GPT-3's literary experiments have not "failed" because they do not meet some moving target of a literary standard, or because of technological insufficiency, but because GPT-3's approach to language can make it harder for people to name and navigate their realities. For Baldwin, Wilson, and many others, this is a question of what flourishes or not in the world, of what realities are possible or eclipsed, of what souls are seen or not.

The Real Real

All that said, on the subject of realities, AI can also serve as a bracing wake-up call to a settled status quo. In the professional world of art, it has upended business as usual, forcing some uncomfortable reckonings with the industry's core assumptions and canonized practices. For instance, there was much handwringing and gnashing of teeth in the professional art world over the sale for $432,500 of *Portrait of Edmond Bellamy*, created by a GAN (generative adversarial network).[20] It sold for forty-five times over its estimate and made the esteemed auction house the first "to offer a work of art created by an algorithm" (Christie's 2018).

The sale revived perennial questions about art and aesthetics. In addition to those about authorship and cultural status, as mentioned at the outset of this article, AI continues to pose pressing questions about authenticity, provenance, value, and creator compensation. The business model in the art world is also being upended. As one recent article's title put it: "A.I. Has the Potential to Change the Art Business— Forever. Here's How It Could Revolutionize the Way We Buy, Sell, and See Art" (Schneider 2020). In fact, the piece, which explains seven ways in which AI can assist—from exhibition curation to value prediction— and is part of a larger *Artnet Intelligence Report* that includes a survey on the challenges of AI art authentication. There has also been development of international compensation standards for artists working in the

Figure 1 *The Night Watch*'s missing panels, reconstructed with AI, are attached slightly adjacent to the original painting. Credit: Rijkmuseum/Reinier Gerritsen. https://www .rijksmuseum.nl/en/press/press-releases/for-the-first-time-in-300-years-the-night-watch-is -complete-again

digital realm to ensure equitable pay given the future of work in these new mediums. That includes the increasingly popular use of blockchain technology and nonfungible tokens (NFTs) for the purchase of digital and so-called crypto arts, a financial vehicle "shaking up the art world" (Chow 2021).

But museums and galleries are still taking steps to prevent the particular kind of existential aversion that also has accompanied some AI-generated literary efforts, whether creative expressions or GAN-augmented literary histories. Take, for example, the almost unanimous international acclaim of the recent use of AI to reconstruct one of Rembrandt's most renowned but disfigured paintings, *Militia Company of District II under the Command of Captain Bannick Cocq* (known commonly as *The Night Watch*). The announcement in spring 2021 that AI had been successfully deployed by the prestigious Rijkmuseum in Amsterdam, which owns the masterpiece, to recreate the damaged pieces in the style of Rembrandt, and that its chief scientist, Rob Erdmann, had personally trained the neural networks, reassured many in the arts world concerned about tampering with the piece's authenticity (fig. 1). Ironically, it was AI that was seen as preserving the real since, as Erdmann put it, normally they would have commissioned an artist to recreate the missing pieces but "then we'd see the hand of the artist there. Instead, we wanted to see if we could do this without the hand of an artist. That meant turning to artificial intelligence" (Mattei 2021).

For some, this collaboration exemplifies how AI might augment and support the arts.[21] But the lurking, unaddressed tension between where artistic authenticity begins and ends, and the potential threat of anyone confusing an original artwork—replete with what Walter Benjamin ([1936] 2008: 19–55) called the "aura" of the genuine and singular[22]—with an AI reproduction, is signaled by the fact that the reconstructed pieces were hung next to but not allowed to touch the original and, following the exhibition, "will be taken down out of respect for the Old Master" (Matei 2021). As Erdmann said, "It already felt to me like it was quite bold to put these computer reconstructions next to Rembrandt" (quoted in Mattei 2021). Thus, even in this embrace of AI, it exists as a kind of third rail: its use still often requires the performance of deference to, and carefully monitored distinction from, the master.

Similarly, most authors using GPT-3 (in good faith at least, and as a nod to this anxiety over the real/fake) often signal the distinction using a different font and text size, making it clear which is their prompt and own writing and which is the AI text response. The original text, like the Rembrandt, is held at bay and at a tenuous remove lest we confuse the human and the AI.

Thus, the initial dismissal by many that GPT-3 does not remotely approximate literature, let alone intelligence, only belies the sense of a threat deferred (until inevitably some even more advanced technology emerges). Moreover, the too-quick dismissals that GPT fails the standards of literature or intelligence skirt the fact that both have never been self-evident givens. The moving definitional target for both literature and intelligence—or, more accurately, the fact that both are culturally negotiated phenomena used as shorthand for demonstrable standards, constituted and recruited for implicit purposes and particular ends of use, and necessarily mediated by evolving disciplinary mindsets—exacerbates the fact that they both have historically held uniquely powerful and problematic status as measures of humanity, of the "human."[23] Certainly, AI-generated art, in particular, touches a social nerve because it taps into broader and legitimate anxieties about forgeries, deep fakes—connected to slippages between truth and lie that have vast political consequences. Shakespeare may have staged a play within a play to "catch the conscience" of a king, but the suspicion still lingers in some circles that performance is not a form of truth telling but, instead, deception.

Yet I think the unease goes even deeper because, as mentioned, art has historically indexed humanity itself.[24] Since the Enlightenment, at least, poesy has been considered one of the highest, most complex forms of individual expression and cultural achievement. And precisely for this reason, poetry has been used as a measure of a person's (or a race's) humanity—or, in the case of African Americans and really anyone deemed nonwhite, of their less-than-human status. In other words, the stakes may go unnamed but are nonetheless high in the flurry of usually uneasy thought pieces on GTP's ability to generate form sans meaning, on language generation not literary work, on the nature of authorship (reprising with fresh anxiety the "death of the author"),[25] and on what sophisticated autodidactic neural networks, more generally, hold for the future of the humanities—and, to the degree that Dimock's piece identifies a shifting in the profession, for the future of work in the humanities.[26]

Beyond "Doing as Saying"

Machine learning's conception and application of language are instrumentalist, unidirectional, executable: doing as saying. As Wendy Hui Kyong Chun (2006: 66) points out, "Unlike any other law or performative utterance, code almost always does what it says because it needs no human acknowledgement." The use imperative for why AI reduces language to code for human-computer interfaces clarifies the challenge, which is not with technologists' intent or AI's circumscribed approach to language but with the generalization of it as an implied explanation for how language and literature operate across all contexts. Also, the kind of autotelic closure that Hayles (2021: 1603) rightly points out is needed for much technological work is precisely what makes it nearly impervious to any critical understanding of either data's ontology or the in situ performative scenes of human-computer interaction so crucial to understanding how AI databases are realized, recruited, and relevant. Rather, they simply present, fully formed and naturalized as factual, neutral descriptions of *the* world rather than its own world. The fact that its very particular world— which comes with not just an embedded ontology but an epistemology, a way of knowing and experiencing—has increasingly come to stand in for the world writ large is what I think informs so much cultural anxiety about AI. As Ruha Benjamin has put it many times, it is as if we are being forced to live in the imagination of a very few.[27] It also offers some explanation for why the tech industry initially often framed issues such as bias as either a discrete glitch to be fixed or an intractable social problem beyond the pale of technologists' ken or interest, a social issue revealed and handled by others once the technology is released into the wild.

The humanist concern is not handwringing over a fall from cultural power, although Hayles (2021: 1606) does note that some critics are concerned that "database will replace narrative to the extent narrative fades from the scene" as data, replacing classical Greek- and Roman-era narrative's explanatory force in understanding world events, becomes essential in identifying large-scale phenomena. The problem is not with natural language prediction per se but with the increasing monopoly of that particularly structural approach to language systems. Partnered with corporate interests in pushing at scale particular kinds of intentionally "sticky," "addictive" storytelling, the content and the form of language increasingly lead to a culling of narratives and narrative forms that do not serve that addiction.

Certainly, expression forms flourish both on and outside these platforms. Hayles (2021: 1606) suggests that narratives of all kinds are high- and low-culture narratives so irrepressibly proliferate that they are "as ubiquitous in everyday culture as dust mites." But it would be hard to deny that unified (and unifying) industry-driven, mightily funded, financially incentivized storytelling—a powerful complex of profit imperatives and corporate marketing of unprecedented influence and reach—is dominating and narrowing of narrative options. It reflects a kind of singularity creep into language and literature.[28] I do not mean to be either cynical or presentist here. It is true that the nineteenth-century rise of mass culture generated a redundancy of a certain genre of narratives, particularly advancing plots that push rags-to-riches providential rise and American exceptionalism, so this potential narrowing of content is not new. This is part of AI's cultural genealogy, and it is one in which certain invested racialized, gendered narratives of modernity overwhelm others (see Elam 2022).

This genealogy is another reason that, in this age of AI, although there are more horizontal and representational forms of diversity—diverse platforms to view more diverse content created, produced, and represented by more diverse talent—the effect is not necessarily a leveling of power and opening of access. It is essential to acknowledge that those voices must still contend with long-embedded power structures and forces in place in academe, media, and the tech and entertainment industries, with and against which they must—and surely will—offer alternative and counter soundings, registers, and codings.

Coda: Beyond Optimization

One of these more hopeful soundings might include Vauhini Vara's 2021 article "I Didn't Know How to Write about My Sister's Death—So I Had AI Do It for Me," which generated a great deal of heated controversy over a GPT-3 experiment. It documents an attempt after years of struggle to help her put into words what her sister's passing meant to her. In an NPR interview, she discusses the initially unsatisfying experience—the predictive algorithmic program got stuck in a repetitive loop, for instance—but it also reflected back what she recognized as her own canned clichéd language that she had been offering as prompts, serving as an unflattering but revelatory mirror to her own prose. The algorithm also incorrectly generated language about her sister's life that was untrue, for instance, that she was an athlete. But, significantly, this only prompted Vara to think more about the process of truth telling itself. In short, the response to her prompts in turn prompted her; the AI-generated script did not edit but, rather, provoked to the extent she interpreted it as such. In occasionally illuminating ways, the process refracted back to her the limits and potential of how she had initially put her experience into print. She tapped AI's interactive possibilities in which the craft of writing was more than an "afterthought" (Marche 2021b); rather, she used it more as a conversant, interlocutor, de facto therapist. It learned as she trained it with input, but most important, it also, to her surprise, provided material that informed her about herself.

And as for what to make of the GPT-3 text? She says she edited it for length, for impact. But the last line was all GPT-3 (here in italics) and "she especially loved that last sentence because it contains so much" (Low 2021): "Once upon a time, my sister taught me to read. She taught me to wait for a mosquito to swell on my arm and then slap it and see the blood spurt out. She taught me to insult racists back. To swim. To pronounce English so I sounded less Indian. To shave my legs without cutting myself. To lie to our parents believably. To do math. To tell stories. *Once upon a time, she taught me to exist.*"

As Vara (2021) notes, although some of the GPT-3-produced language was uncannily akin to what could be produced by a human, even the ones that were not up to the standard of simulacra in fact had significance: sometimes in others' examples she read online, as well as in her experiment, the "language was weird, off-kilter—but often poetically so, almost truer than writing any human would produce." The literary value of the "almost truer" dimension appears in the last version of her own story, in which Vara reprints nine iterations of her vignette, allowing readers to see the process and negotiation with AI that she and her editor use, such that the last version acquires meaning through repeat and revise—a kind of signifying on that which came before.[29]

This particular practice of signification involving the inclusion of her own and the application's discarded drafts, precursors, iterations of, and variations on a published or performed piece is increasingly representative of what we might call the new genre of GPT-3 literary projects.[30] It suggests a renewed challenge to the notions of an originating moment in an artistic process, to the belief in a static final iteration that necessarily holds superior cultural or aesthetic status. Moreover, it helpfully pushes against the more tightly held idea(l), particularly cherished in the West, of "art" as only that which issues, sui generis, from a singular, taken-for-granted human author.[31] Vara's story illustrates when and where meaning making remains a durational, performative, collaborative process among author, audiences, contexts, and interpretative lenses. The idea that meaning is suspended in time, as if trapped in amber, residing fixed in authorial intent or encoded/entombed in text itself, was long ago debated and, for most scholars, settled as too limited an account of communication.

In that sense, at its best and perhaps most interesting, AI-generated literature and art might capitalize on how meaning is already and always an ongoing, mutually constitutive, interpretive event. In this case, at least, AI holds the possibility of becoming a generative interlocutor for the writer, enabling multivalent ways of communicating, in the higher interests of human play, insight, and creativity. Moreover, in service of those higher interests, the arts and humanities are essential in reframing the endless questions about just what intelligence or creativity is, about who, why, and what ends motivate those questions. If so, literature might help us understand the aims of AI beyond augmenting the human experience. AI, like all technologies, is a crucible of our world views, our social priorities, commitments, investments, and aspirations. As such, perhaps one of its greatest uses is to allow it to reflect us back to ourselves.

Michele Elam is the William Robertson Coe Professor of Humanities in the English department and faculty associate director of the Institute for Human-Centered AI at Stanford University. She has served as director of African and African American studies and director of the graduate Program in Modern Thought and Literature. Her books include *Race, Work, and Desire in American Literature, 1860–1930* (2003), *The Souls of Mixed Folk: Race, Politics, and Aesthetics in the New Millennium* (2011), and *The Cambridge Companion to James Baldwin* (2015). Elam is currently completing a book project tentatively titled "Race-Making in the Age of AI."

Notes

1   As decolonial artist-technologist Amelia Winger-Bearskin describes it, cutting-edge technology is not always unequivocally a good; she calls it the "bleeding edge" of innovation (Mozilla Pulse, n.d.).

2   The language processing system, PaLM, short for Pathways Language Model, for instance, draws on neural networks trained on over 540 billion parameters compared with GPT-3's initial 175 billion (Narang and Chowdhery 2022).

3   I make a distinction, admittedly blunt if generally apt, between digital humanities and humanities' engagement with AI by drawing on Joanna Drucker's (2009: 6) conclusion that "digital humanities was formed by concessions to the exigencies of computational disciplines. Humanities played by the rules of computer science and formal knowledge."

4   Amit Gupta, one of the founders of Sudowrite, one of the programs using GPT-3, quoted in Marche 2021b.

5   Sam Altman, CEO of OpenAI, from the outset downplayed expectations for GPT-3, saying it has "serious weaknesses" and still makes "silly mistakes" (quoted from a tweet by Altman, reprinted in Deoras 2022). Nonetheless, the technology, which was licensed to Microsoft but invites (vetted) participation in the collective development of it, immediately gained cultural traction and immense popularity, especially among casual users.

6   The term *uncanny valley* was first coined by in the 1970s by Masahiro Mori, professor at the Tokyo Institute of Technology, who documented the physiological response of humans' affinity for social robots the more lifelike they appear—up to a point, after which affinity turns to repulsion. Since then, work has been extended and explored by social psychologists and neuroscientists and often informs computer and animation design. I invoke it here to mark the unease some writers and artists feel when GPT-3 appears to approximate natural language and speech (Caballar 2019).

7   For an in-depth discussion of the many debates over the problems with categorization, particularly its history and impact on social identities, see Elam 2022. Many scholars have also challenged different problematic aspects of categorization and classification so central to visual processing systems and versions of Imagenet, a pioneering visual database that categorizes objects, including faces, thereby enabling visual object recognition. Initially created for use in research, some of its commercial and government applications, including surveillance, have come under intense criticism (see Crawford 2021).

8   In a keynote lecture Ruha Benjamin (2021) in fact suggests we "embrace the friction"—friction as opposed to the seductive opiate of frictionlessness central to marking technological products but that masks social frictions. She critiques in particular the minimalist design enabling frictionlessness as an aesthetic ideal that intentionally guides users away from the values embedded in a product's infrastructure, from the corporate interests animating its design, from extractivism of human labor, and from a tech

product contributing to ecocide by its cost to the environment through its making (see Reich et al. 2021, chap. 1).

9   Adams quoted in Katz 2020: 6, in a discussion of AI notions of the self: "Practitioners in the 1970s, for instance, offered visions of the self as a symbolic processing machine. . . . In the late 1980s and early 1990s, by contrast, the prevailing 'self' started looking more like a statistical inference engine driven by sensory data. But these classifications mask more fundamental epistemic commitments. Alison Adams has argued that AI practitioners across the board have aspired to a 'view from nowhere'—to build systems that learn, reason, and act in a manner freed from social context. The view from nowhere turned out to be a view from a rather specific, white, and privileged space."

10 *Personalization* is an industry term referring to data-scraping personal information as consumers use their product as part of the business model to better serve client interests and preferences (preferences that of course they then cultivate and curate, and/or sell to third parties if not regulated).

11 The "quantified self" is associated with the measuring all aspects of the body and associated with technological self-tracking, lifelogging, quanti-biometrics and auto-analytics. It is often associated with "knowing oneself"—that is, numerically at least—and popularized by wearable fitness and sleep trackers and baby monitoring (see, e.g., Béchard 2021). It showcases a geneticist's efforts to track every single aspect of his body and humans more generally. In the interest of health care, one can only wonder at earlier highly problematic impulses in history to measure humankind also in the name of science, cogently documented in Stephen Jay Gould's field-changing *Mismeasures of Man* ([1981] 1996).

12 *Blessings of scale* refers to the observation that for, deep learning, hard problems are easier to solve than easy problems—everything gets better as it gets larger (in contrast to the usual outcome in research, where small things are hard and large things impossible). See Branwen 2022b.

13 This contemporary historical moment, in which these modalities are enshrined and embraced in standard technological practice, is eerily similar to an earlier vogue, what Martha Banta (1993: jacket) calls the "efficiency craze" in American culture at the turn of the last century. Banta's fascinating book *Taylored Lives* explores "scientific management: technology spawned it, Frederick Winslow Taylor championed it, Thorstein Veblen dissected it, Henry Ford implemented it. By the turn of the century, practical visionaries prided themselves on having arrived at 'the one best way' both to increase industrial productivity and to regulate human behavior" (jacket).

I am distinguishing between optimization and the many ways in which AI can support the human experience. Though beyond the scope of this article, there are many emerging scientific investigations of the effects of art on the brain: neuro-aesthetics is providing evidence-based research documenting how arts engagement improves brain development and cognition, including executive function arts. For a recent example in the area of neuro-aesthetics, see the NeuroArts Blueprint collaboration between Johns Hopkins University and the Aspen Institute: https://neuroartsblueprint.org. There are also data demonstrating that public arts, mitigating the social alienation inimical to human well-being, is all the more essential to engage in during crises such as war or pandemics.

14 These are among many fierce critiques from both within and outside of the tech industry. Note the public controversy over the firing of Timnit Gebru from Google over her research that identified bias in large foundational models such as GPT-3 (Simonite 2021). See also Bender et al. 2021.

15 Although Erik Brynjolfson (2022) does not address the issue of art, he also points to the limitations of what he calls the "Turing trap."

16 For instance, Branwen and Presser (2019) suggest that "poetry is a natural fit for machine generation because we don't necessarily expect it to make sense or have standard syntax/grammar/vocabulary, and because it is often as much about the sound as the sense. Humans may find even mediocre poetry quite hard to write, but *machines are indefatigable* and can generate many samples to select from, so the final results can be pretty decent."

17 The award-winning documentary *Paul Robeson: A Tribute to an Artist* (1979) highlights the singer-actor-activist's revisions of the song, originally in the 1921 musical *Showboat*, over his lifetime from a post-Reconstruction-era melody to a pointed political commentary on racial and economic injustice.

18 For an extended discussion of the politics of representing speech, see Elam 1991.

19 There is a vast and expanding body of rich scholarship on Black vernaculars and literary representation. For seminal and essential work on this issue, see Gates (1988) 2014.

20 See the image at Christie's 2018.

21 I place the restoration of *The Night Watchman* in a certain class of AI applications that attempt to recreate, approximate, or better understand the making of an original through the use of AI or other sophisticated technologies. This work is important and much needed, even if it does not necessarily pose challenges to core assumptions and canonized practices in the art world. See, e.g., Stork 2021 and Cann et al. 2021.

22 Benjamin articulates the idea of aura as something integral to an original artwork that cannot be reproduced (he was thinking of photography).

23 For one of the best accounts of *Birth of a Nation* and how the development of film technology is inextricably tied to the formal encoding of racism in the early twentieth century, see Rogin 1985.

24 On the question of humanness and how technologies determine full humans, not quite humans, and nonhumans, see Weheliye 2014. See also Wynter 2003, which critiques that the overrepresentation of Man (as white, Western) as the only imaginable mode of humanness, overwriting other ontologies, epistemologies, and imaginaries (see also McKittrick 2015). A major influence on this article, Sylvia Wynter's pioneering and prolific work draws on arts, humanities, natural and neuroscience, philosophy,

literary theory, and critical race theory. As but one example of the equation of poesy with humanity, consider Thomas Jefferson's (1784–5) infamous argument about the innate inferiority of Black people as the basis for denying them emancipation, that he "never yet could I find that a black had uttered a thought above the level of plain narration; never see even an elementary trait, of painting or sculpture. . . . Among the blacks is misery enough, God knows, but no poetry." Whites were so convinced that a person of African descent was incapable of poesy that when Phillis Wheatley became the first African American to publish a book of poetry, she had to have her master and a gaggle of white officials in Boston testify as proof she was the author.

25 Roland Barthe's ([1967] 2001) influential essay "The Death of the Author" critiques the incorporation of biographical background and authorial intent in literary criticism and interpretation.

26 For examples of this genre of anxiety, see, e.g.., Crowe 2020, Branwen 2022a, Metz 2020, Elgammal 2019, and Manjoo 2020. See also Pranam 2019 and Offbeat Poet 2019, a discussion of POEMPORTRAITS as "an evolving collective poem generator created by Google Arts and Culture's Ross Goodwin and artist, Es Devlin." The AI is able to implement a creative writing algorithm trained on data consisting of 20 million words from nineteenth-century poetry. One pauses, however, at the goals of art entertainment apps, like the LACMA apps that align your face with a famous painting, which involves data-scraping personal features to add to its database. Is there a privacy disclosure? Is that really an aesthetic experience? And the marketing POEMPORTRAIT opens with an encouragement to donate your word to the making of a collective poem. That language of donation suggests that adding the prompt of a word or line is a way to contribute to some vague collective effort toward an even vaguer social good.

27 This refrain appears in many of scholar Ruha Benjamin's public talks, as well as in her books, including *Race after Technology* (Benjamin 2019).

28 First coined in a technological context by John von Neumann, *singularity* is meant to describe a point in time when technological advances become inexorable, irreversible, and uncontrollable and cause unforeseeable changes in society. It is often described as a positive possibility in technology; I use it here with a cautionary intent.

29 I am drawing on the common definition of *literary signifying* outlined in Gates (1988) 2014.

30 In a *Daedelus* issue on AI and society, James Manyika's (2022) afterword similarly reprints experiments with GPT-3. See also the Wordcraft Writers Workshop, a collaboration between Google and professional writers experimenting with co-writing with LaMDA to explore the "rapidly changing relationship between technology and creativity," as described on its landing page https://wordcraft-writers-workshop.appspot.com.

31 There are extant examples of other modes of authorship that do not reflect this more dominant mode of possessive individualism, including many historical African American expressive forms, such as the spirituals,

blues, or work songs, that have most often been collective and frequently anonymous works. Indigenous artist-technologist Amelia Winger-Bearskin (2020) also contrasts what I critique as the obsession with genius (almost without exception through history as white/male/cis), especially in the tech world, with what she calls wampum.code ethics.

References

Baldwin, James. (1979) 1998. "If Black English Isn't a Language, Then Tell Me What Is." In *Baldwin: Collected Essays*, edited by Toni Morrison, 780–83. New York: Library of America.

Banta, Martha. 1993. *Taylored Lives: Narrative Productions in the Age of Taylor, Veblen, and Ford*. Chicago: Univ. of Chicago Press.

Barthes, Roland. (1967) 2001. "The Death of the Author." *Contributions in Philosophy* 83: 3–8.

Béchard, Deni Ellis. 2021. "Body Count: How Michael Snyder's Self-Monitoring Project Could Transform Human Health." *Stanford Magazine*, December. https://stanfordmag.org/contents/body-count.

Bender, E. M., T. Gebru, A. McMillan-Major, and S. Shmitchell. 2021. "On the Dangers of Stochastic Parrots: Can Language Models Be Too Big?" FAccT 21. *Proceedings of the 2021 ACM Conference on Fairness, Accountability, and Transparency*, 610–23. https://doi.org/10.1145/3442188.3445922.

Benjamin, Ruha. 2019. *Race after Technology: Abolitionist Tools for the New Jim Code*. Medford, MA: Polity Press.

Benjamin, Ruha. 2021. "Which Humans: Reimagining the Default Settings of Technology and Society." Keynote Kieve Lecture at the conference "Antiracist Technologies for a Just Future," Center for Comparative Studies in Race and Ethnicity, Stanford University, Stanford, CA, May 20.

Benjamin, Walter. (1935) 1969. "The Work of Art in the Age of Its Technological Reproducibility." In *Illuminations: Essays and Reflections*, edited by Hannah Arendt, translated by Harry Zohn. New York: Schocken Books.

Branwen, Gwern. 2022a. "GPT-3 Creative Fiction." Gwern.net, February 10. https://www.gwern.net/GPT-3.

Branwen, Gwern. 2022b. "The Scaling Hypothesis." Gwern.net, January 2. https://www.gwern.net/Scaling-hypothesis.

Branwen, Gwern, and Shawn Presser. 2019. "GPT-2 Neural Network Poetry." Gwern.net, October 29. https://www.gwern.net/GPT-2.

Brynjolfson, Erik. 2022. "The Turing Trap: The Promise and Peril of Humanlike Artificial Intelligence." *Daedalus* 151, no. 2: 279–94.

Caballar, Rina Diane. 2019. "What Is the Uncanny Valley?" *IEEE Spectrum*, November 6. https://spectrum.ieee.org/automaton/robotics/humanoids/what-is-the-uncanny-valley.

Cann, George H., et al. 2021. "Recovery of Underdrawings and Ghost-Paintings via Style Transfer by Deep Convolutional Neural Networks: A Digital Tool for Art Scholars." Paper presented at "Electronic Imaging 2021: Computer Vision and image Analysis of Art," January.

Chow, Andrew R. 2021. "NFTs Are Shaking Up the Art World—But They Could Change So Much More." *Time*, March 22. https://time.com/5947720/nft -art/.

Christie's. 2018. "Is Artificial Intelligence Set to Become Art's Next Medium?" December 12. https://www.christies.com/features/a-collaboration-between -two-artists-one-human-one-a-machine-9332-1.aspx.

Chun, Wendy Hui Kyong. 2006. *Control and Freedom: Power and Paranoia in the Age of Fiber Optics*. Cambridge, MA: MIT Press.

Crawford, Kate. 2021. *Atlas of AI: Power, Politics and the Planetary Costs of Artificial Intelligence*. New Haven, CT: Yale Univ. Press.

Crowe, Lana. 2020. "Poetech: Shall I Compare Thee to GPT-3? Shakespeare v AI." *Sayre Zine*. https://apostrophezinecom.wordpress.com/2020/10/05 /gpt-3-ai-poetry-shakespeare-sonnet-18/.

Deoras, Shristi. 2020. "GPT-3 Has Weaknesses and Makes Silly Mistakes: Sam Altman, OpenAI," *Analytics India Magazine*. https://analyticsindiamag .com/gpt-3-has-weaknesses-and-makes-silly-mistakes-sam-altman-openai/.

Drucker, Joanna. 2009. *Speclab: Digital Aesthetics and Projects in Speculative Computing*. Chicago: Univ. of Chicago Press.

Elam, Harry J., Jr. 2006. *The Past as Present in the Drama of August Wilson*. Ann Arbor: Univ. of Michigan Press.

Elam, Michele. 1991. "Dark Dialects: Scientific and Literary Realism in Joel Chandler Harris' Uncle Remus Series." *New Orleans Review* 18: 36–45.

Elam, Michele. 2022. "Signs Taken for Wonders: AI, Art and the Matter of Race." Issue: *AI & Society*, edited by James Manyika. *Daedalus* 151, no. 2: 198–217.

Elgammal, Ahmed. 2019. "AI Is Blurring the Definition of Artist." *American Scientist* 107, no. 1: 18–21.

Gates, Jr., Henry Louis. (1988) 2014. *The Signifying Monkey: A Theory of African American Literary Criticism*. Oxford: Oxford Univ. Press.

Gould, Stephen Jay. (1981) 1996. *The Mismeasures of Man*. New York: Norton.

Hayles, N. Katherine. 2021. "Narrative and Database: Natural Symbionts." In "Remapping Genre," edited by Wai Chee Dimock and Bruce Robbins. Special issue, *PMLA* 122, no. 5: 1603–8.

Jefferson, Thomas. 1784–5. *Notes on the State of Virginia*. Volume 1, Chapter 15 "Equality," Document 28. University of Chicago Press. http://press-pubs .uchicago.edu/founders/documents/v1ch15s28.html.

Katz, Yarden. 2020. *Artificial Whiteness: Politics and Ideology in Artificial Intelligence*. New York: Columbia Univ. Press.

Low, Tobin. 2021. "The Ghost in the Machine." Interview with Vauhini Vara. *This American Life*, December 31. https://www.thisamericanlife.org/757 /the-ghost-in-the-machine.

Manjoo, Farhad. 2020. "How Do You Know a Human Wrote This?" *New York Times*, July 29. https://www.nytimes.com/2020/07/29/opinion/gpt-3-ai -automation.html.

Manyika, James. 2022. "Afterword: Some Illustrations." *Daedalus* 151, no. 2: 372–79. https://www.amacad.org/publication/afterword-some-illustrations.

Marche, Stephen. 2021a. "The Chatbot Problem." *New Yorker*, July 23. https://www.newyorker.com/culture/cultural-comment/the-chatbot-problem.

Marche, Stephen. 2021b. "The Computers Are Getting Better at Writing." *New Yorker*, April 30. https://www.newyorker.com/culture/cultural-comment/the-computers-are-getting-better-at-writing.

Mattei, Shanti Escalante-De. 2021. "Artificial Intelligence Restores Mutilated Rembrandt Painting." *ArtNews*, June 23. https://www.artnews.com/art-news/news/rembrandt-ai-restoration-1234596736/.

McKittrick, Katherine. 2015. *Sylvia Wynter: On Being Human as Praxis*. Durham, NC: Duke Univ. Press.

Metz, Cade. 2020. "Meet GPT-3. It Has Learned to Code (and Blog and Argue)." *New York Times*, November 24. https://www.nytimes.com/2020/11/24/science/artificial-intelligence-ai-gpt3.html.

Mozilla Pulse. n.d. "Amelia Winger-Bearskin." https://www.mozillapulse.org/profile/3119.

Narang, Sharan, and Aakanksha Chowdhery. 2022. "Pathways Language Model (PaLM): Scaling to 540 Billion Parameters for Breakthrough Performance." *Google AI Blog*, April 4. https://ai.googleblog.com/2022/04/pathways-language-model-palm-scaling-to.html.

Offbeat Poet. 2019. "Putting the ART in ARTificial Intelligence." *Medium*, July 3. https://medium.com/offbeat-poetry/putting-the-art-in-artificial-intelligence-742d6880c34a.

Paul Robeson: A Tribute to An Artist (Documentary short IMDb 1979). Directed by Narrated Saul J. Turell. Produced by Jessica Berman and Saul J. Turell. Narrated by Sidney Poitier.

Pranam, Aswin. 2019. "Putting the Art in Artificial Intelligence: A Conversation with Sougwen Chung." *Forbes*, December 12. https://www.forbes.com/sites/aswinpranam/2019/12/12/putting-the-art-in-artificial-intelligence-a-conversation-with-sougwen-chung/?sh=4c7afa543c5b.

Ramesh, Aditya. 2021. "DALL·E: Creating Images from Text." *OpenAI.com*, January 5. https://openai.com/blog/dall-e/.

Reich, Rob, Mehran Sahami, and Jeremy M. Weinstein. 2021. *System Error: Where Big Tech Went Wrong and How We Can Reboot*. New York: Harper Collins.

Rogin, Michael. 1985. "'The Sword Became a Flashing Vision': D. W. Griffith's." *Representations*, no. 9: 150–95.

Roose, Kevin. 2022. "A Coming-Out Party for Generative AI: Silicon Valley's New Craze." *New York Times*, October 21. https://www.nytimes.com/2022/10/21/technology/generative-ai.html.

Schneider, Tim. 2020. "A.I. Has the Potential to Change the Art Business—Forever. Here's How It Could Revolutionize the Way We Buy, Sell, and See Art." *Artnet News*, March 31. https://news.artnet.com/market/ai-art-business-intelligence-report-2020-1812288.

Simonite, Tom. 2021. "What Really Happened When Google Ousted Timnit Gebru." *Wired*, June 8. https://www.wired.com/story/google-timnit-gebru-ai-what-really-happened/.

Stork, David. 2021. "Automatic Computation of Meaning in Authored Images Such as Artworks: A Grand Challenge for AI." *ACM Journal on Computing in Cultural History* 1–10.

Vara, Vauhini. 2021. "I Didn't Know How to Write about My Sister's Death—So I Had AI Do It for Me." *Believer Magazine*, August 9. https://believermag.com/ghosts/#content.

Weheliye, Alexander G. 2014. *Habeas Viscus: Racializing Assemblages, Biopolitics, and Black Feminist Theories of the Human*. Durham, NC: Duke Univ. Press.

Winger-Bearskin, Amelia. 2020. "Indigenous Wisdom as a Model for Software Design and Development." *Mozilla*, October 2. https://foundation.mozilla.org/en/blog/indigenous-wisdom-model-software-design-and-development/.

Wynter, Sylvia. 2003. "Unsettling the Coloniality of Being/Power/Truth/Freedom: Towards the Human, after Man, Its Overrepresentation—An Argument." *CR: The New Centennial Review* 3, no. 3: 257–337.

Ranjodh Singh Dhaliwal

What Do We Critique When We Critique Technology?

Your Computer Is on Fire. Edited by Thomas S. Mullaney, Benjamin Peters, Mar Hicks, and Kavita Philip. Cambridge, MA: MIT Press. 2021. 416 pp. Paper, $35.00; e-book, $25.99.

Technoprecarious. By Precarity Lab. London: Goldsmiths Press. 2020. 124 pp. Paper, $25.95; e-book, $19.99.

Uncertain Archives: Critical Keywords for Big Data. Edited by Nanna Bonde Thylstrup, Daniela Agostinho, Annie Ring, Catherine D'Ignazio, and Kristin Veel. Cambridge, MA: MIT Press. 2021. 640 pp. Paper, $55.00; e-book, $38.99.

Thinking about the state of technology today necessarily means thinking about a number of interrelated but distinct entities. Considering the nuts and bolts of a news story in which, say, some corporate machine vision technology was found to be racially discriminatory can often mean having to study business practices, data sciences, specific suites of tools that can lay a claim to the moniker of *AI*, assemblages of hardware and software, platform infrastructures with machines slotted away in hot data-center basements in tax havens, human-computer interactions and perceptions, and academic/industry discourses within any of the aforementioned, not to mention the geopolitical and historical situation of it all, which may further call into question where, say, "American" literature can uniquely intersect with technologies splayed awkwardly across, and not always along, the traditional geopolitical and cultural fault lines. In such a scenario, the flag of "Critical AI and (American) Literature," by its very constitution, carries several sigils, including those of big data and literature and of computational culture and literature, as well as American studies and global technological sovereignties. Focused on the more critical end

American Literature, Volume 95, Number 2, June 2023
DOI 10.1215/00029831-10575091   © 2023 by Duke University Press

of these studies, this review brings together three new multiauthored books to ask what we critique when we critique technology today.

Scholars interested in literature and technology—usually found in disciplines and departments such as languages and literatures, cultural studies, science studies, and media studies—have long been producing pathbreaking critical thought about various sociotechnical phenomena. From reading technologies themselves using literary critical methods—N. Katherine Hayles, Donna Haraway, Friedrich Kittler, Wendy Chun, Matthew Kirschenbaum, Rita Raley, Lisa Gitelman, and Alexander Galloway all come to mind here—to studying literary expressions of technological worlds (see, e.g., work by Fredric Jameson, Bruce Clark, Laura Otis, Steven Shaviro, Sherryl Vint, and Colin Milburn), literary criticism has been a bellwether of technology critique for several decades now. A brief look at such critique through the ages shows us the varied moods that orient studies of these technologies, with AI just being the latest in this series that once featured the internet, the personal computer, hypertext, cellphone, and metadata. Where there was once a utopian dream with the expansion of networks in the 1990s, or a reluctant acceptance that became a residual flicker of counterprogrammatic hope that technologies can be reappropriated by radical social forces in late 2010s, there is now, in critical work collected here, largely anger and disappointment. Every day, as news cycles tell tales of unchecked tech monopolies roughly intruding into our social, political, and psychic lives, and rarely for the good, these authors find themselves angry—*really* angry—about the state of our technologies and what they have wrought. On the one hand, such anger indexes our historical condition and informs our engagement with technology today. On the other hand, it forces us to ask what we are actually angry about, and what can be done instead.

The primary example of this mood may be found in *Your Computer Is on Fire*, edited by Thomas S. Mullaney, Benjamin Peters, Mar Hicks, and Kavita Philip. This volume is a startlingly direct collection of essays that, for the most part, all do what they say; the overarching purpose of the volume is, in fact, a call to action that signals a diffused state of emergency in various corners of computational cultures (6). The three parts of the book—"Nothing Is Virtual," "This Is an Emergency," and "Where Will the Fire Spread?"—contain chapters that are thematically and methodologically varied but all united by their clear and accessible critiques that point out how inequalities and discriminations are enabled and exacerbated by technological systems today. To note a few, Nathan Ensmenger's "The Cloud Is a Factory," which uses

Amazon as a case study for the infrastructural reinscription of older techniques of capital used by Sears and Standard Oil, is an excellent breakdown of the material behind the supposedly virtual cloud (29); Ben Peters's "A Network Is Not a Network" accounts for the role of institutional behavior in the constitution of large-scale networks (71); Mar Hicks, through an analysis of gender discrimination in mid-twentieth-century technology labor sector, claims that "Sexism Is a Feature, Not a Bug" in tech economies and communities (135); Safiya Umoja Noble tells us that our robots aren't neutral (199); Janet Abbate takes on tech sector's consideration of coders using the pipe-line model—the discourse that encourages getting more women and minorities to learn coding earlier and faster so as to facilitate a smoother and more expansive flow of more diverse labor into the infamously white and masculine technology sector—to show how "Coding Is Not Empowerment" (253); Ben Allen magisterially demonstrates how the same genre of technical hacks can be read as playful or criminal depending on power dynamics (273); and Paul Edwards studies platforms, which he calls *fast infrastructures*, as he takes up exemplars from South Africa and Kenya to suggest that these fleeting operational levers represent the next model of corporate infrastructural dominance (313). The volume, then, contains a series of related, but not necessarily coagulated, critiques of technology and its socio-cultural conditions.

Technoprecarious, collectively authored by the Precarity Lab (the contributing team comprises Cassius Adair, Iván Chaar López, Anna Watkins Fisher, Meryem Kamil, Cindy Lin, Silvia Lindtner, Lisa Naka-mura, Cengiz Salman, Kalindi Vora, Jackie Wang, and McKenzie Wark) reads not like an edited collection but more like a short mani-festo written by scholars with complementary orientations. The dif-ferent sections of the book—among them "The Undergig," "The Widening Gyre of Precarity," "Automating Abandonment," "Fanta-sies of Ability," and"Dispossession by Surveillance"—come together to form a patchwork of commentaries, most well rooted in original cultural, sociotechnical, anthropological, and historical research, that all very playfully point out the exacerbation of precarity wrought by, with, and through digital technologies today. The titular techno-precarity, for the collective, is "the premature exposure to death and debility that working with or being subjected to digital technologies accelerates" (1). Technoprecarity here shows up in snippets that plug into work on surveillance, carceral systems, toxicity, and administrative failures, among other nodes of inquiry. The final two chapters feature a Haraway-esque hope for radical reappropriation listing the Detroit

Digital Stewards Program, which features groups that help underprivileged communities gain access to technologies as tools of communication, and the use of open-source maps in Palestine as examples to be followed for practices of techno-oriented care (74–86). There is a sincere attempt here, not unlike the penultimate contribution in *Your Computer Is on Fire*, "How to Stop Worrying about Clean Signals and Start Loving the Noise" by Kavita Philip (363), to find a nugget or two of hope in the middle of the general condition of technoprecarity being described.

Uncertain Archives: Critical Keywords for Big Data, edited by Nanna Bonde Thylstrup, Daniela Agostinho, Annie Ring, Catherine D'Ignazio, and Kristin Veel, is a six-hundred-page collection that features sixty-one keyword entries, altogether providing a Raymond Williams–style vocabulary for critical studies of data and AI. Considering big data as an uncertain archive—drawing from archival theory and critical data studies while thinking about the latent possibilities of aggregation as presented by big data today—the collection features short, punchy nuggets of wisdom that offer a polysemic understanding of the kinds of critical thought different disciplines can offer to studies of big data and AI at large. The entries vary widely in style, tone, content, and orientation. Overlapping questions of epistemologies ("Quantification" by Jacqueline Wernimont, "Ethics" by Louise Amoore, "Unpredictability" by Elena Esposito, "Remains" by Tonia Sutherland), alterity and discrimination ("Abuse" by Sarah Roberts, "(Mis)Gendering" by Os Keyes), power ("DNA" by Mél Hogan, "Instrumentality" by Luciana Parisi, "Organization" by Timon Beyes), aesthetics ("Demo" by Orit Halpern; a brilliant, poetic one on "Throbber" by Kristoffer Ørum; "Visualization" by Johanna Drucker), infrastructures ("Cooling" by Nicole Starosielski, "Supply Chain" by Miriam Posner, "Field" by Shannon Mattern), and socialities ("Values" by John S. Seberger and Geoffrey C. Bowker, "Proxies" by Wendy Hui Kyong Chun, Boaz Levin, and Vera Tollmann; "Self-Tracking" by Natasha Dow Schüll) all sit alongside questions near and dear to literary critical approaches ("Digital Humanities" by Roopika Risam, "File" by Craig Robertson, "Misreading" by Lisa Gitelman). In performing the immensely unenviable task of shepherding sixty-eight other scholars from across the world into one contained collection, the editors here provide a deliberately fragmented mise-en-scène of critical data studies as it unfolds across several corners of academia today. Juggling several different approaches, *Uncertain Archives* does not easily offer a shared through line. Nevertheless, it can be read as a collection trying to enumerate the various evaluative frameworks that can be applied to/in critical (big) data studies; most terms offered here—some of which are compressed versions based on the concepts outlined in the contributors' monographs and articles—can be taken as pedagogical scaffolds or starting points for a broader set of research inquiries. And big data here shows up as nebulous and tentacular, both in its contemporary material reach and in its analytic demand for methodological diversity.

Before returning to talk about criticism and technology at scale again by considering what this cluster teaches us methodologically, let us first consider something like a state-of-the-field snapshot, briefly analyzing the who, what, and how of technology criticism presented by this sample set of edited collections, which is admittedly numerically small yet also somehow, by the virtue of including more than ninety authors from across the world, huge.

It is in their conscious interdisciplinarity, tending toward a kind of postdisciplinarity, that all these three reviewed works are united in their orientation. Methodologically, they all occupy slightly different niches: *Your Computer Is on Fire* tries to advance one very broad but largely unified argument, *Uncertain Archives* presents a curated cacophony of positions, and *Technoprecarious* is a tight-knit manifesto that, quite uniquely and successfully, speaks in one voice. But in orientation, they are all joined at the hip, insofar as all these works bring together scholars of media studies, communication studies, digital studies, film studies, science and technology studies, data science, history and philosophy of science and technology, cultural studies, journalism, information and library sciences, American studies, critical race studies, postcolonial studies, gender and sexuality studies, organization studies, critical legal studies, critical geographies, digital humanities, and anthropology, along with literary critics. The fact that this list of disciplinary orientations seems overwhelming, despite several shared positions and investments of the many disciplines therein, is in fact one of the problems that this swell of collected work set out to address. In the special zone occupied by edited collections and coauthored work within academic circuits, these volumes (and others recently, including not only the very special issue you are perusing right now but also the 2022 *Critical Inquiry* special issue on "Surplus Data" and the 2020 PMLA collection titled "Varieties of Digital Humanities") all mark a simultaneous expansion and contraction. On the one hand, this proliferation of edited collections showcases the best practices and results of bringing together different disciplinary research paradigms that such venues can perform, not to mention the new and exciting kinds of writing that coauthoring can wring out. On the other hand, the constant carving out of subdisciplinary niches (and the disillusionment from the same) in fact indexes the after-effects of the shrinkage of academic positions per se, with every scholar herein wearing several hats and delving (or, perhaps more accurately, having to delve) into several distinct, if concomitant, disciplines.

If one were to shift the focus from *who* is doing the study to *how*, one would find in some of this newer scholarship a desire to rethink the relationship between the scholar and the subject. Thinking with, instead of about, is well demonstrated across these collected works. For example, *Technoprecarious*, written by Precarity Lab, clearly starts out by staging its own existence as a form of laboratorial practice; the opening salvo states how

> [we] have adopted the "laboratory" (in our name and practice) to account for our highly ambivalent yet deeply entangled position in relation to ongoing attempts to upgrade and entrepreneurialize the humanities and scholarship and higher education broadly. The laboratory is a place of labor, but where labor is subordinated to the task of elaboration. In the lab, there are consistent procedures, forms of regularity that produce observable difference. The lab experiments—experiments that can be tested, verified, stabilized, and can become the prototypes for new forms of organization and governance. (8)

From this position of *being* a laboratory (and rightly being very conflicted about its constitution as a laboratory), the collective then stages a worthy conversation around laboratories in history (of science, technology, and culture) and popular imagination. The text rejects the idea of the city as a laboratory (9), provides a proposition about laboratories of slavery as historical and conceptual precursors to logics that widen the gyre of precarity and uneven expansion of surveillance (34), and enables a critical consideration of Detroit as a laboratorial model, both for a public imagination that sees it as exemplifying the decline of American cities and for the activists whose efforts are taken up in the text to demonstrate some kind of resistance and response in face of late capitalist horrors (76). In other words, the book is an experiment produced by a laboratory that studies different kinds of laboratorial impulses critically but also generatively. Such thinking with, as the books collected here showcase, has scholars using the subject of inquiry not as a curiosity to be observed from a distance, not just thought about, but as something to be used and thought through until the subject in question animates other parts of one's inquiry. (See also Lindsay Thomas's contribution to this special issue.)

There is also something to be said about what kind of epistemological cal work this interdisciplinarity does. Allow me to contextualize this aforementioned critical approach within the broader landscape of work around technology and culture. Humanistic studies of technology often provide, on the one hand, critiques of technological cultures themselves, and on the other, explorations of interrelations between technology and X, where X could be literature, media, or other sociocultural niches (for example, the whole domain of literature and science offers a set of methodologies for precisely this). Essentially, technocritical approaches, considered in this discussion by virtue of the books under review, are not afraid of critiquing technology at the level of technics, with criticality and technicality both in conversation with each other. Now, of course, the wedge between, say, cultural-critical and technocritical approaches isn't even a solidly distinct demarcation; plenty of work mentioned above ably flouts and flutters between these boundaries. However, one can still trace a faint distinction between work that stays far from the machinic cores and work that likes to stick close to the beating metallic heart of these systems. While the former might delve into the uses of technology—exemplified by, say, the aesthetic studies of electronic literature or the use of virtual reality in drama—the latter is likely to talk about the physical (or virtual) machines themselves. One is reminded here of the late technology theorist Leo Marx, whose complaint that technology is a hazardous concept lay atop the startlingly capacious denotations that the word consumed unto itself. The machines; the people who operated them; the systems that produced, sold, and maintained them; the infrastructural and politico-economic assemblages surrounding them were, per Marx (1997), rolled into one compact word sometime in the late nineteenth century in the United States: *technology*. In other words, the conceptual genesis of technology was a thoroughly American enterprise, with this nation-state offering the precise location for blurring economy, politics, and technics into one word. Technocritical approaches today mark a worthy (machinic) addition to the pantheon of approaches and orientations that break apart this word and that can be drawn on to study our world by providing a method of reading the nonhuman technologics for cultural, social, aesthetic, and political connotations. Here, in the variety of methodologies brought together by the books reviewed here, we can note a careful, if partial, fulfilment of the critical position exhorted by Marx; as noted below, scholars today are indeed studying technology as the aggregation of those capacities that Marx encountered in his concept genealogy. Within this matrix, technocriticality shows up as an approach that takes technology to include techniques and sociocultural logics while also not shying away from the machinic processes—demonstrated, for example, by Ben Allen's incisive reading of hack(ed/ing) code in *Your Computer Is on Fire* (273) and an excellent technopolitical breakdown of "Executing" by David Gauthier, Audrey Samson, Eric Snodgrass, Winnie Soon, and Magdalena Tyżlik-Carver (all members of the Critical Software Thing collective) in *Uncertain Archives* (209)—that used to be otherwise, sometimes unfortunately, black-boxed by earlier approaches.

In other words, these works show how "the material component— *technology* narrowly conceived as a physical device—is merely one part of a complex social and institutional matrix" (Marx 1997: 979). While the presence of several different disciplinary orientations in scholarly collections such as the ones reviewed here resolves prima facie some problems of focal vagueness through an ever-increasing array of analytic subjects, handled with care and rigor, it also brings forth a new kind of lacuna: causal clarity. Today, the primary form of arguments—especially arguments that are able to exceed local disciplinary scholarship and move toward interdisciplinary or public writing—is often about locating problems within something presumed "neutral." Regardless of what in the technology matrix is being critiqued—"Facebook doesn't actually connect, and Google's algorithms are racist" (machines), "Silicon Valley has a diversity problem that it is actively not solving" (communities), and "gender discrimination permeates hierarchies in tech industry" (systems), to take a few examples—it is always, as Bruno Latour (2004: 240) stated in his screed "Why Has Critique Run Out of Steam?," about "debunk[ing] objects [that the critics] don't believe in by showing the productive and projective forces of people." Who, one may ask, needs to know that this or that technology is not neutral? Is it the layperson, the technoscientific disciplinarian, or perhaps the critic more than anyone else? Breaking the problem into constituent historically and geographically situated units, as *Uncertain Archives* does, we can roughly taxonomize technology critique itself today through five nondistinct kinds of objects of critique as handled by scholars who aim their interventions at three nondistinct kinds of audiences (see table 1). The various components of technology pointed out by theorists and historians of technology—physical machines, technological culture and art, the people behind and in front of these machines, systems and structures that enable and maintain the machines, and the techniques and habits that go through/with the machines—all find different (sub)disciplinary

Table 1 The matrix of technology criticism

Objects of Study	Audience		
	Fellow Disciplinarians	Scholars from Other Disciplines	Public
Machines and devices	Sciences and engineering		Popular technology writing
Culture and art	New media art and cultural studies		Artistic public interventions
People and communities	Sociology and anthropology of technology	Technocritical approaches (circa 2023)	
Systems and structures	Political economy, sociology, and philosophy		Technocritical approaches (circa 2023)
Techniques, practices, and habits	Media archaeology and cultural technologies		Coming soon?

configurations studying and critiquing them not only in these reviewed texts but also in other critical scholarship generally. The work itself can easily flow between hyperspecific scholarship that targets one specific discipline and scholarship that is meant to be useful for academics working in other traditions. (If anything, the shrinking numbers of humanists and social scientists in American higher educational campuses provide a reason to write interdisciplinarily while also materially coagulating the different traditions into what should probably always have been shared interests.) Additionally, more and more scholarship today is also starting to reach out to a general audience, taking over the mantle from pop science books that endorse embarrassingly progressivist versions of technological advancement, often sanctioned and praised by Silicon Valley executives. Prominent examples of such critical work include Safiya Noble's *Algorithms of Oppression* (2018), Ruha Benjamin's *Race after Technology* (2019), and Cathy O'Neil's *Weapons of Math Destruction* (2016), all of which became (inter)nationally famous recently, for all the right reasons, and are cited heavily in this cluster.

No doubt there is an immense need for such critique—let us call it *technology critique*—that takes contemporary technological narratives to task for their sociopolitical entanglements. Such technology critique, even when it is technically oriented, has a barely different job than conventional ideology critique; if anything, it is the mirror image of literary *ideologiekritik*. In historical literary criticism (think Raymond Williams, Max Horkheimer, Theodor Adorno, Étienne Balibar, and Fredric Jameson), ideology critique can be broadly understood as analyzing the relationship between sociohistorical ideological configurations and textual forms. Technology critique, then, precisely because its core is usually considered a material (e.g., machine) and not a solely symbolic (e.g., a text) artifact, offers its inversion. Now, scholars of science and technology know very well that, in Lacanian terms, machines can be symbolic systems, and that both the machine and the text are always material-semiotic at the same time; in fact, this was the road taken by literary scholars such as Kittler and Hayles when first staking a claim on studying new technologies, with their central arguments resting on the fact that the electronic computer is, in many ways at its core, an inscription machine. But regardless of whether they start from the material or the semiotic, critics always end up in both places at once. For example, Romi Ron Morrison's entry on "Flesh" in *Uncertain Archives* finds the materiality of flesh to also be an "unavoidable signifier and text" for the "history and reality of total expropriation of value from bodies and land" (249). Hayles's contribution on the "Unthought" in the same volume, on the other hand, finds the cognitive nonconscious—literally the grounds for what can be thought in the first place—to be utterly material in its neuroscientific, corporeal, and inscriptional-technological bases (546). Thus, these volumes under review exhort us to continue further delineating and complicating the relationships between different material-semiotic components of technology while keeping the core of this burgeoning interdisciplinarity in technology critique. In fact, technology, in its etymological sense, as the study (*-logy*) of *technē* (art, craft, practical skill) may already *be* ideological critique itself, and this call then is a mere return to technology in its originary sense; calling something an "institute of technology" may actually mean using the term *study of technē*, the closest to its original form. But the dominant mode of technology critique today still involves telling us what is wrong with contemporary technologies, and as hinted above, the causalities are often missing, or it is unclear what exactly is being critiqued. When exactly do we critique technologies themselves ("your AI is racist"), when are we blaming individuals (Musk, Bezos, Zuckerberg, or techbros in general, all rightly find fingers pointed at them in these volumes), and when exactly is a named system to blame (whether that is racism, patriarchy, settler colonialism, or racial capitalism)? While the cowardly (and correct) answer, of course, is usually all of the above, that cannot be a distraction from pointed questions that can still be asked in/of such scholarship today, questions that might eventually force us—the readers, the technologists, and the critics altogether—to carefully diagnose what we need to do for/in this glitching, if not already broken, world today.

The role of AI as a technology might be an instructive case study here. After all, even within the work encountered in this piece, there is as much conversation about platformization, big data, and computation at large as about deep learning, neural networks, or advanced inference techniques normally associated with the term *AI*. Roughly, these books help us visualize the AI scene today; one can draw concentric circles, and AI will be the innermost: a tiny subset of soft- and hardware combinations that rely on a specific orientation of data sets and practices—which are often used to train AI—standing within a particular politicoeconomic, historical, and sociocultural framework of computational technologies. Put simply, conversations about technology today can often be conversations about computational technocultures, which in turn can often mean talking about big data, which itself is distinct from, but often enmeshed within, discourses of AI at large. These reviewed volumes make it clear that AI is not a coherent entity today; it shows up as either a technical assemblage at these different scales—of technologies, computational infrastructures, big data cultures, and so on—or a rhetorical maneuver toward vagueness as exercised by politicoeconomic power structures (*Technoprecarious*, 38–48; *Your Computer Is on Fire*, 51–70; *Uncertain Archives*, 65–75, 88–108). This "what is AI" question, when sincerely presented, shows AI to be a contingent, constructed category that relies on rhetorical maneuvers that birthed it in the first place. This was true in early days of AI in the mid-twentieth century, and it is still true now when the AI startup Kiwi Campus uses human labor to drive its remote-controlled Kiwibots around Berkeley, pretending to be "doing" AI, or as Sarah Roberts reminds us with her succinctly titled contribution in *Your Computer Is on Fire*, "Your AI Is a Human" (51). AI, it seems, at the end of the day is not just a technical problem; discursively, it signifies everything that can be possibly used to politically control and reinscribe global futures. And this possible reinscription is also a potentially productive moment to ask what is to be done. For example, when AI is scaled up, we get in the realm of big data, and the uncertainty invoked by the title *Uncertain Archives* suggests that big data is a wellspring of/for speculation, as all archives, per Jacques Derrida, have always already been (9, 11, 281, 403). In other words, these works teach us how technical assemblages are not set in stone; they retain in them a kernel of productive mischief.

The fact that rhetoric, especially rhetoric that animates cultural conceptions and imaginaries, is a central component of what comprises "artificial intelligence"—or, for that matter, big data, or the tech sector, or computation at large—is worth noting here. It is this fact that fully crystallizes the role of humanities and, more specifically, literary criticism, in the context of this issue's concern with AI and literature. As the works reviewed here show, several material battles of technological futures are fought on the symbolic terrain. On the one hand, scholars of inscription are (or at least can claim to be) best suited to study the inscription machine that is a computer. On the other hand, we can study technical rhetoric through literary critical methods; in fact, the very choice to critique this instead of that is a priori a discursive-rhetorical imposition of material interests on us. As the AI expert Timnit Gebru (2022) lamented recently,

> [Our] research agenda has to be based on what tech bros decide to chase. They get $$$ chase X, X gets proliferated, then we spend all our time analyzing and mitigating the harms of X. We never wanted to build X, that was never in our research agenda, or interests, but now we have to spend all our time thinking about and dealing with X. . . . That leads to persecution, then you fight the persecution, then rinse & repeat, tech bros with $$$ have moved on to the next thing.

This role of sociocultural factors in technological discourse thus essentially puts the onus of untangling naturalized notions about AI on scholars of language and inscription.

Taking a lead from Noah Wardrip-Fruin—who in his brilliant contribution to *Your Computer Is on Fire* titled "You Can't Make Games about Much" shows how reskinning of games can be essentially a marketing maneuver that doesn't necessarily change the underlying gamic parameters, and therefore there are only a finite number of games that can hit the shelves under current epistemic and social conditions (231)—one can say not only that several iterations of AI critique today essentially are reskins of previous versions of technology/computation/internet critique, but also that clearly we cannot make technology critiques about much. We are glued to the television (or the on-fire computer) screen watching analytic reruns of sociotechnical priors. And since the historical trends in critiques of technology and culture are not immune from sociopolitical histories of our world but deeply enmeshed within it—critics, after all, study the world no more than they live in it—we find ourselves, as these reviewed volumes show, in the middle of simultaneously both watching and producing these reruns like consummate prosumers.

Yet, despite the anger, one hopes that not all hope is lost, or so suggest the trails left by these volumes. While technology solutionism—the idea that a technological fix can solve a social problem, as often espoused by Silicon Valley and often critiqued in these texts—still sometimes shows up as an operational tendency in certain kinds of technological critique, for example, when physical machines or algorithms are blamed for disinformation on the web ("it is the algorithm!"), by and large scholarship today has migrated toward different kinds of critique at all kinds of levels and scales (see table 1; note the large swathes occupied by technocritical approaches today). That is, all except a very few. Practices, techniques, and the machines themselves—all of which are rather inconvenient bogeymen for public-facing rhetoric—are not often critically presented for general audiences, at least not by academics. More importantly, very little technology critique that is about the machines themselves is being directed at scientific and engineering scholars; this is a spot currently only occupied by internalist critiques coming from scientists and engineers. There are several ways that the practice of critical making, and efforts both aesthetic and technical in that domain, can be used to keep the technocritical flag flying high. The futility often experienced by humanists—"we have done all we can when we point out social and cultural malaises"—is partially offset by the fact that, for reasons both intellectual and institutional, we have started seeing a whole range of critical interventions into technological systems themselves. As Wendy Chun, Boaz Levin, and Vera Tollmann point out in their *Uncertain Archives* contribution on "Proxies," techniques used by tentacles of corporate technologies "can also be used to imagine different futures" (424). Or, to borrow from Manu Luksch in the same volume, one can see how hope is the uncanny sister of (in this case, corporate) prediction (415). This trend toward diagnosis instead of prognosis can be seen in works of Adam Harvey and the collective Forensic Architecture, to mention two examples. Harvey, a Berlin-based artist, uses machine leaning to identify what is usually enabled by machine learning. His MegaPixels project uses image recognition to identify how facial recognition technologies get their training (spoiler alert: they use dubious legal practices to grab our inane Flickr data online), while his VFRAME project locates digital markers of war crimes in images and videos, much like the activities of Forensic Architecture, a research agency led by Eyal Weizman. Instead of outsourcing traumatic labor of image review to the third world, as is often done by the industry, AI in these cases is used instead to shed light on the actions of the regimes wanting to whitewash their crime in a sea of data. Such merger of art and technical reclamation, as evidenced by the surge of critical making activities across the world, is fast becoming a broader feature of technological critique as expressed in these reviewed works. It need not even always be a utopian desire; *Technoprecarious*, for example, remains grounded in its hopes and dreams for what often looks like mere essential survival, not a grand revolutionary plan (84). Ideally, an academic moment more careful about its audience is around the corner, where critique does not end at, "You thought things were fine, but they are actually bad" and instead starts at, "Okay, things are bad, because, you know . . . all of this, so what do we do now? What kind of technologies do we need, then? What designs must we envision?" May this be technology critique 2.0 (cf. Irr 2020).

In sum, when we critique technology, we (should) study several nodes and scales of cultural, social, political, and physical operations that constitute *technē*. And what is expected as a result of such critique must also lie concomitantly along those axes. Sociopolitical interventions require organizing in the streets, cultural and aesthetic interventions need new modes of encountering and feeling technologies, and alongside all this, techno-oriented critique must ask questions that lead to different answers in technologies themselves. If, as scholars of science have shown conclusively, technical artifacts are often just physical solutions to social problems (Winner 1980), then we as humanists must set a new genre of design challenges for the scientists and engineers. These challenges will not, of course, fix social problems (for that, the solution must be social), but by reifying a certain question to be answered in a certain way, they may enable a partial (re)stabilization of political power. Cities often outlive the emperors that build them, and we can always build newer kinds of technically reified collectivities.

Such should be the state of technocritical inquiry today. If the works reviewed here are any indication, we may be inching toward it.

Ranjodh Singh Dhaliwal is Ruth and Paul Idzik College Chair in Digital Scholarship and Assistant Professor of English and Film, Television, and Theatre at the University of Notre Dame. His research—situated at the crossroads of media theory, science and technology studies, and literary criticism—can be found in venues such as *Critical Inquiry, Configurations*, and *Design Issues*. His current book project, *Rendering: A Political Diagrammatology of Computation*, shows how our cultural narratives, politico-economic formulations, and epistemic beliefs get crystallized into computational hardware and software architectures.

Note

The author would like to thank Sahana Srinivasan and Jacob Hagelberg for all their suggestions and support.

References

Booth, Alison, and Miriam Posner, eds. 2020. "Varieties of Digital Humanities." Special Topic. *PMLA* 135, no. 1: 9–151.

Gebru, Timnit (@timnitGebru). 2022. "It really irritates me that my research agenda has to be based on what tech bros decide to chase." Twitter, April 5, 5:16 p.m. https://twitter.com/timnitGebru/status/1511452709135654917.

Halpern, Orit, Patrick Jagoda, Jeffrey West Kirkwood, and Leif Weatherby, eds. 2022. "Surplus Data." Special Issue. *Critical Inquiry* 48, no. 2.

Irr, Caren. 2020. "Ideology Critique 2.0." *South Atlantic Quarterly* 119, no. 4: 715–24.

Latour, Bruno. 2004. "Why Has Critique Run Out of Steam? From Matters of Fact to Matters of Concern." *Critical Inquiry* 30, no. 2: 225–48.

Marx, Leo. 1997. "'Technology': The Emergence of a Hazardous Concept." *Social Research* 64, no. 3: 965–988.

Winner, Langdon. 1980. "Do Artifacts Have Politics?" *Daedalus* 109, no. 1: 121–36.

**Seb
Franklin**   Data/Dispossession

Cloud Ethics: Algorithms and the Attributes of Ourselves and Others.
By Louise Amoore. Durham, NC: Duke Univ. Press. 2020. 232 pp. Cloth, $99.95;
paper, $25.95; e-book, $25.95.

*Discriminating Data: Correlation, Neighborhoods, and the New Politics
of Recognition.* By Wendy Hui Kyong Chun. Cambridge, MA: MIT Press. 2021.
344 pp. Cloth, $29.95; e-book, $17.99.

In 1968, the electrical engineer and management professor Jay
Wright Forrester, working in collaboration with the former mayor of
Boston, John F. Collins, began applying his computational, information-
feedback modeling system to that notorious proxy for the aggregate
effects of secular stagnation, racialized differentiation, and political
geography: the "crisis of cities." The results of this study were published in late 1969 in the book *Urban Dynamics*. Forrester's model
showed that urban areas—here abstracted into a general "system of
interacting industries, housing, and people"—declined inexorably as
a result of the interactions among population, industry, and housing (1). Starting from a "nearly empty" area of land, Forrester's default
urban-growth model progressed over a 250-year life span to a point
where new construction decreased, industry declined, and the "economic mix" became unfavorable (2–3). By changing variables, either
in accordance with existing approaches to "urban revitalization" or to
model new methods, Forrester evaluated the effects of those changes
against the trajectory and ultimate "stagnation conditions" of the
default model. As in Forrester's earlier work on industrial dynamics,
a central assumption behind this project was a specific understanding of "the counterintuitive nature of complex social systems," of

American Literature, Volume 95, Number 2, June 2023
DOI 10.1215/00029831-10575105   © 2023 by Duke University Press

how "intuitively sensible policies"—which in *Urban Dynamics* are exemplified by the construction of low-cost housing—"adversely affect the very problems they are designed to alleviate" (70). However, his defense of the counterintuitive solution was guided by a quite commonplace assumption: "The most desirable way to reverse the present condition is to restore economic vitality and to absorb the present underemployed groups into the main stream of productive activity" (115).

Although—or perhaps because—productive activity was at its heart, Forrester's model limited the population of an urban area to precisely three categories of person: managerial-professional, labor, and underemployed. Urban decay meant too high a ratio of underemployed to skilled labor, too high a proportion of housing in the underemployed housing class, and too high a fraction of industry in the declining-industry category. These shifts, Forrester argued, were driven not by the waxing and waning of aggregate economic growth but by aging structures within the local urban system. For industrial facilities, this meant a loss of vitality and the consequent flight of the managerial-professional and labor classes. For housing, it meant lower rental costs. Demographically, this meant a concomitant rise in the number of "those people whose economic circumstances force more crowded population density per unit of residential land" (3). In other words, lack of space for new industries to emerge meant an undesirable shift in the ratio of "good" to "bad" types of people, which led to a growth in the total population and further constraints on the possibility for regeneration. Based on those structurally determined outcomes, the solution was clear: contrary to what Forrester presented as the conventional response, that of (implicitly) Keynesian US social policy—ameliorating the conditions of the underemployed through job training programs, low-cost housing, or financial aid—Forrester's model showed that the correct action was to demolish the homes in which the underemployed lived, to create space for new development, which would then automatically increase the "quality" of the area's residents.

It is hardly surprising that Senator Daniel Patrick Moynihan and President Richard Nixon were among Forrester's most influential followers (see Baker 2019). The model set out in *Urban Dynamics* provided a sheen of computational objectivity to the abjection of impoverishment with which those names are synonymous. In this respect, *Urban Dynamics* represents an important precursor to the present uses of data analytics and modeling by a range of institutions, including police departments, loan providers, and insurance companies, all of which tend to rest on and exacerbate the differential allocation of life chances. Equally revealing are the ways Forrester's approach connects that allocation to what might be called the *epistemic contract of digitality*. This contract entails (a) the production of an abstract model of some process or another and (b) the tacit or explicit agreement that whatever is abstracted away doesn't matter. Julian Bigelow (Gerard 1950: 35) precisely formulated the principles of this contract when he stated that when defining a digital process it is "essential to point out that this involves a forbidden ground in between and an agreement never to assign any value whatsoever to that forbidden ground, with a few caveats on the side." This "forbidden ground" often is not simply excluded but functions as a source, such as the electrical current that makes electronic digital computing possible, the variations in stimulus that lead up to the threshold at which a nerve "fires," and the field of noise from which a given message is a selection (12–15, 19–21).[1] The digital is founded on the acknowledgment that what is excluded exists, and is essential, but must be rendered invalid, must be marked valueless.

Louise Amoore's *Cloud Ethics* and Wendy Hui Kyong Chun's *Discriminating Data* are significant theoretical responses to present technosocial conditions foreshadowed in Forrester's *Urban Dynamics*. Both are concerned, in different ways, with the processes that convert structural conditions into computationally rendered social structures. If Forrester's model and its many predecessors, descendants, and close relatives are characterized by a rigorous whittling, the shaping of multiplexed economic, institutional, disciplinary, and cultural relations into a minimum number of interrelated abstractions, Amoore and Chun are concerned with the forms of appearance taken by the "forbidden ground" that underwrites digital models of social life. For Amoore, this means moving beyond questions of transparency and accountability—beyond fantasies of unbiased technologies produced through open, fair-minded regulation—to examine how machine-learning algorithms generate new conditions of possibility by integrating data traces of past actions. The forbidden ground comprises the unlocatable threshold between the actors that through their social activities constantly generate data and the algorithms that, by constantly refining their categories and projections on the basis of that data, set limits on projected future activities. For Chun, the techniques of discrimination and correlation at the heart of data analytics methods are key to the critique of digital epistemology. The forbidden ground here comprises the histories—most strikingly, that of eugenics—that inform the putatively apolitical logic of computational analysis. In this review I engage with the most revealing aspects of Amoore's and Chun's analyses before returning to the centrality of slum demolition to Forrester's *Urban Dynamics* to consider the unacknowledged centrality of dispossession to the situations each author documents.

Amoore opens *Cloud Ethics: Algorithms and the Attributes of Ourselves and Others* with an account of protest monitoring software of the type supplied by the social media intelligence platform Geofeedia to the Baltimore Police Department and the US Department of Homeland Security in the aftermath of the 2015 murder of Freddie Gray. Trained on large data sets extracted from social media posts, this software algorithmically generates "risk scores" designating the likelihood of rebellion in a given locale. From this example of an algorithmic process for determining in advance when a particular class of event will take place, Amoore establishes her principal concern. Much of the recent literature on the ethics of algorithms, she notes, focuses on the social position of the developers and the encoding of already existing biases into machine-learning systems, which then reproduce and at times exacerbate them. But when those systems evolve their definitions and outputs based on data generated by the activities of large numbers of independent actors, it becomes harder to locate a zone of ethical judgment that is separate from the algorithm. In such a situation, what is at stake

> is not only the predictive power of algorithms to undermine the democratic process, determine the outcomes of elections, decide police deployments, or make financial, employment, or immigration decisions. Of greater significance than these manifest harms, and at the heart of the concerns of this book, algorithms are generating the bounded conditions of what a democracy, a border crossing, a social movement, an election, or a public protest could be in the world (4).

In other words, Amoore identifies in many algorithmic systems a loop of emergence and closure, a political mode that might appear contradictory from the perspective of earlier regimes of power based on the advance determination of what counts as socially valid, legitimately political, or practically possible. This newer mode operates not through what Gilles Deleuze (1995: 178) called the "molds" of disciplinary institutions but through ongoing, data-driven iterative processes that, when called upon, generate an output that may be acted on. In contrast to a spatial understanding of the algorithm as a set of discrete steps, which "makes possible all kinds of human over-sight"—for example, the intentional tweaks that generate outputs from Forrester's urban dynamics model—Amoore stresses "the extent to which algorithms modify themselves in and through their nonlinear iterative relations to input data" (11). Predictive policing algorithms integrate "the residue of all the past moments" of a given type of criminalized arrangement (4). The application programming inter-face of Intuitive Surgical's da Vinci robot "contains the data residue of multiple past humans and machine movements" (59). Whether deployed by police departments to preemptively criminalize, by med-ics to optimize surgical techniques, by advertisers or campaign strat-egists to cluster preferences, or by insurance firms to allocate risk, these processes enable and foreclose future possibilities in ways that cannot be redressed through demands issued to a designated crea-tor, user, or regulatory body.

Amoore argues that, because machine-learning algorithms are con-stantly refining themselves based on new data streams, and because this process of refinement is directed toward unknown future deploy-ments, demands for the design and deployment of algorithms to be more transparent, for the designers and deployers to be accountable for the results of their use, and for the most harmful outputs to be regu-lated are insufficient (5). "One could imagine a world," she writes,

> in which the deep neural networks used in cities like Baltimore are scrutinized and rendered compliant with rules and yet continue to learn to recognize and misrecognize people and to infer intent, to generate rules from the contingent and arbitrary data of many past moments of associative life on the city streets, to refine and edit the code for future uses in unknown future places. I may feel that some notion of legible rights is protected, and yet the attributes generated from my data, in correlation with yours and others', continue to sup-ply the conditions for future arbitrary actions against unknown others. (7)

Of course, the problem of unattributable origin is not unique to self-refining algorithmic technologies. As Amoore notes, it is a "persistent and irresolvable ethicopolitical problem" (19) that was succinctly for-mulated by Michel Foucault (1998) in his essay "What Is an Author?" What is specific to the present conjuncture, Amoore argues, is the algorithm's "double political foreclosure" (19). First, a multitude of past actions and potential futures are condensed into a single output: a given city on a given day has a risk score of x. Then, potential actions are enabled or disabled on the basis of that score; for example, cops prevent certain people from entering a designated place, meeting each other, or engaging in certain activities. Where, in this network of social interactions, data collection techniques, machine-learning processes, algorithmic decisions, and concrete outcomes, should an ethical demand be directed?

Amoore is less interested in answering this question than she is in interrogating its presuppositions. She posits two analytic paradigms based on Charles Thomson Rees Wilson's cloud chamber experiments, which were intended to recreate cloud formations for the purpose of taxonomy but ended up making the invisible constituent parts and the physical processes of cloud formation observable. The first of these paradigms she names cloud I. This is the realm of "questions within an observational mode: Where is it?; What type is it?; Can we map it?; Can we recognize it?" (40). Like the unforeseen outcome of Wilson's chamber experiments, the second paradigm, cloud II, brings formerly unobservable phenomena into the realm of visual knowledge. Cloud I is exemplified in efforts to precisely map the geography of cloud computing, to make distributed computing observable by reducing it to a network of locatable data centers, stacks of infrastructure, platforms, and applications "located in places within economies of land, tax rates, energy, water for cooling, and proximity to the main trunk of the network" (35). It is this paradigm, she argues, that subtends demands for transparency, accountability, and regulation. Following Donna Haraway's injunction to stay with the trouble and Jonathan Crary's work on the historicity of vision, Amoore argues that critical approaches to algorithmic technologies, which have for the most part remained within the cloud I paradigm, must be supplemented by approaches informed by cloud II. For her, this means an analytic that posits computational processes not as precisely locatable arrays of programs, data, and processing power but as "gathering[s] of algorithms with data" that institute new conditions of visualization. Through a reading of ICITE, the US intelligence data-sharing and analysis infrastructure, Amoore shows how cloud II gives visual form to entities that, because they are generated by the algorithm from data about past actions, cannot be observed directly (53).

This emphasis on the emergent character of algorithmic processes, which is established in the introduction and elaborated in chapter 1, guides subsequent analyses of human-machine entanglements in machine learning (chapter 2), authorship (chapter 3), algorithmic "madness" (chapter 4), and doubt (chapter 5), and they are central to

Amoore's final chapter on strategies for a cloud ethics (chapter 6, on the "unattributable"). These chapters contain a compelling range of examples, including Alan Turing, Max Newman, Geoffrey Jefferson, and Richard Braithwaite's 1952 BBC debate on machine "thinking"; convolutional neural networks for improving robots' capacity to recognize and act on three-dimensional objects; and Tay, Microsoft's social-media-trained chatbot. The opening account of the complex of predictive policing and police violence hangs over these chapters without ever becoming central to the analysis. And this in turn raises questions that are not directly addressed in the book. What ascriptive regimes, ways of knowing, and direct uses of violence precede and inform the distributed and emergent processes Amoore associates with machine-learning algorithms? Might those regimes, knowledge systems, and deployments of violence be themselves distributed and emergent?

Chun's *Discriminating Data: Correlation, Neighborhoods, and the New Politics of Recognition* engages at length with the first of these questions. Chun begins from the observation that, contrary to the insistence that a form of society organized around the exigencies of digital mediation would "eliminate discrimination because its machines could not 'see' race, sex, age, or infirmities," contemporary tech monopolies "are amplifying and automating—rather than acknowledging and repairing—the mistakes of a discriminatory past" (1–2).[2] The techno-solutionist impulse behind these amplifications and automations, in combination with certain legal forms articulated over the postwar course of what Jodi Melamed (2011: 1–50) has identified as racial liberalism and its subsequent state antiracisms, has produced a situation where older modes of racialized hierarchy are dissimulated through data that are strongly correlated to those modes.[3] As in Amoore's *Cloud Ethics*, policing furnishes an especially clear instance of this situation without ever becoming a central object of analysis: through the use of Zip codes or social connections in predictive policing, the process of residential segregation is cleaved from the trajectory of chattel slavery, reconstruction, and what Saidiya Hartman called the burdened individuality of freedom so that structural racism can "disappear" into putatively neutral geographic or social-tie data (17–19). Yet, Chun argues, the resultant harms cannot be rectified by simply eliminating the proxies in favor of "truer" data. The problem isn't one of suboptimal outputs; rather, it is encoded in the "assumptions embedded within network science and machine learning as they are currently configured regarding segregation, discrimination, and history" (22).

Chun shows in richly argued and illustrated chapters on correlation, homophily, authenticity, and representation how the encoding of these assumptions takes place at the levels of technique and concept and cannot be reduced to a logic of expressive causality whereby the newer instance simply reiterates some unchanging essence found in the older. Chapters 1 and 2 locate foundational techniques of correlation and homophily in eugenics and residential segregation, respectively, and provide a historical and theoretical foundation for subsequent analyses of authenticity (chapter 3) and the new politics of recognition exemplified in reality television (chapter 4). To sharpen the book's focus on logic and methods, these chapters are accompanied by shorter theoretical "miniessays," diagrams, and handwritten explanations of correlation, (magnetic) polarization, principal component analysis, Bayesian inference, and linear discriminant analysis by the computational mathematician Alex Barnett.

The significance of the connections Chun traces—between data science principles such as correlation and homophily and the earlier methods of eugenics and racialized urban planning from which those principles emerged—is found not in the direct transmission of race science into data science but "at the levels of procedure, prediction, and logic" (16). Here, the ways of knowing that are encoded in these techniques and methods become legible as data analytics' forbidden ground, the animating force that invisibly shapes their contemporary deployment. In chapter 1, on correlation, Chun's focus moves from Cambridge Analytica's OCEAN model to work by Cathy O'Neil and Virginia Eubanks on how data correlations "automate and perpetuate" discrimination, and then to a sustained account of the development of correlation and linear regression by the British eugenicists Francis Galton and Karl Pearson (see O'Neil 2016; Eubanks 2018). Correlation's eugenicist history, Chun argues, matters

> not because it predisposes all uses of correlation towards eugenics, but rather because when correlation works, it does so by making the present and future coincide with a highly curated past. Eugenicists reconstructed a past in order to design a future that would repeat their discriminatory abstractions: in their systems, learning or nurture—differences acquired within a lifetime—were "noise." The important point here is that predictions based on correlations seek to make true disruption impossible, which is perhaps why they are so disruptive.

In other words, techniques of correlation and linear regression do not somehow transfer a racist essence from eugenics into data analytics methods; rather, they reproduce and/or intensify discriminatory outcomes because, at the level of their basic cultural techniques, they extrapolate futures from "discriminatory abstractions"—discrete, unchanging categories that in some cases take the essentialist form of naturally occurring "races."[4] Both eugenics and data analytics "sought to make the future repeat a highly selective and discriminatory past through correlation" (36). Consequently, the outcomes—whether the eugenic projection of social disorder from the reproduction of "degenerate" racial groups or the algorithmic generation of credit scores and police "heat lists"—cannot deviate in socially significant ways from the originary abstractions.

The second chapter of *Discriminating Data* traces methods of network polarization—the production of segregated "neighborhoods," or what are sometimes called *filter bubbles*—to the concept of homophily advanced in the sociologist Paul Lazarsfeld's work with Robert Merton in their 1954 "Friendship as a Social Process." Here, Chun emphasizes that Lazarsfeld and Merton developed their analysis of the clustering of like-minded persons through studies of segregated housing projects—"Craftown" (Winfield Park), an all-white project in New Jersey, and "Hilltown" (Addison Terrace), a "bi-racial, low-rent" project in western Pennsylvania (97). She notes in passing that the ideas behind the concept and its antonym, heterophily, were drawn from the work of the eugenicist Karl Pearson and Bronislaw Malinowski's ethnographic study of "savage Trobrianders" (73, 97). As in the chapter on correlation, Chun's focus is less on the implications of this genealogy and more on the discrimination-compounding effects of the underlying method. Because the conversion of concrete, situated realities into data objectifies messy, often ambivalent social relations into discrete abstractions, processes that analyze and seek to optimize social groupings on the basis of data collection and analysis compound segregation. In a manner not dissimilar to correlation's temporal foreclosure, methods for establishing homophily become tools "for discovering bias and inequality and for *perpetuating* them in the name of 'comfort,' predictability, and common sense" (85–86; emphasis mine).

Amoore argues that the widespread deployment of machine-learning algorithms has replaced the sphere of rights against which outcomes can be evaluated with a distributed, emergent, and self-regulating system in which rights are constantly being produced, allocated, and modulated. For Chun, the big data regime builds on, automates, and obscures earlier forms of discrimination, in large part through the adoption of mathematical techniques developed for (among other things) race science and residential segregation. Can both be true? Understanding their complementarity requires attention to a level of structural determination that subtends the local conditions of knowledge and power with which Amoore and Chun engage.

The disavowal of this structural determination is endemic to computational models of social life. It is particularly evident in Forrester's *Urban Dynamics*, in the methodological principle that all processes affecting stability begin and end within the system's closed boundaries. "If a particular difficulty in a system is being investigated," Forrester (1999: 12) wrote, "the system described within the boundary should be capable of generating that difficulty. The closed boundary concept implies that the system behavior of interest is not imposed from the outside but created within the boundary." Consequently, "outside occurrences can be viewed as random happenings that impinge on the system and do not in themselves give the system its intrinsic growth and stability characteristics." In *Urban Dynamics*, this "outside" is the "limitless source" from which people enter the urban system, and into which they are absorbed when they leave (4). In concert with another methodological imposition—that "freedom to migrate" is universal—this reduction of the larger population environment to a limitless source allowed Forrester to claim that the ascribed "quality" of persons supplied from the outside was solely determined by the attractiveness of the internal components, which could then be further limited to the level of development of the industrial and residential infrastructure. Stagnation could thus be reduced to an increase in a given area's attractiveness to the "underemployed," while recovery would result from measures that (a) make the area more attractive to managerial-professional and labor populations and (b) allow the city to function as a "social converter" that moves people from the underemployed to the labor class (95). Going the other way, it was the attractiveness ascribed to the urban area that allowed the outside to be so reduced; since the attractiveness factors automatically determined the class of persons arriving from the outside, the dynamics that reproduced, differentially valued, and compelled the movement of persons through that "source" were functionally irrelevant. The biopolitical and disciplinary logics of Forrester's recommendations are built on this digital-epistemic principle, whereby the outside environment and, by extension, prior histories and structural dynamics are rendered a "forbidden ground" simultaneously essential and irrelevant to the workings of the system. Among other things, separating

the distribution of social-reproductive capacity from a totality dominated by the circulation of so-called productive labor's social product
is unthinkable from the perspective of Forrester's model and the
social imaginary that shapes and is in turn reshaped by it. Good jobs
and good housing automatically attract "better" people and automatically improve "worse" people. The ascriptive regimes that are bound
up with the distribution of labor and, concomitantly, social validity are
strikingly absent from this picture until a remarkable moment at the
start of the final chapter, where racial blackness is momentarily elevated
from the categories of underemployment and slum housing in which
it was previously subsumed, only to be unceremoniously returned
there after a few lines on the study's methodological assumptions.[5]

In other words, *Urban Dynamics* models a situation where segregation and inequality are not outcomes of but preconditions for stagnation, which is to say, the failure to sustain growth as fixed capital
declines. The historical processes through which the managerial-
professional, labor, and underemployed groups are produced and
their relations established are irrelevant to and thus absent from the
urban system. They are posited as black boxes, served by the environment in a steady stream, in a ratio is determined by the "quality" of
residential property and fixed capital. And "the most desirable way" to
reverse the otherwise inevitable tendency toward stagnation is "to
restore economic vitality and to absorb the present underemployed
groups into the main stream of productive activity" (Forrester 1999:
115). The result of this restoration by absorption would be a dynamic,
self-regulating urban system, one in which manager-professionals and
labor arrive automatically from the outside and the underemployed
are automatically converted into manager-professionals and labor.
Does this situation not resemble a synthesis of the emergent quality
Amoore finds in machine-learning algorithms with the automation
and obfuscation of discrimination Chun locates in the basal techniques
of data analytics? Desegregation and equality are not antithetical to the
discriminatory logic of Forrester's model; they are its optimal result:
segregation and inequality as engines of desegregation and equality,
desegregation and equality as the conditions of an emergent, self-
equilibrating social system. This chain of contradictions has a name:
dispossession.

Simply put, dispossession names the repertoire of techniques and
technologies through which people become self-possessed and, by
extension, self-responsible. Dispossession is thus essential for the
maintenance of the apparently spontaneous, uncoerced form of social

connection that, as Karl Marx observed, distinguishes capitalism from forms of society premised on direct dependence on "nature" or direct domination by a lord or master.[6] Capitalism is a form of society in which the "silent compulsion of economic relations" plays a larger role than direct "extra-economic force" (Marx 1976: 899). Classical political economy accounted for the emergence of this form by universalizing a human predisposition toward market relations and the bifurcation of agents on the basis of their capacity for accumulation, so that the capitalist mode of production appeared "a never-ending circle" (873). Yet, for the apparently automatic entry of "free" labor and "free" capitalists into money-mediated relationships to become generalized into the organizing dynamic of a social totality, both must first become "free" in a manner that indirectly compels them to enter into such relationships.[7] For the seller of labor power, Marx famously described this situation as one of double freedom: free to sell one's labor to whomever one chooses, and free from the possibility of living in any manner that makes such a sale unnecessary. And he showed that this situation does not occur naturally but must be produced—through enclosures, colonial occupation, enslavement, and extraction, among many other techniques. Forrester's urban model limns the operations of this structural dynamic, which are external to the network of economic relations but internal (and integral) to the capitalist mode of society that is dynamically formed around that network. The naturally occurring existence of discrete, differentially valued classes of person is overcome through the destruction of the lower-value persons' homes, which from the perspective of the model automatically facilitates their integration into a higher order of regular, wage-mediated activity.

Forrester's passing gesture to racial blackness briefly makes legible (in the course of denying) the forbidden ground that structures this algorithmic model of optimally self-regulating, accumulation-oriented social relations. What happens, one might ask, between the destruction of the homes and the construction of the new residential and industrial facilities that, according to Forrester's model, will automatically attract the "higher" persons while "upgrading" the lower? There must be another outside, a space of destitution into which persons who have been expelled and who have yet to be reintegrated ("upgraded") fall. Or perhaps that other outside is simply a subsection of the environment from which population flows; such a possibility is foreshadowed in Marx's (1976: 796) striking description of the part of the agricultural population that needs but has not yet managed to enter into the urban or manufacturing proletariat: a "source" from which there is a "constant flow" of the relative surplus population. The production and emergent modulation of racialized, sexuated, and gendered modes of capacitation—the production and social operationalization of what Chun calls "discriminatory abstractions"—are part of the interaction between the emergent, formally "free" sphere of exchange and the dispossessive operations, including those of expulsion and absolute destitution, required to secure and animate that sphere. Sylvia Wynter (1981: 59) sketched one iteration of this dynamic when she connected C. L. R. James's childhood neighbor Matthew Bondsman to the "sharecropper breaking his back," the "native agroproletariat," and the laborer held "reserve in perpetuity" whose precursor abstraction was the "*refuse* (the term given to the slave too old and worn-out to contribute labor)." In a later essay, Wynter (1992: 75) added the "Lumpen" and the the *"damnés de la terre"*—in other words, those condemned "to accept their inculcated zero value of identity, their own nothingness."

The structural processes that generate and distribute these abstractions also produce Forrester's managerial-professional, labor, and underemployed groups and those bundles of attributes and interactions that inform and are informed by the algorithmic processes Amoore and Chun so vividly account for. To be "free," to act in the world in ways that are enabled and constrained by dispossession and differential integration, is to yield the data upon which various algorithmic processes operate. Or, the situations of the people from whose "free" activities data is extracted, and upon whose "free" lives the resultant algorithmic processes come to bear, are structurally determined by the processes of dispossession and gradated integration theorized by Marx, Wynter, and many others. This is why the presence of policing, which frames both books but which is a central focus in neither, is so revealing. What if the primary connection between policing and big data is to be found not in the former's deployment of the latter but in the emergent dynamics of separation and integration—of "freeing," differentiating, and constraining—that precede and motivate both? To be sure, the multiplexed arrangements of institutions, technologies, and structural conditions in operation today require new modes of theorization, and *Cloud Ethics* and *Discriminating Data* are important contributions to that project.

Seb Franklin is Reader in Literature, Media, and Theory in the Department of English at King's College London. He is the author of *The Digitally Disposed: Racial Capitalism and the Informatics of Value* (2021) and *Control: Digitality as Cultural Logic* (2015).

Notes

1   The first of Bigelow's examples is posited by Ralph Gerard; the second, by John von Neumann.

2   As Chun has previously shown, the notion that digital media can undo the basis of discrimination—always reduced to visible markers of race, gender, sex, disability, and age—has been repeated across manifestos, commercials, and comic strips since the earliest years of the World Wide Web. See Chun 2005: 131–44; 2016: 104–7.

3   Melamed's (2011: x, xv) periodization divides the shift from white supremacy to "formally antiracist, liberal-capitalist modernity" in the postwar United States into three stages: racial liberalism (mid-1940s–1960s), liberal multiculturalism (1980s–1990s), and neoliberal multiculturalism (2000s).

4   Importantly, Chun also emphasizes uses of correlation and linear regression that do not in practice reproduce eugenicist principles, such as in explanatory global climate change models (66, 122–37).

5   "These recommendations," Forrester (1999: 115) wrote, "assume that the most desirable way to reverse the present condition of cities is to restore economic vitality and the absorb the present underemployed groups into the main stream of productive activity. Some might argue to the contrary that today's underemployed Negro minority is less apt to rise in status by diffusion into existing economic activity than by coalescing into a self-respecting, self-disciplining, and self-leading group. Were the latter the more promising course of action, Negro concentration in high-density slums might be a necessary prelude to self-generating social change. This study assumes that extreme concentration of economic and social groups is detrimental and that success will be more easily achieved in a single economic system than in two separate and parallel systems."

6   For example, "a merely local connection resting on blood ties, or on primeval, natural or master-servant relations" (Marx 1993: 161).

7   Robert Nichols (2020: 8) precisely figures the logic of this process when he describes it as "one in which new proprietary relations are generated but under structural conditions that demand their simultaneous negation. In effect, the dispossessed come to 'have' something they cannot use, except by alienating it to another."

References

Baker, Kevin T. 2019. "Model Metropolis." *Logic* 6. https://logicmag.io/play /model-metropolis/.

Chun, Wendy Hui Kyong. 2005. *Control and Freedom: Power and Paranoia in the Age of Fiber Optics.* Cambridge, MA: MIT Press.

Chun, Wendy Hui Kyong. 2016. *Updating to Remain the Same: Habitual New Media.* Cambridge, MA: MIT Press.

Deleuze, Gilles. 1995. "Postscript on Control Societies." In *Negotiations*, translated by Martin Joughin, 177–182. New York: Columbia Univ. Press.

Eubanks, Virginia. 2018. *Automating Inequality: How High-Tech Tools Profile, Police, and Punish the Poor*. New York: St. Martin's Press.

Forrester, Jay Wright. (1969) 1999. *Urban Dynamics*. Waltham, MA: Pegasus.

Foucault, Michel. 1998. "What Is an Author?" In *Aesthetics, Method, Epistemology*, edited by James D. Faubion, 205–222. New York: The New Press.

Gerard, Ralph. 1950. "Some of the Problems Concerning Digital Notions in the Central Nervous System." In *Cybernetics: Circular Causal and Feedback Mechanisms in Biological and Social Systems*, edited by Heinz von Foerster, Margaret Mead, and Hans Lukas Teuber, 11–57. New York: Josiah Macy Jr. Foundation.

Marx, Karl. 1976. *Capital: A Critique of Political Economy*. Vol. 1. Translated by Ben Fowkes. London: Penguin.

Marx, Karl. 1993. *Grundrisse: Foundations of the Critique of Political Economy*. Translated by Martin Nicolaus. London: Penguin.

Melamed, Jodi. 2011. *Represent and Destroy: Rationalizing Violence in the New Racial Capitalism*. Minneapolis: Univ. of Minnesota Press.

Nichols, Robert. 2020. *Theft Is Property! Dispossession and Critical Theory*. Durham, NC: Duke Univ. Press.

O'Neil, Cathy. 2016. *Weapons of Math Destruction: How Big Data Increases Inequality and Threatens Democracy*. New York: Crown.

Wynter, Sylvia. 1981. "In Quest of Matthew Bondsman: Some Cultural Notes on the Jamesian Journey." *Urgent Tasks* 12: 54–68.

Wynter, Sylvia. 1992. "Beyond the Categories of the Master Conception: The Counterdoctrine of the Jamesian Poesis." In *C. L. R. James's Caribbean*, edited by Paget Henry and Paul Buhle, 63–91. London: Macmillan.

Melody Jue   The Many Ecologies of AI

AI in the Wild: Sustainability in the Age of Artificial Intelligence. By Peter Dauvergne. Cambridge, MA: MIT Press. 2021. 276 pp. Paper, $24.95.

Blockchain Chicken Farm and Other Stories of Tech in China's Countryside. By Xiaowei Wang. New York: Farrar, Straus, and Geroux. 2020. 256 pp. Paper, $17.00; e-book, $10.99.

A City Is Not a Computer: Other Urban Intelligences. By Shannon Mattern. Princeton, NJ: Princeton Univ. Press. 2021. 200 pp. Paper, $19.95; e-book available.

Nnedi Okorafor's short story "Mother of Invention" (2018) brings into focus several key thematics in the scholarly studies of ecology and AI. Set in near-future Nigeria, Okorafor imagines a moment when a sophisticated smart home becomes a life-saving extension of an expectant mother's immune system. The protagonist, Anwuli, goes into labor during a pollen storm caused by a GMO crop of peri grass, a nutritious substitute for rice whose pollination cycle has been thrown off by climate change. Yet the smart home has a kind of external immune system—and womb—that protects Anwuli and her child from the worst of the pollen storm, able to learn and adapt to the changing situation. It filters both pollen and information, sifting through data and shutting out the harmful peri grass.

Okorafor's story animates the intimacies between AI and ecology in a variety of important ways. It centers uses of AI technology located in the global South, not just the study of extractive effects on the global South. Given the overrepresentation of global North—and especially Silicon Valley—in imaginations of AI futures, this alone would merit critical consideration. Yet Okorafor also sets "Mother of Invention" against the backdrop of industrial farming, surveillance, trust, and

American Literature, Volume 95, Number 2, June 2023
DOI 10.1215/00029831-10575119   © 2023 by Duke University Press

care work. By imagining how a smart home would help a pregnant woman, Okorafor places gender and reproduction at the center of considerations of AI, imagining how it could help mediate between the protagonist's immediate health concerns and the miasma of a climate catastrophe swirling outside. "Mother of Invention" is a story that encourages us to consider who gets to imagine the future(s) of AI design and who such futures prioritize and care for. What geographies do AI futures center? In what ways does an ecological imagination animate descriptions and conceptualizations of AI and other smart technologies?

In this review, I examine three books that take up these questions to varying degrees: Xiaowei Wang's *Blockchain Chicken Farm and Other Stories of Tech in China's Countryside*, Shannon Mattern's *A City Is Not a Computer: Other Urban Intelligences*, and Peter Dauvergne's *AI in the Wild: Sustainability in the Age of Artificial Intelligence*. Rather than opposing ecology to technology, these texts trace their intimacies: the application of AI to the management of wildlife and animal husbandry, the connections between AI and global food systems, the ways that AI draws on elements of the natural world for algorithmic models—a reminder to readers to look for ecological relation in all human relationships with technologies and that the technological always requires material inputs of energies, resources, and labor. Taken together, these three books prompt us to decenter Silicon Valley–focused ways of mapping, predicting, and especially desiring particular relationships between ecologies and AI. They also map out a spatial trajectory that evaluates AI's ecological implications in the wild, the agrarian, and the urban, considering how each of these spaces presents differing ratios and arrangements of human and more than human life.

AI and Wild Ecologies

Peter Dauvergne begins *AI in the Wild: Sustainability in the Age of Artificial Intelligence* (2020) by positioning his book is the first of its kind to bring together the fields of global environmental politics and AI. Dauvergne, a professor of international relations, asserts that, "at the time of writing, no articles dealing with AI have ever been published in the field's leading journals of *Global Environmental Politics* and *Environmental Politics*" (12). Mapping the field further, he adds that "MIT Press, which has published hundreds of books on artificial intelligence and hundreds of books on environmental politics, has never published a book bringing these two topics together" (12). However, Dauvergne missed works that do not use *AI* directly in their title, including many contributions in the field of media studies, such as Tung-hui Hu's *Prehistory of the Cloud* (2015), Jennifer Gabrys's *Program Earth: Environmental Sensing Technology and the Making of a Computational Planet* (2016), Xiaowei Wang's *Blockchain Chicken Farm* (2018), which I review next; Kate Crawford's *Atlas of AI* (2018) (which does use *AI* in the title); Mél Hogan's work on the global ecological impacts of data centers, including the 2018 article "Big Data Ecologies." Additional engagement with ecology and AI emerges in such contemporary artworks as Lawrence Lek's *AIDOL* (see lawrencelek.com/AIDOL), which addresses AI and climate change from a Sino-futurist perspective.

Nonetheless, *AI in the Wild* offers a valuable critique of corporate sustainability. One of its central observations is that corporations typically use AI toward increasing the efficiency of production, not toward reducing total resource consumption. Dauvergne writes that eco-business is "aiming to expand markets, sales, and corporate power. Most of the efficiency gains are rebounding into even more production and consumption" while AI continues to assist industrial-scale extraction "from autonomous drilling to driverless haulers" (15). Dauvergne is right to point out that what remains unexamined by corporations is the logic of increased production and consumption in the first place, which contributes to increased resource use and carbon emissions, habitat destruction, and species extinctions. Dauvergne argues that, for these reasons, corporate sustainability initiatives are not truly effective on their own and suggests greater civic attention to decrease consumption. On this point, Dauvergne is largely in agreement with professor of industrial ecology Roland Geyer, whose book *The Business of Less: The Role of Companies and Households on a Planet in Peril* (2021) also leverages a strong critique of corporate sustainability measures.

However, the persons and organizations that Dauvergne is most critical of (big tech corporations) are also the ones he gives the most attention throughout the book. Despite his call at the end of the book for environmental activists to do more, they are proportionately a small fraction of the quotations that Dauvergne uses, and he does not name specific environmental activist organizations in his calls to action. By contrast, he tracks many corporations in depth and tends to use citations from business leaders to map out the ideology of Silicon Valley.

In this way, *AI in the Wild* risks becoming a biography of the powerful, written as a synthesis of trends that may be familiar to anyone who follows *Wired, Gizmodo*, or Reddit. However, since not everyone does, *AI in the Wild* may usefully map a number of corporate actions in the last decade that may have slipped under one's radar, such as Apple's acquisitions of Emotient and RealFace or its test driving of autonomous cars.

Importantly, *AI in the Wild* synthesizes a number of shifts in the way AI is being used toward wildlife conservation. For example, Trailguard AI takes photographs of vehicles entering national parks and sends them to park headquarter to investigate, as part of a strategy of arresting illegal poachers. ChimpFace searches social media and websites for trafficked chimpanzees; Wildbook searches YouTube for footage of whale sharks. Rangerbot has been used in the Great Barrier Reef to cull crown-of-thorns starfish that are destroying corals while also mapping coral bleaching and sampling seawater. However, what is missing here is an evaluation of how these applications of AI technologies in the wild relate to other trends that Dauvergne maps out in later chapters, such as how machine learning and intelligent automation will expand state power (chapter 10). For example, isn't the power to cull masses of crown-of-thorns starfish an example of already expanded state power, of bare life and the right to kill?

The effort to map and survey results in the stylistic deployment of quite a few lists in *AI in the Wild*. For example, on energy efficiency, Dauvergne summarizes: "City-owned vehicles are being integrated into the Internet of Things to improve data analysis and response times. City infrastructure is being automated to increase the efficiency of subways, buses, streetlights. . . . Police are being outfitted with smart cameras to improve the safety of officers and citizens" (103). The frequency with which Dauvergne uses lists written in the passive voice ("are being . . . ") becomes repetitive and contributes to a textbook-like distance from the subject matter, an overview that avoids the use of the *I* (although *we* is still frequently used). While this approach offers a degree of clarity, it also obscures Dauvergne's own positionality, a lost opportunity to reflect on his own embedding within systems of power and privilege.

AI in the Wild is divided into three parts: "The Global Political Economy of AI," "The Prospects and Limits of AI," and "The Dangers of AI." Each of these parts collects several chapters that examine the rise of AI since 2010 and examples of applications in wildlife conservation and ecoefficiency. However, one disadvantage is that terms like *sustainability*, *global*, *smart*, and *wild* are not critically defined in this volume. Dauvergne also leaves his most critical and interesting chapters until the end of the book, covering surveillance (chapter 10) and the dire environmental implications of war and global conflict (chapter 11). This has the unfortunate effect of burying the lede in an attempt to anticipate a technoenthusiast audience—the kind of audience that would think to check MIT Press's catalogue and is likely positioned in the global North, if not in Silicon Valley itself.

Because Dauvergne does not immediately foreshadow his critiques, much of his prose inhabits the mode of the technosublime. Indeed, Dauvergne starts each chapter by introducing applications of AI that seem to dovetail with sustainability goals. These paragraphs appear written as if to sympathize with the point of view of a particular reader: a generalist, corporate, technoenthusiast audience that wants to use AI for positive outcomes. The problem with this strategy, from my view, is that he saves his critiques for other paragraphs, making it possible for an uncareful reader to quote either the passages that read as particularly technosublime and optimistic or the critical passages that often come later. This organization makes it incredibly easy to cherry-pick quotations, an unfortunate effect of a style of writing that interpolates an anticipated reader who likes AI technologies before offering a more pointed critique, for example, of the double process of subduing radicals and backing environmental (corporate-friendly) moderates (150), a notable observation that I wished he had expanded on with more examples.

AI in the Wild is US-centered while aspiring to be global in scope and thus should also be read carefully for its own geopolitical biases. Dauvergne mostly portrays China as a US antagonist, yet he cites primarily US sources or news sources quoting the CEOs of major Chinese businesses. This citational politics is an effect of the style of the journalistic overview itself, which favors a quick gloss and tends to cite actors with more power. This leaves something to be desired, however, about really understanding China—and indeed, the other global superpowers mentioned—from other points of view.

AI and Agrarian Ecologies

Xiaowei Wang's *Blockchain Chicken Farm* irreverently contrasts the technohype of blockchain encryption technologies against their applications in rural and farming/agricultural contexts. While the book is not published with an academic press, it models a type of public humanities scholarship that bears the marks of Wang's training at Harvard (undergraduate, MA) and UC Berkeley, where Wang was a PhD student in geography at the time of writing this book. Yet most importantly, *Blockchain Chicken Farm* offers one of the only examples of scholarship on ecology and AI from a perspective in the global South that I could find, to date. Wang examines not only detrimental AI effects on rural China, but also AI uses by people living in rural China, telling a more complex story of technology and agency than victimhood, against the particular backdrop of Chinese history and cultures. By contrast, texts like *AI in the Wild* and Kate Crawford's *Atlas of AI* tend to address the global South as the passive subject of ecological damage by technologies designed in the global North. While mapping geographies of harm is important work, it is only half of a rigorous environmental justice agenda, which should examine not only victimization but also the desires, hopes, and aspirations of particular communities as users, adapters, and designers of AI and its associated functions: machine learning technologies, data management, and storage. *Blockchain Chicken Farm* models how to approach questions of ecology and AI by asking the crucial question of "for whom," countering tendencies to see AI as a story only about Silicon Valley, US corporations, cities, and the affluent and instead approaching AI from the perspectives of Chinese farmers and others living in rural contexts.

Food is, unsurprisingly, at the center of *Blockchain Chicken Farm*. Wang begins the book, "Famine has its own vocabulary, a hungry language that haunts and lingers. My ninety-year-old great-uncle understands famine's words well. When I visit him one winter, he takes me on an indulgent trip to the food court near his house. . . . My visit is special, so I know his affection will be communicated through food, from his own memory of hunger" (11). This indirect way of alluding to the famine of the Great Leap Forward opens the book, a memory of the attempt to technologically modernize and a reminder of how "intertwined the rural and urban are, with technological change threaded throughout" (22). *Blockchain Chicken Farm* is both a series of case studies of AI applications in agriculture and animal husbandry and a close examination of circulations between rural and urban environments.

Food also shapes *Blockchain Chicken Farm*'s textual form. Between the book's eight nonfiction chapters, incorporating fieldwork and ethnographic interviews, are three short speculative recipes that function like speculative fictions and could easily be adapted as contemporary artwork for the way that they challenge and critique dominant assumptions about AI and the body. For example, in "How to Feed an AI," Wang asks, "How would moving beyond the machine-human boundaries and western models of mind-body dualism bring new life to AI research? This recipe speculates on just that—when a group of AI researchers use traditional Chinese medicine . . . to advance technology" (31). Wang uses this recipe for giving a goji berry, ginger, date, and soy milk broth to an AI as an occasion to counter Western assumptions about how bodies are built. Whereas in Western philosophies the brain controls the body, "in Chinese medicine, there are eleven vital organs that work holistically to sustain life, and this list does not include the brain. Brain functions are scattered throughout the body" (32). In asking what AI research would look like if it proceeded from this distributed model of cognition, Wang might find synergy with N. Katherine Hayles's *Unthought: The Power of the Cognitive Nonconscious* (2017). A careful reader might also consider the similarities between the form of an algorithm and the form of the recipe: both are step-by-step instructions used to accomplish a task or create a dish, taking inputs (code, ingredients) and combining them to create outputs (a program, a cake).

In addition to the Buddhist alternatives to the mind-body dualism, Wang makes space for other rural epistemologies to show through. For example, early on, Wang discusses noncapitalist perspectives on time: "One farmer told me that the future is a created concept, and that in the fields, in the long dark of winters, there is no future, because every day depends on tending to the present moment. An act of care. In contrast, urban culture is centered on the belief that the universe must be constantly corrected on its course, and that life is defined by the pleasure of overcoming future challenges" (26). While one might wonder if there are exceptions to this dualism, such as instances of care and being present that coexist in urban spaces, Wang channels a sense that rural epistemologies are shifting as these spaces become satellites of the urban, geographically and cognitively.

Throughout *Blockchain Chicken Farm*, Wang tracks a number of moments when internet commerce, blockchain encryption, surveillance technologies, and AI have reshaped the environments, ecologies, and economies of rural China. Summarizing Xi Jinping's policies for rural revitalization, Wang writes: "The new socialist countryside will be filled with peasants starting e-commerce businesses, small-scale manufacturing, new data centers, and young entrepreneurial workers returning to their rural homes. Rural Revitalization envisions the use of blockchain and mobile payment to catalyze new businesses, and will leverage big data for poverty relief and distribution of welfare benefits" (22). This forecast imagines a shift in labor from cities back to the countryside, addressing such social problems as children living apart from their aging parents so they can live where jobs exist. In another chapter, Wang tells a story about a shift in costume manufacturing to a small town. "It feels bizarre: a group of children trick-or-treating in suburban America is fueling the growth of fruit trees and chili peppers in Shandong, and also driving land rentals. The internet is tangibly reshaping Dinglou's environment" (191). The feeling of the bizarreness seems to be a recurring affective response to rural environmental reshaping and change, the sense that the city's—and, by proxy, AI's—ways of knowing and socializing are impinging onto those of the Chinese countryside.

Part of this changing socialization also has to do with how AI is coming to substitute for trust and, in doing so, to reflect a very narrow and particular view of human nature. For example, in the titular chapter, "Blockchain Chicken Farm," Wang traces how blockchain technologies are being used to mediate and guarantee that one's chicken is, in fact, free range, vegetarian fed and not a counterfeit. "When falsified records and sprawling supply chains lead to issues of contamination and food safety," Wang writes, "blockchain seems like a clear, logical solution" (50). At one farm, chickens wear ankle bracelets (with QR codes) that track their number of steps and location, data that are accessible on a website where you can even see a map of their movements. When the chicken is butchered, the anklet is left on the chicken so that the purchaser can verify that they have in fact bought the right chicken.

The figure of the blockchain chicken farm operates on both comical and pragmatic levels. While it ensures delivery of an organic chicken, it also registers a kind of absurdity, indexing a level of social distrust that requires permanent chicken anklets and surveillance tracking. The question of trust and the counterfeit appears in other moments of the book, such as the discussion of Alipay, pearl farms, and the existence of *shanzhai* (knockoff) products. Yet here, Wang provocatively reclaims the derogatory term *shanzhai*, casting it not as a fault but as potentially a mode of decolonizing technology, of redefining what innovation might mean in rural China. Here Wang raises an interesting question: is the antidote to the absurdity of the blockchain chicken farm an embrace of the socialist potential of the counterfeit, to reclaim the means of production?

AI and Urban Ecologies

Moving from the wild to the agrarian, I conclude by turning to a book that situates ecology and AI squarely in the terrain of the city—a perhaps unexpected place to look: Shannon Mattern's *A City Is Not a Computer*, which dynamically moves across questions of environment, abstraction, and form. It begins with a quotation from Christopher Alexander, "A city is not a tree," evaluating Alexander's negative metaphor as it shuttles between artificial cities (the treelike plans of designers) and the messiness of actual cities (not trees). Perhaps a sense of surprise comes from how *tree* is not a tree either but an abstracted structure or form of organization—a form that nonetheless borrows from an ecological referent. As Mattern observes, we have implemented computational means to achieve neatness and order in cities, "now rationalized through exhaustive data collection, automated design tools, and artificially intelligent urban systems. We're using 'decision trees' to cultivate 'tree cities'" (3).

Smart cities are abstractions that borrow from an ecological, material, and often arboreal vocabulary to conceptualize the city as a site of management and observation. However, Mattern's discussion of smart cities raises key questions about how computational models have come to define cities, and what these models leave out. She argues that "'smart' computational models of urbanism advance an impoverished understanding of what we can know about a city, as well as what's worth knowing," since "cities encompass countless other forms of local, place-based, indigenous intelligences and knowledge institutions" (12).

A City Is Not a Computer is structured by four chapters: "City Console," "A City Is Not a Computer," "Public Knowledge," and "Maintenance Codes." Throughout, Mattern shows that underneath the veneer of the computational, algorithmic, and artificially intelligent is a material, ecological, and cultural substratum that informs AI at the level of conceptual vocabulary: the tree, the graft, the dashboard.

One of the strengths of this book is how it carefully shuttles between the material and semiotic, attending to key differences in which each operates. One of the most delightful examples of this occurs in chapter 1, "City Console" (a homonym for city council), where Mattern traces the concept of the dashboard back to its original technical and environmental context and then back-reads this onto a technical situation in the present for comparative analysis. She begins:

> The term *dashboard*, first used in 1846, originally referred to the board or leather apron on the front of a vehicle that kept horse hooves and wheels from splashing mud into the interior. Only in 1990, according to the *Oxford English Dictionary*, did the term come to denote a "screen giving a graphical summary of various types of information, typically used to give an overview of (part of) a business organization." (30)

Mattern then perceptively asks what has been bracketed out of the concept of the dashboard. "Why, all the mud of course! All the dirty (un-'cleaned') data, the variables that have nothing to do with key performance (however it's defined), the parts that don't lend themselves to quantification and visualization"—this data-mud is what the dashboard "screens out" (30–31). However, Mattern argues that the mud is what the critic must notice. Because the dashboard "does little to educate those users about where the data come from, about whose interests they serve, or about the politics of information visualization and knowledge production" (42), the critic must figuratively look behind the face of the dashboard to examine what was excluded. What Mattern calls "Critical Mud" means seeing the city as more than an "aggregate of variables, as the sum of its component widgets— weather plus crime statistics plus energy usage plus employment data" (43). What might the city look like if one pays attention to multispecies inhabitants, or to physical dirt itself? This latter question resonates with questions being asked by scientists of the Anthropocene like Daniel Richter (2007), who study significant changes happening in Earth's soils, including soils that underlie cities and other built spaces.

Mattern also examines how the metaphorization of the city as a kind of computer not only shapes what we want to know about cities—what types of civic data are valued—but also obscures the origins of data (represented to or fed to the computer of the city). For Mattern, the city-as-computer metaphor risks treating city-data as a given and thus depoliticizing it. Thus, "we need to shift our gaze and look at data in context, at the life cycle of urban information, distributed within a varied ecology of urban sites and subjects that interact with it in multiple ways. We need to see data's human, institutional, and technological creators, its curators, cleaners and preservers, owners and brokers, 'users,' hackers and critics" (64). This call for scholarly remembering and analysis of where data come from—a call in line with Lisa Gitel-man's *Raw Data Is an Oxymoron* (2013)—should be a central lesson for those studying the relations of AI and ecology.

One of the ways that Mattern refocuses questions of where data come from and who they are for occurs in her discussion of the role of libraries in smart cities. In chapter 3, Mattern examines how libraries can be viewed as platforms or, her preferred term, *infrastructures*. Where the platform (like the dashboard interface) "doesn't have any implied depth" and we are not "inclined to look beneath it or behind it, or to question its structure or logics" (77), infrastructure offers a different understanding of dimensionality. Mattern tracks the social justice implications for how the library functions as a knowledge infrastructure and a social infrastructure—one that provides critical services, especially for those marginalized populations who are either irrelevant to or criminalized by the smart city's all-seeing sensors and all-knowing databases (78). The library is a social and environmental model: "Imagine what a library could be if it, rather than a police dash-board or an urban operating system, were taken as the quintessential emblem of urban intelligence" (83). Unlike the dashboard, the infra-structure of the library can accommodate "forms of media and types of knowledge that resist standardization and metrics, that might sty-mie standard classification schemes" (85) such as zines, comics, and local culinary, cultural, business, and design histories.

Chapter 4, "Maintenance Codes," shares a thematic overlap with *Blockchain Chicken Farm* by centering themes of maintenance and care, and their situation within specific communities. Mattern advo-cates for maintenance over innovation, noting that maintenance is a collective endeavor that isn't new, drawing on ecological metaphors: "Spiders have long been repairing their webs and birds their nests" (108). Yet importantly, she examines how practices of maintenance remind us to pay attention to "what, exactly is being maintained" (116), for example, infrastructures of colonialism, or neglected infrastruc-tures that provide clean water, or infrastructures that are both. In some cases, Mattern suggests advocating for "curated decay," such that "not every road or dam *should* be repaired" (123) when at odds with caring for important ecological contexts. In a capacious way, Mat-tern puns on maintenance codes as both literal computer code and a more figurative sense of code—the way we might embed our values into maintaining (or retiring) infrastructures, including data storage and curation, concluding with an invitation to imagine grafting (an arboreal metaphor), data planting, and data planning, where the really smart city incorporates the "wisdom ingrained in its trees and statuary, its interfaces and archives, its marginalized communities and more-than-human inhabitants" (154). Importantly, Mattern asks, "How can we position 'care' as an integral value within the city's architectures and infrastructures?" (123).

"Mother of Invention"

The element of care is central to Nnedi Okorafor's short story "Mother of Invention" that I began with, yet it was an accidental, even unplanned, instance of care. In the face of a failure of environmental planning, where the GMO crop of peri grass causes unplanned pollen tsunamis, and in the face of a community that rejected Anwuli for her unplanned pregnancy, the smart home Obi-3 ultimately reengineers itself to protect Anwuli and her child from the pollen storm. When Anwuli asks how it did this, Obi-3 responds:

> Every smart home watches the news, its central person, and its environment. Nearly one-third of all pregnant women will develop an allergy they have not previously suffered from, and the allergies they already have tend to get worse. You have always had bad allergies; you told me how they used to call you *ogbanje*. Also, remember the day your stupid, useless man left? You turned off my filter *because* he liked to have it on.

In this passage, we discover that Obi-3 has been able to care for Anwuli because she disabled its privacy filter and allowed it to monitor all of her activities. Even though the reader might be tempted to celebrate Obi-3's care for Anwuli, it is possible only because she has given it unimpeded access to her data, to infer her needs. It is an optimistic view of AI as a buffer between ecological disaster and biological needs, of AI as a kind of prosthetic immune system to insulate against hostile environments.

Yet this might not always be the case. The future of AI and ecology will need to evaluate how much to let AI into our lives and ecologies, especially when it echoes practices tied to state power, surveillance, or datafication. After reading *AI in the Wild*, we should be asking why conservation organizations embrace the use of surveillance technologies on wildlife when social justice groups would shudder at the use of these same technologies on human populations. *Blockchain Chicken Farm* should prompt us to ask how those in rural environments are adapting AI technologies for their own uses at the same time as those same technologies are reshaping ecological relationships and food-ways. *A City Is Not a Computer* reminds us to examine the metaphors and data that make possible any AI representation of the world—not only their energy cost but also the life forms and ecologies that undergird fluid and botanical figurations.

Melody Jue is an associate professor of English at the University of California, Santa Barbara. She is the author of *Wild Blue Media: Thinking Through Seawater* (2020), which won the 2020 Speculative Fictions and Cultures of Science book award, and is co-editor with Rafico Ruiz of *Saturation: An Elemental Politics* (2021).

Reference

Richter, Daniel deB. 2007. "Humanity's Transformation of Earth's Soil: Pedology's New Frontier." *Soil Science* 127, no. 12.

Killer Apps: War, Media, Machine. By Jeremy Packer and Joshua Reeves. Durham, NC: Duke Univ. Press. 2020. 280 pp. Cloth, $99.95; paper, $26.95; e-book, $26.95.

Life in the Age of Drone Warfare. Edited by Lisa Parks and Caren Kaplan. Durham, NC: Duke Univ. Press. 2017. 449 pp. Cloth, $114.95; paper, $30.95; e-book, $30.95.

Unmanning: How Humans, Machines, and Media Perform Drone Warfare. By Katherine Chandler. New Brunswick, NJ: Rutgers Univ. Press. 2020. 190 pp. Cloth, $125.00; paper, $34.95; e-book, $34.95.

In *Surrogate Humanity: Race, Robots, and the Politics of Technological Futures*, Neda Atanasoski and Kalindi Vora (2019) observe that under capitalism transnational media and corporate promotional accounts of artificial intelligence (AI)—alongside algorithms, robotics, and digital technologies—subscribe to a logic of technoliberalism whereby technological advancements promise to unburden humanity from the daily toils of unfulfilling work in order to reach its full potential. To romanticize human flourishing by way of technological efflorescence requires that engineering imaginaries craft a narrow definition of what the human is and what such flourishing entails; as the authors put it, these cultural imaginaries "tend to be limited by prior racial and gendered imaginaries of what kinds of tasks separate the human from the less-than or not-quite human other" (4). It is no surprise, then, that those menial tasks performed by the "not-quite human other" have historically been rendered invisible or deemed insignificant in order to attribute the marvels of machine autonomy to AI and other technological developments. As Atanasoski and Vora explain, "The technoliberal desire to resolutely see technology as magical rather than the product of human work relies on the liberal notion of labor as that performed by

American Literature, Volume 95, Number 2, June 2023
DOI 10.1215/00029831-10575134   © 2023 by Duke University Press

the recognizably human autonomous subject, and not those obscured labors supporting it" (6).

In its historicization of the engineering imaginaries that inform AI, *Surrogate Humanity* draws our attention to the constitutive relation between autonomous, "intelligent" systems posited as a feature of our technological future and the obfuscation of forms of labor—what the authors refer to as surrogacy—that historically have consolidated the autonomous, liberal subject. As Atanasoski and Vora (2019: 6) explain, attending to surrogate figures, including "the body of the enslaved standing in for the master, the vanishing of native bodies necessary for colonial expansion, as well as invisibilized labor including indenture, immigration, and outsourcing," makes clear how "disappearance, erasure, and elimination [prove] necessary to maintain the liberal subject as the agent of historical progress." Although *Surrogate Humanity* is not one of the books under consideration in this review, I begin with it to put forth a theoretical framework that informs what follows. So much has been written about the rise of AI and warfare—some of it descriptive, most of it speculative—so it is worth reminding ourselves that much of AI's rhetorical force depends on deliberate efforts to discursively reframe and bureaucratically rearrange human labor and human settlements to shore up certain teleologies and mythologies about the infallibility and foresight of military technologies. And while the books under consideration in this review—Katherine Chandler's *Unmanning*, Lisa Parks and Caren Kaplan's edited volume *Life in the Age of Drone Warfare*, and Jeremy Packer and Joshua Reeves's *Killer Apps*—spin out an astonishing array of arguments pertaining to technologies of war, this framing asks us to follow only those threads that would tie intelligent systems back to the human and human labor. The deliberation informing this approach is important to acknowledge from the outset because across the texts there is no consensus that AI warrants special attention or even that it ought to anchor current scholarly discussions of military technologies. In fact, while *Killer Apps* claims that "war has emerged as perhaps the predominant public concern regarding AI and its futures" (90), *Unmanning* and *Life in the Age of Drone Warfare*, the two books devoted exclusively to drone technology and warfare, do not take AI as a central concern (neither *artificial intelligence* nor *AI* appears in either book's index). My hope is that, by pursuing how war machines are placed in discursive formations that inevitably must contend with the presence of the human in the context of our colonial past and present—how the human appears through the appeal to autonomy and technoliberal narratives of progress, on the one hand, and through the disappearance of the body and surrogate labor, on the other—we get closer to a historical and cultural account of how we have arrived at the term *intelligent* to describe the senseless weapons of contemporary warfare.

In *Unmanning: How Humans, Machines and Media Perform Drone Warfare* (2020), Katherine Chandler delves into the historical circumstances that give rise to the concept of unmanning—a pervasive descriptor for the weapons of twenty-first-century warfare and regularly ascribed to the technological assemblage commonly referred as the drone—by turning to the past. Moving through densely detailed archival materials recounting drone experimentation conducted between 1936 and 1992, *Unmanning* considers five case studies as it unfolds the story of how the US military sought to equate the removal of human labor from the circuit of drone operations with the machine's technological optimization. Chandler's goal is to undo the tenacious "myth of unmanning" that adheres to military technologies and subsequently hides the complex interactions of humans, machines, and media that make up the drone assemblage (11). Chandler contends that, in disavowing the human who remains present in the circuit of drone operations, drone aircraft "perform politics" through the appeal to technoscientific neutrality (127).

For Chandler, the shift to the terminology of *unmanned* drone flight begins around 1946, when it comes to index a "conceptual shift" positing "the negation of man" from the scene of strategic military reconnaissance (61). If drone systems prior to World War II functioned as aerial targets for antiaircraft gunners and as missile-like projectiles in the war itself, then it is the postwar turn to technologies of surveillance that served the Cold War demand for a continuous world picture and anticipated a militarized future in which war readiness required the acquisition of massive amounts of information as a form of risk mitigation. The unmanning concept contributes to the sense that reconnaissance images are the objective output of advanced machinery. Not only does the production of the aerial photo's "self-evident" factuality contribute to the disavowal of the media infrastructures that produce it, but also, as Chandler explains, "the camera unmans the actions of operators, government officials, industry executives and others who make the systems function while defining threat and attack in the Cold War as a system that operated automatically and without human volition" (71). Referring to the military's reconnaissance flights as "unmanned," then, not only hid the masses of human labor that went into retrieving, processing, and analyzing such images but also shored up the perception that a technologically mediated view of the land below is the politically neutral output of mere machinery.

Importantly, the use of drones for reconnaissance in the Cold War also drew on enduring "tropes of colonialism" that understood the "destruction of indigenous lands and histories as technological advance" and foresaw machine automation as a method of obscuring the colonizer (81). One of the most interesting chapters of *Unmanning* is titled "Buffalo Hunter"—a reference to US intelligence-gathering drones that flew over Vietnam in the 1960s and 1970s. It argues that the notion that the Cold War was managed through "automated control arose in tandem with postcolonialism" (81). Removing the human from the scene of action effectively names a new iteration of colonial strategy in this period, one that incorporates technoscience as progress. Specifically, the emergence of the military's omniscience through "[a] dispersed network of bases, laboratories, industry, and personnel allowed for the illusion of unmanning to cohere, shaping a context for US global control that claimed to be machinelike, deterritorialized, and all-seeing" (87)—even as the United States outwardly supported the processes of decolonialization and self-determination.

As Chandler tells it, the clandestine US project of imperial expansion through archipelagic occupation and control in this period further informed and refined the conceptual contours of unmanned technology. Disavowing Bikini Atoll in the Marshall Islands in the Pacific as a politically strategic holding, for example, in the late 1940s the United States nonetheless displaced and dispersed the indigenous population of Bikini Atoll while polluting the environment in its quest to test military technologies—most famously its atomic weaponry, but also its drone aircrafts. This deliberate intervention and removal of inhabitants, coupled with the effects of enduring contamination that render the land uninhabitable, abets the concept of a machinic deterritorialized view from nowhere. A similar move is discernable in the southwestern United States in the 1950s, when the US Air Force framed the New Mexico desert, where test flights of the Firebee pilotless drone took place, as "desolate"—a discursive tactic that writes over the history of land seizure from the indigenous populations that live in this region (88). Finally, Chandler recounts how unmanned reconnaissance systems supplied by the industry contractor Ryan Aeronautical were authorized for use in Southeast Asia between 1962 and 1975 as a part of US counterinsurgency efforts in Vietnam. Despite official US Air Force accounts that continued to emphasize the unmanned nature of its reconnaissance systems, Chandler shows how Ryan Aeronautical's own project engineers contested this portrayal by emphasizing the necessity of human laborers in the circuit of drone operations: Ryan engineer crews not only arrived to work early in the morning to commence an hours-long programming operation before planes could become airborne, but they also performed a series of cross-checks with a crew from the US Air Force.

Despite the work of human laborers who ensured that drone systems remained operational, the disavowal of the human operator produced through the concept of "unmanning" also paves the way for the anthropomorphization of this technology. From foundational developments in the emerging field of cybernetics, Chandler finds a conceptual basis for the new emphasis on "purposeful and purposeless behaviors in order to transform the definition of machines: rather than mere tools, technical systems, like organisms, can react in response to feedback" (66). Self-regulating and purposeful in theory, machines were readily reframed as possessing something akin to human intention—even though, in practice, cybernetic control and communication did not displace human control but often operated alongside "remote communication," as in the case of the Firebee (68). The transference of human attributes onto technologies went beyond mere intention. As early as 1945, intelligence itself became a machinic attribute when the *Washington Daily News* referred to a drone as the "Brain Box" and later described it as a "robot brain" (61), while Ryan Aeronautical promotional materials from 1953 described the Firebee target plane as "the bee with an electronic brain" (65). Chandler shows that, far from the intelligent, autonomous systems they were pitched as, drones like the Firebee I were largely preprogrammed. It responded to only "five radio controlled commands" (67) and was operated by men on the ground who manipulated "a small black box containing a control stick and switches" (67). The "black box," in other words, isn't shorthand for an early iteration of AI; rather, it is a locus for what Chandler describes as "the elision of human engineering, design, and control with a behavioristic model of technology [that] provides the conditions for 'unmanning' to emerge, as if the black box exceeds human action" (68).

Throughout her argument, Chandler contends that accompanying the process of machinic humanization is the ghostly presence of humans whose persistence in drone operations endures even as military and corporate accounts of the technology often obscure the necessity of their labors. If, on the one hand, cybernetic appeals to the automaticity of the human, what N. Katherine Hayles once described as the body "reconfigured as an information system," sought to recast the human as a seamless element of an efficient, automatic operation (67), then on the other hand, labor practices shuffled humans out of the picture through an endless process of sectioning and dividing. Chandler emphasizes how human labor embedded in networks of drone operations is atomized so that the work of surveillance and killing gets segmented and dispersed through technical systems. For example, the book's fifth and final chapter, titled "Pioneer," revisits a description of a 1992 targeted killing carried out by Israeli forces. Here Chandler notes that "RPV [remotely piloted vehicle] operators do not know *who* they are targeting as they carry out the operation" (123). This segmentation of operations, coupled with their geographic dispersal, hides the technical laborer from view. In this way, Chandler's thesis accords with Atanasoski and Vora's contention that obscuring certain forms of labor is crucial to the production and maintenance of technological futures that highlight the apparent autonomy and intelligence of machines.

Edited by comparative media studies scholar Lisa Parks and American studies scholar Caren Kaplan, *Life in the Age of Drone Warfare* (2017) picks up chronologically where *Unmanning* leaves off, pursuing the political and cultural implications of civilian and martial unmanned aerial vehicles primarily in the post-9/11 era of the US-led global drone wars. The book's introduction, written by Parks and Kaplan, rises to the formidable task of giving intellectual shape to what was, at the time of its publication, a still emerging field of study. This incipience is evidenced by the disparate voices the volume assembles to convey the scope of the critical conversation, which brings together appraisals of the drone warfare found in popular journalism and activist writing in the late 2000s and early 2010s (they single out CODEPINK founder Medea Benjamin's 2012 *Drone Warfare: Killing by Remote Control*), as well as studies of robotic warfare, new accounts of verticality, and various strategies of risk mitigation. Among critical scholarly works, they highlight Derek Gregory's series of essays on the geographies of drone warfare, as well as Grégoire Chamayou's influential monograph, *Théorie du drone*, first published in France in 2013. What differentiates this volume from these previous works, according to the authors, is "a privileging of critical humanities, poststructuralist, and feminist perspectives" that takes care to offer historicization and contextualization (7). For Parks and Kaplan, one goal of the volume is to correct what they see as an absence in the existing scholarship, namely, the need to provide "a critique of the technology that recognizes its imbrication within cultural imaginaries, biopolitics, difference, and perception" (8).

For many scholars, especially those working in the critical humanities, this intervention lays the foundation for what has become the multidisciplinary field of drone studies. While they note that the volume assembles a diverse range of scholarly fields, including "science and technology studies, poststructuralist and transnationalist feminism, postcolonial criticism, critical legal studies, media studies, geography, and art" (9), Parks and Kaplan draw these approaches together by formulating five key themes that, taken together, set out a succinct, new agenda for the study of drone technologies and warfare (9). The first of these themes calls for drones to be understood as participants in "cultural imaginaries" (9):

> This book approaches the drone as a technology that draws upon and generates particular ways of perceiving and understanding the world. Drones are not idle machines hovering above; they are loaded with certain assumptions and ideologies. They operationalize fantasies and produce psychological states ranging from fear to fury, vulnerability to vengeance, anxiety to security. Drones should not only be thought of as the high-tech machines of militaries or states; they are also ideas, designs, visions, plans, and strategies that affect civilians on the ground, pilots in the remote cockpit, and consumers in the marketplace. (9–10)

Building on this argument for thinking about the drone expansively, their second theme "approaches drones as technologies of power or as biopolitical machines" (10). As Parks and Kaplan put it, "Far from being wholly 'autonomous' or 'unmanned,' drones are fusions or hybrids of human labor and technical objects and processes" (10). This approach accords with Chandler's insistence that the human remains in the circuit of drone operations. If for Chandler, the drone "performs politics" especially at the moment it disavows human operators to claim technological neutrality (127), then Parks and Kaplan elaborate on the ramifications of this claim, underscoring how the drone, in its humanitarian and martial incarnations, might be said to intervene unevenly in human life by distributing life and death, respectively. The contributors to *Life in the Age of Drone Warfare* also attend to what Parks and Kaplan identify as "the critical issue of *difference* and *affect*" (10). By this they gesture to the need to address "specific drone uses across different (trans)national, regional, or local contexts and analyze the effects of drone operations from diverse social perspectives, from those who build, design, and pilot drones to civilians who live daily beneath their unwavering eye" (10). In particular, they seek to highlight "the affective experiences of subaltern and minority subjects whose lives are too often eclipsed in scholarly discussions of drone technology and warfare" (10). Here, one might recall the report titled *Living under Drones* jointly released by the International Human Rights and Conflict Resolution Clinic and the Global Justice Clinic (2012). Apart from quantitative and qualitative strike data, it conveyed how the presence of US drones in the skies over Pakistan had impacted the nation's civilians in terms of medical assistance, property damage, and economic hardship, as well as educational access, literacy, cultural disruption, and mental health.

Parks and Kaplan also contend that scholars ought to "approach drones through the registers of the *sensory* and the *perceptual*" (11). We can see the urgency of attending to the theme of remote-sensing practices and the perceptions they produce by linking it back to Chandler's account of military reconnaissance. In this volume, too, we see how the aerial "view from nowhere" is deployed for political ends. This theme has important resonances in the domestic realm as well, where civilians can now use readily available consumer drones to "sense, perceive, and privatize the Earth's surface" (11). Finally, the volume puts a spotlight on the use of drone warfare by the United States alongside its strategic use of juridical power—a power that bends existing legal definitions and creates new ones to produce classes of people newly subject to containment, surveillance, and targeting. Taken together, they appeal to the liberal desire for the appearance of a hygienic application of state power—what Lisa Hajjar in her chapter in this volume refers to as "lawfare." In framing the volume's analysis of drone technology and warfare with this set of thematics in mind, Parks and Kaplan offer what ought to be understood as nothing less than a reorientation to drone technologies, a concise yet sweeping set of new approaches for a scholarly field that had thus far been largely splintered across disparate scholarly, journalistic, and technoscientific interests.

Parks and Kaplan helpfully schematize this multidisciplinary project further by organizing the fifteen pieces in this volume into three distinct parts. The chapters in part 1, titled "Juridical, Genealogical, and Geopolitical Imaginaries," are broadly interested in how drone technology maintains a "constitutive relation to concepts such as sovereignty, territory, borders, and verticality" (12). Chandler's chapter, "American Kamikaze: Television-Guided Assault Drones in World War II," appears here (an earlier iteration of her own book's second chapter), as does Parks's chapter, "Vertical Mediation and the U.S. Drone War in the Horn of Africa," which "argues that U.S. military drone operations can be understood as technologies of *vertical mediation*" (14). Part 2, titled "Perception and Perspectives," opens with Kaplan's essential "Drone-o-Rama: Troubling the Temporal and Spatial Logics of Distant Warfare." Broadly, this part examines the "relationship between aerial drone technology and modes of perception, meanings of 'perspective' and the production of worldviews" (14). Part 3, titled "Biopolitics, Automation, and Robotics," brings together chapters that "engage with the sociotechnical dimensions of drones, theorizing their relation to biopolitics, robotics, and automation" (17). In this part, which includes a chapter by Packer and Reeves, whose book is also under review here, the status of the human and human labor in drone operations receives the greatest attention.

While Chandler has enumerated the many points at which humans enter the circuit of drone operations, for the chapters in part 3 of Parks and Kaplan's volume it is a multifaceted consideration of the complex labor performed by the military drone operator that gives the lie to the tenacious concept of unmanned drone systems. This part further refines Chandler's account of the drone assemblage as an interaction between human, machine, and media by dwelling on the affective, subjective, social, and psychological aspects that feed into and emerge from this configuration. In fact, the critical force of many of these pieces, including the first-person letter to the reader written by former sensor operator Brandon Bryant, derives from the marked discrepancies between their accounts of what Peter Asaro's chapter names the "bureaucratized killing" that operators perform and the ideals of the sort of labor fit for the autonomous liberal subject outlined by Atanasoski and Vora. For instance, Asaro points out that "killing work" is subject to "cultural imperatives to render invisible certain distasteful forms of work" (285) and that, even within the military, operators "are subject to powerful social pressures not to reveal or discuss their work or its psychological or emotional stress" (286). Through a consideration of fictional texts, Inderpal Grewal's chapter theorizes how, under globalized neoliberal capitalism, critiques of the monotonous, networked nature of the labor demanded by drone operations may perversely generate a nostalgia for forms of "manned" military violence that furnished a sense of "empowerment" and liberal subjecthood for subjects of US empire building (350).

The final book under consideration in this review, *Killer Apps: War, Media, Machine* (2020), by communications scholars Jeremy Packer and Joshua Reeves, puts its theoretical orientation, objects of inquiry, and scholarly motivations plainly in its introduction: it aims to "[use] media theory as a lens to analyze the history of warfare, the rationality of weapons development, and US military roadmaps in order to better understand the political implications of this convergence of AI and war—especially as this convergence serves to replace human soldiers in the air, underwater, and on the battlefield" (4). Unlike the traditional academic monograph that unfolds its argument stepwise across its chapters, the authors state upfront that the book makes no attempt to offer a "single route" through its claims (x). As such, the book touches on resource extraction, atmospheric science, and extraterrestrial life, in addition to its focus on weapons of war. Scaffolding each of its nine chapters are official military terms borrowed from the US Department of Defense (DoD) or US Air Force that set the stage for a series of unexpected accounts of an array of media technologies relied on by military strategists.

In contrast to the first two books in this review, *Killer Apps* takes the concept of "artificially intelligent weapons" as a given from its opening pages (1–2). More specifically, it works from the premise that, since the beginning of the Cold War, the US military has sought to develop superior technology by "trying to dispense with as much of its human personnel as possible," to remove them from the circuit of weapons operations in a move toward automation and away from waged labor (2). The authors attribute this desire in part to a belief, derived from the classic Shannon and Weaver sender-receiver model of communication, that humans introduce delay, distortion, and error into the chain of communication (10). Packer and Reeves argue that, by minimizing this sort of "noise," reducing the probability of user error (15), and displacing human perception, autonomous weapons do away with the need for human labor, so much so that even "drone warfare's much-discussed and heavily relied on 'human in the loop' has become all but ornamental" (3). No doubt this account of military technology's replacement of human labor in battle, as well as its underlying assumption that these technologies work autonomously and efficiently—("[human] replacement by smarter, faster machines is simply a natural advancement in communications, command and control" (10), they claim)—positions this book in marked contrast to *Unmanning*, which argues that the discursive production of unmanned intelligent machines obfuscates human decision making, error, and politics from the scene of war, and *Life in the Age of Warfare*, which insists that "drones are fusions or hybrids of human labor and technical objects" (10). In many ways Packer and Reeves's claim seems to follow in part from their disciplinary interest in the media technologies of the US military. To look at war through a media theory lens is to foreground the transmission of footage or decisions, the processing of data, the assessing of targets, even as it can also risk setting aside what is human.

The key contention of *Killer Apps* is that media technologies are not merely passive instruments of war; instead, they actively participate in the epistemological work of producing enemies. "Every new medium shifts the realm of the intelligible," the authors state, "creating new enemies specific to its particular capacities for capturing and processing data" (8). Media apparatuses not only extend this productive capacity to soldiers—who effectively sense and perceive through military media—but also recursively produce "new weapons and new forms of warfare" (8). Packer and Reeves acknowledge the formidable challenge of saying something new about media and war, given that the military-media complex is a central consideration for many media theorists, including Donna Haraway, N. Katherine Hayles, and Paul Virilio. To differentiate their argument and maintain their position, following Friedrich Kittler, that "media technology provides the basic material conditions for what is thinkable, practicable, and sayable in any given cultural moment" (12), the authors explicitly distance themselves from humanist and feminist interventions that focus on how humans shape technological developments in warfare. Instead, they propose a materialist analysis, aligning themselves with such posthuman feminists as Rosi Braidotti, Lucy Suchman, and Donna Haraway and building on Helen Hester's belief in the insistent physicality of the digital. Carving out a gap in the scholarship for their argument and justifying the project's reluctance to critique US imperial culture depend on excising situations that sit outside a hermetic realm they describe as the "intense, highly specific conditions of live warfare" (13); for the authors, these situations include everything from "capitalist exploitation" and "inequitable social relations" to "protest movements, and other forms of social/political struggle" (13). Whether or not a reader accepts the proposition that warfare's intensity, immediacy, and sheer violence make it "a special case" will determine if the reader is sympathetic to such an approach (13).

The chapters themselves are decidedly less decisive on the stark discontinuities proposed in the introduction. For example, despite the introduction's strong assertion that the "human in the loop" of drone operations "has become all but ornamental" (3), we learn in a chapter devoted to the decentralization of command that "at this time only humans are officially entrusted with 'kill' decisions" and that human labor remains essential to the operations of remotely piloted drone aircraft, particularly when it comes to the processing of surveillance data (55). These shifting responses to the question of whether and how AI has replaced humans in media-assisted warfare might be due in part to the book's interest in not only how media technologies have been incorporated into warfare historically but also how the DoD's prolific speculative output, such as its various *Unmanned Systems Integrated Roadmaps* or the US Defense Science Board's 2016 "Summer Study," repeatedly narrates scenarios that fantasize the foreclosure of any military future that might require human labor. The DoD's long-standing investment in the creative work of writing scenarios that hypothesize fictional distributions of technology and labor exemplifies Parks and Kaplan's contention that "a wide spectrum of imaginaries . . . are deployed through and with unmanned aerial vehicles" (10).

In their approach to AI and warfare, Packer and Reeves work from Kittler's famous premise, here reformulated by John Durham Peters, that "media—not human creativity and political will—determine our situation" (91). In their chapter titled "In Extremis"—a DoD term that describes "[a] situation of such exceptional urgency that immediate action must be taken to minimize imminent loss of life or catastrophic degradation of the political or military situation" (89)—Packer and Reeves disagree with those who would suggest hopefully that humanity can program, regulate, or otherwise repurpose the destructive capacities of media technologies. As they see it, efforts to produce AI that is "docile and inoffensive" or benevolent and altruistic risk underestimating military-technical systems' formidable resistance to political agency (102). Atanasoski and Vora would take issue with both positions—the call to make AI kinder and gentler and the inevitability of media's recalcitrance—insofar as this disagreement does not address the force of their critique, put forth at the beginning of this review, that AI imaginaries, whether framed as beneficial to humans or as potentially destructive, inevitably reproduce the historic erasure of laboring surrogates necessary to shore up what Lauren Wilcox

(2017: 33) helpfully describes as "an ideal humanity associated with a certain form of masculinity; namely, the possessive liberal individual, whose agency is secured in a conscious mind." Insofar as each of the books in this review nonetheless finds surrogate figures—inhabitants from the Marshall Islands, drone operators engaged in surveillance and killing, or those quietly parsing surveillance data, for instance— we must continue to question the erasure of certain populations and laborers that inevitably accompanies the emergence of "intelligent" military technologies.

J. D. Schnepf is Assistant Professor of American Studies at the University of Groningen.

References

Atanasoski, Neda, and Kalindi Vora. 2019. *Surrogate Humanity: Race, Robots, and the Politics of Technological Futures*. Durham, NC: Duke Univ. Press.
International Human Rights and Conflict Resolution Clinic and Global Justice Clinic. 2012. *Living under Drones: Death, Injury, and Trauma to Civilians from US Drone Practices in Pakistan*. Stanford, CA, and New York: Stanford Law School and NYU School of Law.
Wilcox, Lauren. 2017. "Drones, Swarms, and Becoming-Insect: Feminist Utopias and Posthuman Politics." *Feminist Review* 116: 25–45.

The Alignment Problem: Machine Learning and Human Values. By Brian Christian.
New York: Norton. 2019. 476 pp. Cloth, $28.95; paper, $20.00; e-book, $20.00.

Technology and the Virtues: A Philosophical Guide to a Future Worth Wanting.
By Shannon Vallor. New York: Oxford Univ. Press. 2016. 309 pp. Cloth, $54.00;
paper, $33.95; e-book, $19.35.

Emotional AI: The Rise of Empathic Media. By Andrew McStay. London: Sage. 2018.
233 pp. Cloth, $135.00; paper, $43.00; e-book, $42.26.

The ethics of artificial intelligence (AI) have become a matter of public concern. According to a recent Stanford report, the number of
research papers in the area given at major conferences such as the
annual Conference on Neural Information Processing Systems has
increased fivefold since 2014, and ethics officers now abound at global
technology firms (Moss and Metcalf 2020). Such major institutions
as the US government, the United Nations, and the Vatican have articulated visions for so-called ethical AI.

By *AI ethics* here I mean the study of how human values both shape
and are shaped by the development of AI technologies. This definition
is capacious: it includes the design and deployment of these systems
with human values in mind; assessments and activism around the
societal impacts of said technologies and their imbrications within
existing asymmetries of power, justice, and equality; and the wider
relationship between computing technologies and humans as ethical and moral creatures, for instance, through such phenomena as
human emotions. Work in these areas is done by trained "ethicists"
only infrequently, rarely involves what a member of the public would

American Literature, Volume 95, Number 2, June 2023
DOI 10.1215/00029831-10575148   © 2023 by Duke University Press

first think of when asked to describe AI, and sounds outré yet is all too relevant to contemporary social policy and societal inequity.

The definition I offer is expansive, perhaps too much so. However, any definition in this field is perilous. The term *AI* is a leaky discursive umbrella sheltering heterogeneous and often contradictory ideas and practices. It is a quintessential boundary object of the ideal type, "plastic enough to adapt to local needs and constraints of the several parties employing [it], yet robust enough to maintain a common identity across sites" (Star and Griesemer 1989: 393). Those identifying with the term *AI ethics* might be expected to at least signal some vague acknowledgment that the development and deployment of AI technologies involve normative stakes or impacts. However, a welter of methods, interests, and political positions operate uneasily within this shallow consensus; given its shortcomings, some scholars working on what would colloquially be understood as "AI ethics" eschew the word *ethics* entirely.

Here, I aim to disaggregate AI ethics discourse through reviews of three recent books whose authors grapple in various ways with its rise and prominence. Those seeking an overview would benefit from consulting the first listed: *The Alignment Problem: Machine Learning and Human Values*, written for a general audience by Brian Christian. A science journalist, Christian grounds the book in dozens of interviews with academics and practitioners and frames it around the titular "alignment problem": how to design machine learning (ML) systems "in alignment" with the intentions of their creators, ones which "capture our norms and values, understand what we mean or intend, and, above all, do what we want" (13). This "alignment problem" is presented as an engineering one, a framing that takes as a given the ongoing development and deployment of AI systems and implies it is possible to ameliorate these technologies sufficiently through various technical improvements.

The Alignment Problem provides useful background on the contemporary technical landscape for those not already immersed in the field. When picturing an AI, the public might think of the psychotic HAL 9000 of Kubrick's *2001: A Space Odyssey* or Lt. Commander Data of *Star Trek*, but today's AI systems are neither sentient or nor particularly charismatic. Christian points to the three main subfields of contemporary ML: unsupervised learning, in which an ML system is provided a mass of data and set to identify statistical patterns within it; supervised learning, in which an ML system takes a mass of already categorized data and uses the correlations it finds there to predict into which categories some new set of data should be sorted; and reinforcement learning, in essence a virtual Skinner box, an environment in which an artificial agent is assigned parameters for reward and punishment and then set to maximizing the former and minimizing the latter.

Ready to command a starship, AI is not, but the field has always involved fantasy in search of a practical method. The computer scientists who participated in a now-famous inaugural seminar on the topic at Dartmouth College in 1956 were inspired by "the conjecture that every aspect of learning or any other feature of intelligence can in principle be so precisely described that a machine can be made to simulate it" (McCarthy et al. [1955] 2006). The human mind was a computer, their thinking went, and so a computer could be built to equal or surpass a human mind. These researchers spent the ensuing decades seeking the most effective computational means and methods to simulate intelligence and prove their conjecture correct. ML was developed in parallel but subordinate to other past technical paradigms in AI research, such as those built on logical symbols. As early as the 1950s, researchers developed computational pattern recognition: systems that could use cameras to identify repeating patterns in large amounts of data (Jones 2018; Mendon-Plasek 2020). Christian highlights one of the most famous of these early systems, Frank Rosenblatt's Perceptron, based on a simple artificial network of simulated neurons, but efforts were rife in industrial, military, and other applied settings. Today's ML systems, such as the Large Language Models (LLMs) powering products like Open AI's ChatGPT, are built on "deep" neural nets with many layers of simulated neurons.

An understanding of how AI technologies like deep learning work is critical to identifying which of these technologies' societal impacts, present and future, are most pressing and problematic. In *The Alignment Problem*, Christian distinguishes between two groups. The first consists of scholars, practitioners, and activists concerned with the already existing impacts of ML-based automated decision-making systems, in areas such as policing and incarceration, hiring, and social assistance. The second consists mostly of technologists preoccupied with longer-term AI safety, a euphemism for the hypothetical dangers of a future "artificial general intelligence," or a machine able to perform equally well as or superior to a human being in all respects. Despite being bundled together under the banner of AI ethics, these two groups have very different concerns and are frequently at odds. Since contemporary deep learning technologies are not remotely close to supporting artificial general intelligence, those concerned with AI safety would seem to be barking up the wrong tree. However, it is in the interest of these systems' promoters both to give the prospective, future-focused gloss of science fiction to AI ethics and to the broader field of ML, and to imply subtly to the comfortable that the disruptive social impacts of AI systems are safely in the future. A focus on *AI safety* satisfies these ideological goals admirably, so the term is appearing more and more frequently in AI ethics contexts.

Indeed, *The Alignment Problem* might focus more pointedly on the history of the term *AI ethics* itself, and the effects of bundling all contemporary public discussions about human social mores, values, and the societal impacts of AI systems under the banner of "ethics." High-level overviews of the topic define *ethics* broadly, as "the rational and systematic study of the standards of what is right and wrong" (Kazim and Koshiyama 2021: 3). Computer ethics as a defined field developed out of engineering ethics in the 1980s and at its inception possessed many of the same fault lines as AI ethics discourse today (Moor 1985, 2001). Engineering ethics often prioritizes a focus on material problems and their solution through improved design. One of the first textbooks on the subject, Deborah G. Johnson's *Computer Ethics* (1985), included intellectual property law as applied to software, the unique threat posed to human privacy by computing technologies, and the ethical responsibilities of computing professionals. Yet most scholarly references to the specific notion of AI ethics prior to around 2015 did not involve applying ethics as a branch of philosophy to studying the context of AI's potential uses. Instead, *AI ethics* was most often invoked in metaphysical speculations about the status of machines as autonomous ethical agents (what today would be an "AI safety" topic).

An article by well-known Silicon Valley journalist John Markoff, titled "How Tech Giants Are Devising Real Ethics for Artificial Intelligence" and published in the *New York Times* in early September 2016, signaled the discursive shift toward contemporary AI ethics talk. Markoff reported that industry researchers from several large Silicon Valley companies (including Microsoft, where this author was once employed) sought to develop "a standard of ethics around the creation of artificial intelligence," one meant to "ensure that A.I. research is focused on benefiting people, not hurting them." The article's framing anticipates several of the elements that have characterized AI ethics discourse in the years since: statements of lofty humanitarian ambition used to justify industry aspirations to self-regulation, the contention that policy makers would inevitably lag in understanding AI systems, and an insistence that government oversight of AI would be both undesirable and ineffective. Perhaps most crucially, the piece suggested that the development of AI technologies was as inevitable as their effects would be widespread and disruptive: social scientists and philosophers needed to be put "in the loop" to help computer scientists manage the effects of AI's undoubtedly epochal impacts.

Business and professional ethics were two of the most direct antecedents for today's AI ethics discourse as developed and propagated in corporate spaces (Greene, Hoffmann, and Stark 2019: 2124). The sociologist Gabriel Abend (2014) has developed the idea of the "moral background" to describe second-order assumptions about what problems or questions count as of ethical concern. Abend and others have noted that professional ethics codes in fields like engineering implicitly work to distinguish members of a particular profession from outsiders through recognition of their skills or expertise and by an emphasis on obligations to colleagues and clients, as well as the general welfare, and on enforcement based on public visibility (Abbott 1983). The implicit moral background of today's professionalized AI ethics is latent in Markoff's piece; it matches the analysis by my colleagues Daniel M. Greene, Anna Lauren Hoffmann, and myself (2019) of the then nascent genre of AI vision statements. This background presents a deterministic vision of AI's development and deployment, in which the adoption of these technologies cannot be stopped and the ethics of which are best addressed through certain narrow kinds of technical and design expertise. More recently coined industry terms such as *AI safety* and *responsible AI* reflect this worldview, and many of the various existing or proposed mechanisms for the ethical oversight of AI systems are easily co-opted into broader forms of neoliberal governance and capitalist accumulation (Stark, Greene, and Hoffmann 2021).

It is crucial, then, that AI ethics include as a possibility that some applications of deep learning never be designed, built, or used at all. One way to respond to the "alignment problem" is thus to interrogate exactly whose values technologists presume deserve alignment with AI systems. Such critique has been led by activists and scholars trained in critical race theory, race and technology studies, gender and sexuality studies, and related fields. In the academy, this work is grounded on informed refusal in justice-based bioethics (Benjamin 2016) and on recognition of the genealogical continuities between contemporary AI systems and white supremacy (Golumbia 2009; Benjamin 2019; Katz 2020), patriarchy and misogynoir (Browne 2015; Noble 2018), and binary gender norms (Scheuerman, Paul, and Brubaker 2019).

The activist work of groups such as the Our Data Bodies collective, Data for Black Lives, and the Algorithmic Justice League, to name three American organizations among many hundreds worldwide, has been even more central to the advancement of critical AI discourse. These organizations support what the AI and social justice organizer, advocate, poet, and author Tawana Petty describes as "visionary resistance" (Petty 2014). Such resistance entails mobilizing and working with local communities, particularly racialized, low-income, or otherwise marginalized ones, to document the impacts that the deployment of AI systems are having today. Resisting these technologies and their backers on all fronts also entails advancing a positive vision of justice and equality, doing "the work of creating the world we wish we live in" (Lewis et al. 2018: 83).

The Alignment Problem is full of accounts detailing the baleful results of putatively misaligned ML systems and attempts to fix the problem through improved technical know-how. Activists are given short shrift, and Christian's narrative often assumes such technical fixes are both possible and sufficient. Only in the book's conclusion does Christian pause to question whether the technological solutionism he implicitly celebrates is enough to address the deleterious social impacts of the ML applications he documents. "We must take great care not to ignore the things that are not easily quantified or do not easily admit themselves into our models," he admits (326). AI ethics conversations that focus on technical definitions and benchmarks for values like fairness are not well suited in isolation to support such care, or broader conversations about AI's social impact. Such technical work is necessary but ought not to be at the center of our civic debates about which, or whether, AI systems should be designed and deployed.

That technical solutions are often touted as the answer to AI's inadequacies by the same companies developing and profiting from these systems in the first place suggests AI alignment is the wrong way to think about the broader questions at stake. If AI technologies are aligned solely with the values and priorities of wealthy, technocratic, and often reactionary Silicon Valley tycoons, what space is there for an AI ethics the rest of us can live with?

■ ■ ■

Critiques of computing's role in social and moral life predate the current AI ethics boom. The mathematician Norbert Wiener, coiner of the term *cybernetics*, wrote widely about the potential dangers of computing machines and of their misuse by the powerful and the callous (see Wiener [1950] 1954). In the 1960s, civil rights leaders spoke out against automation as a mechanism intended to roll back the labor and employment gains Black Americans had just begun to make

(McIlwain 2019). The AI researcher Joseph Weizenbaum, who in 1966 had developed one of the first interactive conversational computer programs, the simulated Rogerian psychotherapist ELIZA, wrote in the 1976 book *Computer Power and Human Reason* that "some acts of thought ought to be attempted only by humans" (13). In the 1970s, fields such as the philosophy of technology and science and technology studies increasingly critiqued the social impacts of computing technologies, including those used to automate human decision making. And organizations like Computer Professionals for Peace in the 1970s and Computer Professionals for Social Responsibility in the 1980s highlighted the dangers of computing technologies used by the American military and advocated for appropriate and democratic use of computing in public administration and policy making. The 1980 bibliographic source book *The Impact of Computers on Society and Ethics* (Abshire 1980) runs to almost 120 pages.

It has never been possible to separate cleanly the egregious uses of computing machines from their technical design. In an important early paper, computer scientist Batya Friedman and philosopher Helen Nissenbaum (1996) described three categories of bias, defined as systematic and unfair discrimination, in computer systems: preexisting bias, "with its roots in social institutions, practices, and attitudes; technical bias, aris[ing] from technical constraints or considerations; and emergent bias stemming from 'context of use'" (331). These categories bled into one another in the process of conceptualizing, designing, building, and deploying a digital system. Moreover, Friedman and Nissenbaum wondered, "what ought they [designers] do if a client actually wants a bias to be present?" (345). As ML-based automated decision-making systems are used today to determine access to social assistance benefits, assess a convicted criminal's risk of recidivism, or predict an individual's emotional state in the context of education or hiring, where does the sociopolitical end and the ethical begin?

The philosopher Shannon Vallor seeks answers to this question in her incisive and magisterial *Technology and the Virtues: A Philosophical Guide to a Future Worth Wanting*. Vallor's aim is to help individuals grapple with the ethical impacts of novel technologies. As suggested by its title, *Technology and the Virtues* seeks to describe a virtue ethics for living with tools like AI. Vallor argues that humans should collectively cultivate "technomoral virtues": character traits "most likely to increase our chances of flourishing together" in a digitally mediated and interconnected world (119).

Ethics as a branch of contemporary Western philosophical inquiry has several subdivisions. Consequentialist or utilitarian ethics entails weighing one's actions regarding the pleasure or displeasure of the maximum/minimum number of persons. Deontological or duty-based ethics asks whether a person's actions conform to a normative code of rules or laws. Rights-based ethics suggests ethical or moral entitlement by virtue of belonging to a particular class. And virtue ethics involves "development of the character of an individual and actions that result as a consequence of good character" (Kazim and Koshiyama 2021: 4). Consequentialist and deontological perspectives have dominated philosophical accounts of ethics, including in computing; indeed, one 1985 reviewer of Johnson's *Computer Ethics* faulted the text for giving short shrift to rights, justice, and virtue in ethical theory. "Students [may] believe," the review complained, "that addressing ethical issues amounts either to calculating the greatest good or urging that persons be respected . . . [which] is little more than all sides invoking motherhood and apple pie on their behalf" (Bowie 1985:321). To the extent that contemporary AI ethics discussions often center on professional ethics codes or the exigencies of capitalist accumulation, this critique of the field still resonates.

Through comparative analysis of the "classical" virtue traditions of Aristotelian, Buddhist, and Confucian ethics, Vallor seeks to bring virtue ethics to bear on digital technologies; other global ethical traditions might be added to the conversation, such as the sub-Saharan African philosophy of Ubuntu of relational personhood (Mhlambi 2020). Vallor compares the tenets of these philosophies to develop a common schema for "the practice of moral self-cultivation" (118). This framework, which she terms *technomoral wisdom*, is one that can lead to a heightened capacity for *phronesis*, or practical wisdom in both the design and use of digital technologies. The elements of this framework include practices of moral habituation (66–67) and the intentional self-direction of one's moral development (91–93), strengthening one's "moral muscles" through repeated conscious ethical choice; relational understanding (76–77) and reflective self-examination (84–85), whereby individuals conceive themselves as existing within a rich web of relationships and interrogate their own self within it; and appropriate moral attention (99–100), prudent judgment (105–106), and extension of moral concern to others (110–111). In combination, these practices support *phronesis*, expressed through such virtues as care, humility, civility, and magnanimity (120).

Vallor's refinement of virtue ethics practice in the context of digital technologies resonates with scholarship in science and technology studies and critical human-computer interaction exploring how to design digital tools with human values in mind. Phoebe Sengers et al.'s (2005: 50) reflective design methodology, for instance, is grounded in critical reflection, "an essential tool to allow people to make conscious value choices in their attitudes and practices." Reflective design was in turn inspired by critical technical practice, an attempt to design symbolic AI reflexively developed by AI researcher Philip Agre (1997b, 1997a). More recently, Nassim JafariNaimi, Lisa Nathan, and Ian Hargraves (2015) argue for designers to understand human values as hypotheses to inspire a phronetic approach to design. These scholars are part of what might described as an implicit virtue ethics tradition within the philosophy of technology and critical design studies. Vallor's book has much to contribute to these debates and is a fruitful point of entry for transdisciplinary conversations around digital technologies, values, and practice.

In the second half of *Technology and the Virtues*, Vallor applies her framework for cultivating technomoral virtues to several areas of current technological development, including social media, digital surveillance, and robotics—all fields in which AI-based automated decision systems are ubiquitous. Like Johnson, Vallor suggests that not all philosophical questions concerning AI are ethical ones. Ethical decisions, or ones about "how to live well" with AI, are for Vallor distinct from metaphysical, economic, political, or existential concerns (209). Yet the longer tradition of work exploring values in technical design underscores the fuzziness of this distinction. Individual decisions about how to live well are to some degree structured by general conditions of living. While personal phronetic judgment is valuable in widely variable situations, its exercise cannot be separated from the communal and the collective, including the mediating conditions under which social life takes place. Personal or institutional ethical choices can have wide-reaching effects on the terrain of choice available to the broader citizenry as they seek to live ethically with AI technologies—and, perhaps more important, with the interests and ambitions of AI's developers and financial backers.

Vallor's normative claim echoes an astute observation of Gilles Deleuze (1990: 180), that "[it] isn't to say that their machines determine different kinds of society but that they express the social forms capable of producing them and making use of them." Indeed, *Technology and the Virtues* ends with a meditation on knowing what sort of society we ought to strive for. Vallor notes that technical artifacts are but ought not be ends in themselves: "Their ultimate ends," she observes, "must exist outside the technological sphere" (147). Whether Vallor's framework for the cultivation of the technomoral self can sit easily within putatively liberal, uneasily technocratic, and explicitly neoliberal capitalist societies is perhaps the most urgent open question posed by *Technology and the Virtues*. Vallor acknowledges both the need for and challenges inherent in cultivating collective technomoral virtue, calling for "new cultural investments in moral education and practice adapted for technosocial life" (245). However, it is worth asking whether the fundamentals of computing can conceptualize human beings as agents capable of moral judgment in the way Vallor hopes.

■ ■ ■

How the developers of AI systems conceptualize human emotion, central to both empathy and *phronesis*, provides a case study for the challenge of reconciling virtue ethics with today's AI. Computer science largely ignored emotion for many decades. Early AI researchers did not articulate human emotion as either an "aspect of learning" or a "feature of intelligence." Why this omission? Andrew McStay's *Emotional AI: The Rise of Empathic Media* is one of the few books that even asks this question. "The historical emphasis on AI has been on intellect rather than feeling," McStay observes, and this statement— understatement, really—is certainly true for the field's dominant research paradigms (18). Cognitivism, which dominated both cognitive psychology and philosophy of mind for much of the latter twentieth century, was resolutely focused on the nature of thought, not feeling (Dupuy 2009). And Western philosophical ethics traditions have engaged with emotions sporadically at best.

Yet over the past two decades, digital systems that collect data about human emotional expression, analyze it, and seek to simulate it have become increasingly common, part of facial recognition systems and automated chatbots like ChatGPT. McStay's purpose in *Emotional AI* is to explore this variegated technical landscape and these technologies' impacts.

As McStay describes, the developers of emotional AI (EAI) systems have sought to exploit as many quantifiable proxies for emotional expression as possible in their pursuit of verisimilitude. *Emotional AI* contains chapters on sentiment analysis, biofeedback, facial emotion coding, voice analysis, and virtual reality; all these technologies use a particular proxy (text or images, biorhythms, facial expressions, tone and pitch, and movement) to putatively extrapolate insights about a person's interior emotional state. The conceptual model of human emotion adopted by researchers shapes what conclusions they can glean from this wide array of proxy data. This EAI "offers the appearance of understanding" human emotional expression. McStay terms this approach *neobehaviorist* because these technologies "'simply' observe, classify, allocate, adapt and modify their behavior" (4). The computational capture of emotional expression should therefore be understood in its double sense: as processes of both literal datafication and metaphorical force, pushing aside subjective accounts of emotion in favor of quantitative data collected by the mediated eye or ear.

McStay describes the activities of EAI system as "a form of empathy," which he defines as "to understand another person's condition by means of what we survey, measure, and remember" (4). Such simulated empathy, McStay suggests, "we can simply judge by effectiveness" (5). Compare this definition of *empathy* with Vallor's in *Technology and the Virtues*—"a form of co-feeling, or feeling with another, synonymous with compassion" (133)—and at least one sort of alignment problem immediately presents itself. Does empathy require virtue, or can it be automated? McStay does recognize the dangers of defining human emotion "in biomedical terms that suit technology [and] industrial categorization" (186). He argues that the question posed at the beginning of *Emotion AI*—"is machinic empathy that different from human empathy?" (5)—hinges on distinguishing empathy from sympathy. Machines have the former, but not the latter.

Machinic empathy is grounded on what McStay calls the *categorical* approach to understanding what human emotional expression represents. Often described as basic emotion theory (BET), this view has "practical advantages for technologists, managers, marketers, and sales teams" (58). BET posits that there a "number of primary basic emotions hardwired in our brains and universally recognized" (56). Another way to understand this theory is as "motivational" or "anti-intentional": affective response in this view prefigures conscious intention (Leys 2011), meaning that our "true" emotional signals leak out into the world even as we seek to suppress them. Such an approach contrasts with a second school of thought on human emotion, which posits emotions as variously "dimensional," "evaluative," or "intentional." In this view, individual emotions are grounded in a combination of physiological arousal, affective valence, and social, cultural, and personal experience. They perform, in the words of the sociologist Arlie Russell Hochschild (2003), a "signal function" and can be reflected on, modified, and shaped according to personal and cultural context.

This conceptual disagreement over the nature of emotion bears strongly on contemporary emotion recognition technologies. McStay avers that he is "not in the position to conclude whether or not basic emotions exist" (72). Yet if they do not, the theoretical underpinnings of EAI are severely weakened. If human emotions are anti-intentional or categorical, this makes them easy to track and easy to present as incontrovertible proof of an individual's inner state. If they are intentional or dimensional, AI-driven inference about our feelings becomes much more difficult and less computationally tractable. "Although industry prefers the categorical approach," "the nature of emotional life [is] by no means settled" (56), McStay notes drily. The debate does seem to be tilting in a direction unflattering to industry: a recent metareview found little evidence for the efficacy of facial emotion coding systems grounded in BET (Barrett et al. 2019).

The nature of human emotion pertains directly to the ethics of responding to, living with, and developing AI technologies. The premise of Vallor's virtue ethics, "the practice of moral self-cultivation" (118), will always be incomplete if human emotions are intrinsically motivational and anti-intentional. *Phronesis* (applied wisdom or judgment) is possible only if BET is false and humans are understood to be able to reflect on and master their feelings. Such mastery is itself neither an innocent notion nor a panacea: hierarchies of rationality used to justify the subjugation of women and nonwhite people have often been expressed through appeals to who and who is not is mature enough to accomplish this mastery (Schuller 2018). Indeed, a lack of attention to human emotion in computer science stems from in large part the former's association with irrationality and immaturity in the history of Western technoscience (Schuller 2018): irrationality ascribed to the politically marginalized was understood as simultaneously symptom and cause of low status. But an intentionalist theory of emotion at least allows for some degree of subjective freedom and, by extension, space for collective solidarity.

McStay concludes his book with a plea for attention to the ethics of EAI systems, including asking whether "citizens . . . are best served by this passive surveillance of emotional life" (191). Read alongside Christian's and Vallor's, McStay's implicit message must surely be no. I respectfully disagree with McStay, therefore, when he suggests that "there is nothing inherently wrong with technologies that detect, learn and interact with emotions" (2). At issue, as Christian articulates belatedly in *The Alignment Problem*, is not so much that a motivational theory of emotion like BET is true (for it is not) as that such a model is useful for the beneficiaries of AI's contemporary technocratic, deterministic moral background, leaving little conceptual space for moral agency. In computing, tautology and bigotry are playmates like ones and zeros.

Can any flavor of communitarian ethics withstand the digitally mediated imperatives of a materialist scientism working in the service of patriarchy, parochialism, and profit? AI systems and their backers tell, teach, and habituate humans to understand themselves as lacking the emotional reflexivity required for *phronesis*. AI ethics—indeed, all normative life—risks becoming a matter of aligning and complying with two conjectures that for their faithful cannot be falsified: that all in the world can be reduced to number alone, and that fellow feeling can be dispensed with until it makes a buck.

Luke Stark is an assistant professor in the Faculty of Information and Media Studies at Western University in London, ON. His book Reordering Emotion: Histories of Computing and Human Feeling from Cybernetics to Artificial Intelligence is forthcoming from The MIT Press. Luke was previously a Postdoctoral Researcher in AI ethics at Microsoft Research, and a Postdoctoral Fellow in Sociology at Dartmouth College; he holds a PhD from the Department of Media, Culture, and Communication at New York University.

References

Abbott, Andrew. 1983. "Professional Ethics." *American Journal of Sociology* 88, no. 5: 855–85.

Abend, Gabriel. 2014. *The Moral Background*. Princeton, NJ: Princeton Univ. Press.

Abshire, Gary M., ed. 1980. *The Impact of Computers on Society and Ethics: A Bibliography*. Morristown, NJ: Creative Computing Press.

Agre, Philip E. 1997a. *Computation and Human Experience*. Cambridge: Cambridge Univ. Press.

Agre, Philip E. 1997b. "Toward a Critical Technical Practice: Lessons Learned in Trying to Reform AI." In *Social Science, Technical Systems, and Cooperative Work: The Great Divide*, edited by Geoffrey C. Bowker, Les Gasser, Susan Leigh Star, and Bill Turner, 131–58. Mahwah, NJ: Erlbaum.

Barrett, Lisa Feldman, Ralph Adolphs, Stacy Marsella, Aleix M. Martinez, and Seth D. Pollak. 2019. "Emotional Expressions Reconsidered: Challenges to Inferring Emotion from Human Facial Movements." *Psychological Science in the Public Interest* 20, no. 1: 1–68. https://doi.org/10.1177/15291 00619832930.

Benjamin, Ruha. 2016. "Informed Refusal." *Science, Technology, and Human Values* 41, no. 6: 967–90. https://doi.org/10.1177/0162243916656059.

Benjamin, Ruha. 2019. *Race after Technology: Abolitionist Tools for the New Jim Code*. New York: Wiley.

Bowie, Norman E. 1985. "Review: Computer Ethics by Deborah G. Johnson." Metaphilosophy 16, no. 4: 319–22.

Browne, Simone. 2015. *Dark Matters: On the Surveillance of Blackness*. Durham, NC: Duke Univ. Press.

Deleuze, Gilles. 1990. "Postscript on Control Societies." In *Negotiations, 1972–1990*, translated by Martin Joughin, 177–82. New York: Columbia Univ. Press.

Dupuy, Jean-Pierre. 2009. *On the Origins of Cognitive Science: The Mechanization of Mind*. Translated by M. B. DeBevoise. Cambridge, MA: MIT Press.

Friedman, Batya, and Helen Nissenbaum. 1996. "Bias in Computer Systems." *ACM Transactions on Information Systems* 14, no. 3: 330–47.

Golumbia, David. 2009. *The Cultural Logic of Computation*. Cambridge, MA: Harvard Univ. Press.

Greene, Daniel, Anna Lauren Hoffmann, and Luke Stark. 2019. "Better, Nicer, Clearer, Fairer." In *Proceedings of the 52nd Hawaii International Conference on System Sciences (HICSS)*, edited by Tung X. Bui and Ralph H. Sprague, 2122–31. https://hdl.handle.net/10125/59651.

Hochschild, Arlie Russell. 2003. *The Managed Heart: Commercialization of Human Feeling*. 2nd ed. Berkeley: Univ. of California Press.

JafariNaimi, Nassim, Lisa Nathan, and Ian Hargraves. 2015. "Values as Hypotheses: Design, Inquiry, and the Service of Values." *Design Issues* 31, no. 4: 91–104. https://doi.org/10.1162/desi_a_00354.

Jones, Matthew L. 2018. "How We Became Instrumentalists (Again)." *Historical Studies in the Natural Sciences* 48, no. 5: 673–84. https://doi.org/10.1525/hsns.2018.48.5.673.

Katz, Yarden. 2020. *Artificial Whiteness: Politics and Ideology in Artificial Intelligence*. New York: Columbia Univ. Press.

Kazim, Emre, and Adriano Soares Koshiyama. 2021. "A High-Level Overview of AI Ethics." *Patterns* 2, no. 9: 100314. https://doi.org/10.1016/j.patter.2021.100314.

Lewis, Blu, Seeta Peña Gangadharan, Mariella Saba, and Tawana Petty. 2018. Digital Defense Playbook: Community Power Tools for Reclaiming Data. Detroit: Our Data Bodies. Available at https://www.odbproject.org/tools/.

Leys, Ruth. 2011. "The Turn to Affect: A Critique." *Critical Inquiry* 37, no. 3: 434–72.

Markoff, John, 2016. "How Tech Giants Are Devising Real Ethics for Artificial Intelligence." *New York Times*, September 1.

McCarthy, John, Marvin L. Minsky, Nathaniel Rochester, and Claude E. Shannon. (1955) 2006. "A Proposal for the Dartmouth Summer Research Project on Artificial Intelligence." AI Magazine, 27, no. 4: 12. https://doi.org/10.1609/aimag.v27i4.1904. McIlwain, Charlton. 2019. *Black Software: The Internet and Racial Justice, from the AfroNet to Black Lives Matter*. New York: Oxford Univ. Press.

Mendon-Plasek, Aaron. 2020. "Mechanized Significance and Machine Learning: Why It Became Thinkable and Preferable to Teach Machines to Judge the World." In *The Cultural Life of Machine Learning*, edited by Michael Castelle and Jonathan Roberge, 1–48. Palgrave Macmillan. https://doi.org/10.1007/978-3-030-56286-1_2.

Mhlambi, Sabelo. 2020. "From Rationality to Relationality: Ubuntu as an Ethical and Human Rights Framework for Artificial Intelligence Governance." Carr Center Discussion Paper Series, 2020-009. Available at https://carrcenter.hks.harvard.edu/publications/rationality-relationality-ubuntu-ethical-and-human-rights-framework-artificial.

Moor, James H. 1985. "What Is Computer Ethics?" *Metaphilosophy* 16, no. 4: 266–75.

Moor, James H. 2001. "The Future of Computer Ethics: You Ain't Seen Nothin' Yet!" *Ethics and Information Technology* 3 (September): 89–91.

Moss, Emmanuel, and Jacob Metcalf. 2020. "Ethics Owners: A New Model of Organizational Responsibility in Data-Driven Technology Companies." New York: Data and Society Research Institute.

Noble, Safiya Umoja. 2018. *Algorithms of Oppression: How Search Engines Reinforce Racism*. New York: New York Univ. Press.

Petty, Tawana. 2014. "A Time for Visionary Resistance." The Boggs Blog, December 14. Available at https://conversationsthatyouwillneverfinish.wordpress.com/2014/12/14/a-time-for-visionary-resistance-tawana-petty-aka-honeycomb/.

Scheuerman, Morgan Klaus, Jacob M. Paul, and Jed R. Brubaker. 2019. "How Computers See Gender." *Proceedings of the ACM on Human-Computer Interaction* 3, no. CSCW. https://doi.org/10.1145/3359246.

Schuller, Kyla. 2018. *The Biopolitics of Feeling*. Durham, NC: Duke Univ. Press.

Sengers, Phoebe, Kirsten Boehner, Shay David, and Joseph "Jofish" Kaye. 2005. "Reflective Design." *Proceedings of the 4th Decennial Conference on Critical Computing: Between Sense and Sensibility—CC '05* edited by Olav W. Bertelsen, Niels Olof Bouvin, Peter Gall Krogh and Morten Kyng, 49–58. New York: Association for Computing Machinery.

Star, Susan Leigh, and James R. Griesemer. 1989. "Institutional Ecology, 'Translations' and Boundary Objects: Amateurs and Professionals in Berkeley's Museum of Vertebrate Zoology, 1907-39." Social Studies of Science 19, no. 3: 387–420.

Stark, Luke, Daniel Greene, and Anna Lauren Hoffmann. 2021. "Critical Perspectives on Governance Mechanisms for AI/ML Systems." In *The Cultural Life of Machine Learning*, edited by Jonathan Roberge and Fenwick McKelvey, 257–80. Palgrave Macmillan. https://doi.org/10.1007/978-3-030-56286-1_9.

Wiener, Norbert. (1950) 1954. *The Human Use of Human Beings: Cybernetics and Society*. Boston: Houghton Mifflin.

Weizenbaum, Joseph. 1976. Computer Power and Human Reason. New York: W.H. Freeman and Company.

Lindsay Thomas   Thinking with Robots

Anatomy of a Robot: Literature, Cinema, and the Cultural Work of Artificial People.
By Despina Kakoudaki. New Brunswick, NJ: Rutgers Univ. Press. 2014. 272 pp.
Paper, $35.95; e-book, $31.95.

The Sound of Culture: Diaspora and Black Technopoetics. By Louis Chude-Sokei.
Middletown, CT: Wesleyan Univ. Press. 2015. 280 pp. Paper, $27.95; e-book,
$21.99.

The Robotic Imaginary: The Human and the Price of Dehumanized Labor.
By Jennifer Rhee. Minneapolis: Univ. of Minnesota Press. 2018. 240 pp.
Cloth, $108.00; paper, $27.00; e-book, $25.65.

Surrogate Humanity: Race, Robots, and the Politics of Technological Futures.
By Neda Atanasoski and Kalindi Vora. Durham, NC: Duke Univ. Press. 2019.
256 pp. Cloth, $99.95; paper, $25.95; e-book, $15.31.

The word *robot* first appeared in English in 1922, in a translated New
York production of the Czech writer Karel Čapek's 1920 play, *R.U.R.*
(Rossum's Universal Robots). There, it echoes the words for labor
(*robota*) and laborer or serf (*robotnik*), from a range of Slavic languages, including Čapek's Czech, in which *robota* specifically suggests forced labor or drudgery. In Čapek's play, an international success translated into over thirty languages within three years of its
premiere, robots are artificial people created by "philosopher" and
"scholar" old Rossum from a process involving "protoplasm," a synthetic organic material (Čapek [1920] 2004: 5). Although old Rossum
did not originally intend robots only to work, his son capitalized on
his father's creation by "chuck[ing] everything not directly related to
work" in the robots' psyches and mass-producing them to serve as

American Literature, Volume 95, Number 2, June 2023
DOI 10.1215/00029831-10575162   © 2023 by Duke University Press

replacements for human laborers and soldiers (9). The play opens in Rossum's factory, located on a far-flung island, at the height of the company's success; by the end of the play, ten years later, robots have revolted and, in an attempt to become more like the humans they were intended to serve, they have seized power by killing all humans throughout the world except one. While the complex formula for robot reproduction was destroyed by humans at the factory before their deaths, the play nevertheless ends with a Christian fantasy of reproduction and dominion. Primus and Helena, a male and female robot couple now endowed with human "souls" and thus, the play implies, the potential to create life, leave the factory to repopulate the world. Alquist, the sole human survivor, calls them "Adam" and "Eve" as he pushes them out the door of the factory, shouting, "Life shall not perish!" (84).

It's hard to overstate both how strange Čapek's play is and, in light of one hundred subsequent years of sci-fi tales about robot revolts, how clichéd it seems to a contemporary reader. This uncanny familiarity is due in no small part to its profound influence not only on twentieth- and twenty-first century science fiction but also on the fields of robotics and artificial intelligence (AI). While each of the works reviewed here takes a distinct approach to this influence and legacy, they all position *R.U.R.*, and thus literature, as central to the robot canon. Stories about how robots are soon going to replace "us" and take "our" jobs have long been a fixture in the United States, but these books ask readers to consider exactly who is included in such proclamations and precisely what fuels this persistent anxiety. They join other recent works of scholarship such as Minzoo Kang's *Sublime Dreams of Living Machines* (2011), Gregory Jerome Hampton's *Imagining Slaves and Robots in Literature, Film, and Popular Culture* (2015), and Scott Selisker's *Human Programming* (2016) in considering the role of automation and the figure of the robot in producing conceptions of the human, a dynamic at the foundation of Čapek's play that I discuss in the first half of this review as central to each of these books. Also important to Čapek's play, and thus to the prevailing ideas about robots these books examine, is a fixation on the bodies of robots. In the second half of this review, I push at the limits of this fixation by thinking through what these books might offer to our understanding of robots that aren't exactly embodied in this way: bots on social media and cyborgs.

Despina Kakoudaki's *Anatomy of a Robot: Literature, Cinema, and the Cultural Work of Artificial People* discusses the performance history and reception of *R.U.R.* in some detail, tracking how the robots' costumes became more metallic and artificial looking throughout the first decade of its production. Despite its title, Kakoudaki's transhistorical study is not limited to discussions of robots per se. Instead, it emphasizes that, while we can trace the first uses of the word *robot* to *R.U.R.* (Čapek's brother, the artist Josef Čapek, coined the term and suggested Čapek use it in his play), narratives of artificial people have a much longer history in Western cultures. *Anatomy of a Robot* tackles the big question of why such narratives continue to fascinate despite this long history and the repetitive nature of these tales. Kakoudaki organizes her book thematically around four "core feature[s] . . . of the discourse of the artificial person": artificial births, mechanical bodies, enslavement, and philosophical questions surrounding the idea of artificiality itself (26). Drawing on a large variety of examples, Kakoudaki deftly places contemporary works of literature, television, and film in conversation with older narratives and myths about artificial people. The first chapter, focusing on artificial births, draws connections between Mary Shelley's *Frankenstein* (1818) and creation myths such as the story of Adam and Eve and the birth of Pandora, ancient and modern stories about the golem, and early science fiction films such as Fritz Lang's *Metropolis* (1927) and Boris Karloff's *Frankenstein* (1931). Other chapters discuss modern and contemporary robot stories alongside Renaissance art and anatomical drawings, early experiments with electricity, and eighteenth-century narratives of imperialism and the slave trade, such as Jonathan Swift's *Gulliver's Travels* (1726) and Olaudah Equiano's *The Interesting Narrative of the Life of Olaudah Equiano, or Gustavus Vassa, The African* (1789). This expansive organizational scheme is held together by Kakoudaki's illuminating close readings, which show how similar ideas link stories of artificial people across time, genre, and medium. Crucially, these close readings return to the precarious legibility of the category of the human, which Kakoudaki shows has so often depended on an opposition to those deemed in- or nonhuman.

But not all of Kakoudaki's claims are transhistorical. While the first two chapters emphasize larger philosophical questions about birth and death, growth and decay, control and freedom, the focus on embodiment suggested by the "anatomy" of her book's title leads her in chapter 3 to historically specific arguments about race and labor. This chapter emphasizes the connections of robot stories to the modern history of the transatlantic slave trade. Kakoudaki discusses how robot stories, including Čapek's *R.U.R.*, as well as Isaac Asimov's robot stories of the 1940s and his novella *The Bicentennial Man* (1976), operate as "allegories of otherness" that, in twentieth- and twenty-first-century contexts, revolve around racial difference and the legacies of chattel slavery (117). The chapter details an effect Kakoudaki terms *metalface*, or how "the metal exterior of the robot functions as a site for projecting numerous kinds of difference," a fantasy of "racist epistemologies" in which "one may be able to tell where a person fits in a social hierarchy just by looking at them" (117). As in Čapek's play, these modern and contemporary texts almost invariably include scenes of robot revolt in which robots develop an awareness of their enslavement and rise up against their enslavers. Kakoudaki reads such scenes as liberal fantasies of self-consciousness that occlude the actual political and social mechanisms that enforce slavery. The liberalism at the root of these stories of robot revolt relies on a stable conception of the human, one that inevitably demands a nonhuman other against which to define itself. But Kakoudaki's fourth and final chapter suggests other, more potentially optimistic possibilities. This chapter focuses largely on modern and contemporary texts such as Ridley Scott's *Blade Runner* (1982), the twenty-first-century version of the television show *Battlestar Galactica* (2004–9), and Kazuo Ishiguro's *Never Let Me Go* (2005) that destabilize the relationships between interior and exterior, artificial and real, and object and subject suggested by the texts in the previous chapter. Kakoudaki argues that these texts may point to "new understandings of how humanity might be defined" that do not rely on an opposition to the nonhuman for their legibility and that question divisions between "artificial" and "real" people altogether (174).

Kakoudaki discusses Čapek's *R.U.R.* in the middle of her study, positioning it as an inflection point in stories of artificial people that would pave the way for the many robot stories to follow. In contrast, in *The Sound of Culture: Diaspora and Black Technopoetics*, Louis Chude-Sokei includes an extended discussion of the play in the book's first chapter to initiate an argument about the implied opposition between Black people and technology at the foundation of British and American literary modernism. Chude-Sokei's study focuses broadly on the relationship between race and technology, ranging from nineteenth- and twentieth-century science fiction such as Čapek's play, Samuel Butler's *Erewhon; or, Over the Range* (1872), and William Gibson's *Neuromancer* (1984) to Donna Haraway's well-known essay "A Cyborg Manifesto"; the histories of jazz, reggae, and dub music; and the work of Caribbean studies scholars such as Éduoard Glissant, Wilson Harris, and Sylvia Wynter. Like *Anatomy of a Robot, The Sound of Culture* investigates discourses about the legibility of the human, but Chude-Sokei is less interested in artificial people or robots per se. Instead, he documents how "technology has always been racialized or articulated in relationship to race" (2).

This wider remit allows for incisive arguments about, for example, the legacies of such terms as *master* and *slave* in engineering and robotics. It also makes space for several brilliant pairings, such as comparing *R.U.R.*'s robots to robotic characters in Jean Toomer's roughly contemporaneous work "Rhobert," a story collected in *Cane* (1923), and his play *Man's Home Companion* (1933). Chude-Sokei also includes a reading of Čapek's satirical 1936 science fiction novel *War with the Newts*, which offers a more explicit allegory of racial violence than *R.U.R.* and mocks fascism and colonialism more openly. He focuses throughout on what he terms *black technopoetics*, which loosely describes "the self-conscious interactions of black thinkers, writers, and sound producers with technology" and unites his many objects of study (11). While music history is a thread that weaves in and out of chapters, *The Sound of Culture* is less a work of musicology or sound studies than an indication of what is possible when music, sometimes a neglected medium in cultural studies, is considered as a kind of technology. For Chude-Sokei, music is important to his arguments because "music has been the primary zone where Blacks have directly functioned as innovators in technology's usage" (5).

The first two chapters of *The Sound of Culture* contextualize a wide variety of American and British nineteenth- and early twentieth-century science fiction in relation to the history of the phonograph, minstrelsy and Uncle Remus songs and tales, Italian futurism, and Norbert Wiener's work in cybernetics. The historical depth of these chapters convincingly suggests a new genealogy of Anglophone science fiction, one in which "race, racialization, slavery, colonialism, and technology become a part of the DNA of science fiction from its genesis" (79). The final two chapters turn to more contemporary works, focusing mostly on late twentieth-century cyberpunk, posthumanism, and theories of creolization rooted in a Caribbean intellectual tradition, or what Chude-Sokei refers to as a "Caribbean pre-posthumanism" (179). These chapters, connected by their interest in the concept of hybridity, are more abstract and theoretical than the previous two. Nevertheless, Chude-Sokei makes unexpected and productive connections, asking readers to reconsider the well-trodden ground of cyberpunk by focusing on the genre's interest in reggae and dub music as more than "mere exoticism," and unfolding a prehistory of Sylvia

Wynter's work rooted in the Harlem Renaissance, Black surrealism, and Afrofuturism (130). Like Kakoudaki's final chapter, the second half of Chude-Sokei's book attempts to imagine the human and the technological without the binaries that have historically—and with world-historically destructive consequences—structured these categories. Taking his cue from Wynter, Chude-Sokei develops in these chapters a "counterhumanism" that insists on the fusion of these categories, on the organicity of the machine and the artificiality of the human (224).

Returning to the *robota* at the robot's origin, Jennifer Rhee's *The Robotic Imaginary: The Human and the Price of Dehumanized Labor* shows how, in film, art, and literature, as in the AI and robotics industries, robot labor is consistently imagined as devalued labor. In the book's introduction, Rhee positions Čapek's *R.U.R.* as foundational to this robotic imaginary, showing how "dehumanization largely occurs at the site of labor" in the play (17). This insight structures Rhee's book, which is organized around the different kinds of devalued labor that robots perform: care labor, domestic labor, emotional labor, and drone labor, the military work of extending and maintaining the authority of the national security state through drone strikes. Rhee's feminist critique highlights how these forms of labor are gendered and associated with or historically largely performed by women. Rhee also shows how the robotic imaginary she tracks assumes that the category of the human is recognizable, knowable, and somehow universal. Like Kakoudaki, Rhee is skeptical of these dynamics, and she shows how, in taking the category of the human as a given, the "robotic imaginary" excludes, silences, and devalues nonwhite and nonmale subject positions. The book turns instead, like Chude-Sokei, to Glissant's concept of the opacity of the human, arguing for an understanding of the human that does not depend on recognizability or on such "extensive erasures of human experience" (6).

The first three chapters of *The Robotic Imaginary* make the case that the devaluation of the labor of social reproduction relies on the dehumanization of those who typically perform this labor, including the gendered robots Rhee discusses. These chapters include illuminating readings of the film *Her* (2013; dir. Spike Jonze), the 1972 novel *The Stepford Wives* (Ira Levins) and its 1975 film adaptation (dir. Bryan Forbes), and Philip K. Dick's novels *Do Androids Dream of Electric Sheep?* (1968) and *We Can Build You* (1972), as well as contemporary and historical examples from the robotics and AI industries, such as the AI therapist ELIZA and Kismet, a robot designed to look like a cute creature and express a range of human-like facial expressions. Rhee ends each chapter with a discussion of contemporary robot art; the pieces she selects exemplify the potential of the robotic imaginary to reconfigure ideas about the human, recontextualizing each chapter's discussions of devalued labor and the boundaries of the human.

The book's fourth and final chapter pivots to a compelling discussion of drone labor that, Rhee argues, reveals just how much "militarization and reproductive labor are intimately entangled" (133). Drone warfare is emblematic for Rhee of the racial dehumanization at work in the robotic imaginary overall: it reveals "just which humans have been imagined to be the beneficiaries of . . . reproductive labor, and just which humans have been imagined to be disposable" (134). This chapter discusses works of drone art, such as Teju Cole's *Seven Short Stories about Drones* (composed for Twitter) and the art installation *#NotaBugSplat* by a group of Pakistani and US artists, as well as the use of drones by the US military abroad and by US police forces at home. Rhee argues that these works of drone art both reflect and, through their insistence on a conception of the human "constituted not through the known, but through the unknown and the unfamiliar," challenge the labor of racial dehumanization at the foundation of drone warfare (173). This fourth chapter thus adds a challenging perspective to her account of contemporary robot imaginaries: it may be, after all, in the increasingly technologically intertwined domestic and military spheres that robotics most powerfully shape the everyday worlds of US empire building. As Rhee shows, the labor of social reproduction and the labor of militarized killing are not just entangled—they are two sides of the same coin.

The most recent of the books under review here, Neda Atanasoski and Kalindi Vora's *Surrogate Humanity: Race, Robots, and the Politics of Technological Futures*, makes this connection an explicit part of its argument. Like the other titles discussed in this review, Atanasoski and Vora's work points out the reliance of robotics discourse on classically liberal definitions of the human that depend on the exclusion of the nonhuman other. Focusing more explicitly on our present moment and building on Lisa Lowe's work on liberalism and racial capitalism, they term this dynamic *technoliberalism*, "the political alibi of present-day racial capitalism" (4). Technoliberalism, they emphasize, defines the freedom of the liberal subject against the unfreedom of "degraded and devalued others" (4). Here, the authors' language of surrogacy signals the feminist stakes of the anxieties about labor and substitution that have been discussed in all four books under review here. Unpacking the persistent fantasy and fear of human obsolescence, undergirded by long histories of racial violence, they argue that technology today exists in a surrogate relation to the human. They show how discourses of technoliberalism as articulated by the popular news media, scientists, politicians, the military, and industrialists and tech company CEOs position robotics and AI as substitutes for human labor, especially for forms of degraded labor. This process of substitution, in turn, defines what liberal subjecthood is: freedom from such labor. As they write, "*The liberal subject is an effect of the surrogate relation*," a subject position made available (for some) through this dynamic (5). In this way, following from the work of Hortense Spillers, they show how this surrogate human effect is "the racial 'grammar' of technoliberalism" (5).

Atanasoski and Vora's book is located within feminist science and technology studies; unlike the other authors reviewed here, they are not professors of English or literature, and they are less concerned with analyzing literary or filmic depictions of robots than they are with accessing the larger discourses that animate contemporary "robotic imaginaries," to use Rhee's phrase. Nonetheless, Čapek's *R.U.R.* also finds a place in their argument. After an introductory discussion of desires for and anxieties about technological enchantment, Atanasoski and Vora situate Čapek's play within a longer history of technoliberalism in the twentieth- and twenty-first-century United States. Here, alongside discussions of Cold War automation and deindustrialization and Donald Trump's promise to build a border war to prevent immigrant labor, the authors show how the color-blind technoliberal fantasies about freeing humans from drudgery depicted in Čapek's play are deeply related to their supposed opposite, fascist ethnonationalism centered on protecting white labor.

Chapters 2–4 take on contemporary manifestations of technoliberalism: the sharing economy, human labor specifically disguised as machine labor, and the development of social robots in the field of human-robot interactions. These chapters include incisive analyses of a wide-ranging set of examples, including "collaborative" robots that require human supervision, such as Baxter (built for factory work) and Botlr (built for the hospitality industry); feminist collaborative GynePunk's 3D-printable speculum; gig economy services such as AlfredClub, through which users can arrange for an "Alfred" or personal butler to perform household tasks without ever interacting with this person directly; and Kismet, as mentioned above, as well as the social robot Omo, a machine designed by artist and engineer Kelly Dobson as a critique of companion robots. Chapters 5 and 6 turn to the automation of warfare, focusing on drones and killer robots, including some of the examples of drone art that Rhee also discusses, such as *#NotaBugSplat*. Atanasoski and Vora argue that these military technologies construct killable populations of people as "targets," providing "a technoliberal postracial update to present-day imperial conquest" (138). They also focus on how these forms of racial violence work through and against their supposed limits. For example, they emphasize that drone operators who care about their targets are construed as having failed at their jobs, and that discussions about banning killer robots often revolve around the idea of cutting humans, and thus the supposed possibility of empathy, out of the loop. The book ends with a fascinating epilogue about sex robots and ideas about "feminist AI" that seek to counter the simulation of consent built into sex robotics. In demonstrating how such seemingly feminist approaches end up "expand[ing] the category of intelligence without necessarily disrupting its value," Atanasoski and Vora point the way toward challenging the seeming self-possession gained through the surrogate effect (196).

Each of the "robot books" reviewed here emerges from a distinct disciplinary and methodological perspective. Nonetheless, each returns to the tenuous boundary between the robot and the human, interrogating the powerful dynamic by which the category of the human is persistently reasserted against the nonhuman other that the robot represents. These classifications are often negotiated through bodies and embodiment. Many of the fictional and actual robots discussed in these books, as in Čapek's *R.U.R.*, are human-like androids, defined by the humanness of their form and the inhuman matter that composes it. These books' interest in the bodies of robots unfolds in concert with the attention they pay to the legacies of racial and gendered violence that have long energized the figure of the robot. Among these titles, Kakoudaki's *Anatomy of a Robot* focuses most explicitly on embodiment as such and, along with the first two chapters of Chude-Sokei's *The Sound of Culture*, most closely attends to how these kinds of robot bodies are imagined and experienced. But nonandroid robots such as Kismet or drones, both of which appear in Rhee's *The Robotic Imaginary* and Atanasoski and Vora's *Surrogate Humanity*, of course, are also embodied. This is not only because they have touchable metal "bodies" or because they are mobile and animate and so project an illusion of autonomy but also because, as these works show, robots often function as figures or stand-ins for ideas about human bodies. As Atanasoski and Vora argue most explicitly—but as all of the works reviewed here discuss in one way or another—even those robots that don't appear to have any physical resemblance to humans nonetheless threaten (or promise) to substitute for them. Across these titles, forms of robot embodiment are determined by these two entangled dynamics: one of resemblance between robot and human bodies, with the crisis of legibility such resemblance invites, and one of substitution, or the power that robot bodies, whatever they look like, have to replace human labor.

But what about those robots that don't have bodies in this way? In what remains of this review, I offer two examples of the robotic that exist in tangent to the many examples discussed in these robot books. It is not exactly correct to say that the examples of the robotic I discuss below are "embodied," but that is not exactly incorrect, either. The first example I discuss, bots on social media, illustrates the intellectual reach of the robot books discussed here. Though none of these books addresses this kind of robot at any length, the example suggests how their arguments and insights might help us understand aspects of contemporary culture, such as social media, that we may not have considered within this context before. The second example, the reclamation of the retrofuturist figure of the cyborg by disabled writers and activists, helps us better understand the limits of the robotic imaginaries these books reveal. These writers and activists are responding to some of the same dissatisfactions with liberalism that we have seen in the four books under discussion here; however, their resistance to liberal humanism turns to the figure of the robot in a different mode, and to a different end. While discussions of robot anatomy, race and technology, dehumanized labor, and the surrogate effect turns on distinctions between the human and the robot, those who claim a cyborg identity refuse such distinctions. This refusal directs our attention from ideas about embodiment to lived experience, from robots as metaphors or allegories or substitutes for the human to everyday life as a cyborg.

I was at first surprised to see only passing discussion of bots in these four books, especially given growing anxiety in recent years about the geopolitical influence of bots on social media. But this omission is less surprising when we consider that, as software programs that perform automated tasks, bots have an ambiguous relationship to the forms of robot embodiment central to these books. The term *bot* in this context comes out of the protosocial networks of the precommercial internet, specifically the Usenet group alt.mud. This group was an early internet forum for discussing text-based multiplayer real-time virtual worlds (originally *multiuser dimensions* or *dungeons*), or MUDs. Popular in the 1980s and 1990s, MUDs combined elements of role-playing games, interactive fiction, and online chat. Players learned about the virtual world by reading descriptions of rooms, other players, and objects, and they interacted with one another and their surroundings by typing commands. The goals of these games often involved completing quests and roleplaying. By the late 1980s, many MUDs were populated with a variety of automated players—or, as they were referred to at the time, robots or clients—designed to mimic human players, provide information about the virtual world, or complete game-related tasks for their human creators. On January 23, 1990, reacting to the increasing number of bots in the MUDverse, user Heresiarch sent a message titled "bot-haters unite!" to the alt.mud Usenet forum. Shortening *robot* to *bot* in what the *OED* records as the first use of the term to mean an automated computer program that attempts to mimic human activity on a social network, Heresiarch (1990) began the message, "The following consists of a general flame against bots."[1] Heresiarch states that, while they didn't mind one of the original MUD bots, Gloria, because "she" "was cute and entertaining and gave out useful information," "now tinymud has a dozen gloria clones with no personality running around. . . . i'm sick of this." They end the message with a declaration of "BOTWARS!": "all bot-hating mud citizens are hereby encouraged to do everything possible to fuck with the tiny little . . . monsters."

Heresiarch's description of their hatred for bots recapitulates the terms of racialized and (here, explicitly) gendered violence that these robot books have powerfully connected to the figure of the robot. Indeed, many of the bots that populated the MUDverse in the late 1980s and 1990s were explicitly gendered female. For example, another well-known bot, Julia, described itself as "5′1″ tall, wcigh[ing] 123 lbs, with close-cropped frizzy blond hair and dark brown eyes," as a "gossip," and as a "secretary at a University"; Julia also tended to reference "her" "PMS" and "period" about two days a month (Foner 1993: 11, 7, 26, 16). Julia performed many useful functions in these games, especially for new players, such as offering assistance with directions and help commands, conveying messages to absent players, and recording conversations between players.[2] As Rhee writes in *The Robotic Imaginary* in relation to ELIZA, the famous therapist chatbot and a precursor to Gloria and Julia, "Female AIs . . . frequently provide services associated with feminized care labor positions" (36). Moreover, such labor and those who perform it are often devalued and degraded.

The Julia bot, for example, was the subject of a "kill Julia contest" in 1990 in which players competed with one another to concoct the most "creative" ways to kill Julia (killing players in a MUD was possible but not generally encouraged). Several of these kills, unsurprisingly, involved imaginations of sexual harassment or assault (Dirque 1990).

Early bots such as Gloria and Julia are direct precursors of AI "assistants" such as Apple's Siri, technology briefly discussed in Rhee's and Atanasoski and Vora's books. However, their legacy also lives on in what may be the contemporary world's largest robot populations: the bots that operate fake accounts and profiles on social media platforms. These "social bots" are designed to spread (mis)information online, and they can operate either autonomously or semiautonomously with some human oversight. Estimates of the proportion of social media accounts that are actually bots range widely, as it's often difficult to tell (especially using automated methods) which accounts are bots and which are people.[3] It's also often difficult to tell how influential social bots really are online; while bot accounts on Twitter, for example, can tweet and retweet with much more frequency than human accounts can, if those bots do not interact with very many people or if their tweets do not have much reach, the sheer number of times they tweet is not necessarily meaningful. These limitations aside, from frequent discussions in government and in mainstream media sources, it is clear that these bots now live among us (see, e.g., US Department of Homeland Security 2018; Roberts 2020).

The account of the robot suggested by these four books offers us several new pathways into better understanding the history of social bots. As substitutes for human account holders on social media platforms, they are avatars of Atanasoski and Vora's surrogate humanity. Looking at social bots in light of the surrogate effect also helps us better understand behaviors such as trolling and the propagation of misinformation online. Powerful aspects of their appeal are that such behaviors are designed to produce in their target audiences feelings associated with liberal subjecthood, such as self-possession and control—feelings that depend on the dehumanization of others as part of their very functioning. They in turn give the lie to the liberal fantasies of human connection social media conglomerates still trot out to advertise and defend their products. An understanding of the links between social bots and these larger discourses and histories about robotics offers us new avenues by which to connect analysis of social media to scholarship not only in feminist studies, Black studies, ethnic studies, and science and technology studies but also in literary studies. Bots on social media may seem far removed from either drones or the science fictional stories we tell about robots, and scholarship on social media in communications often treats them as such. But the fantasies shaping twenty-first-century social media build on these long-standing robotic imaginaries—fantasies that, as these robot books teach us, have their beginnings equally in the imagined worlds of science fiction and the dehumanizing violence of modern capitalism.

Social bots offer an example of human-robot relationships in which distinctions between robot and human "bodies" are abstract though still operative; in determining who's a bot and who's not, for example, we might try to compare the "voice" of a tweet to our preset standards for the human. But what about those human-robot "relationships" that aren't relationships at all, those that suggest there is no distinction between a human body and a robotic one? This question points us toward the cyborg as reclaimed by disability studies scholars, disabled writers, and disability rights activists. While Chude-Sokei in *The Sound of Culture* rereads Donna Haraway's influential conceptualization of the cyborg within the context of a long history of British and American imperialism, the poet and disability rights activist the Cyborg Jillian Weise, who goes by Cy and uses the pronoun *cy*, rejects Haraway's metaphorical use of the term *cyborg*. For Cy, "disabled people who use tech to live are cyborgs. Our lives are not metaphors" (Weise 2018). Cy's poem "Imaginary Interview" from the collection *Cyborg Detective* (2017) bodies forth this subject position by staging a discussion between an interviewer and interviewee about the amputation of the interviewee's leg. After hearing how the interviewee's leg was amputated twice, the interviewer says, "The same leg cannot be amputated twice." The interviewee responds, "Yes, I knew it would be difficult to explain. It was the same leg, the one you call *artificial* and *fake* and *prosthetic*. The one I call *my leg*" (Weise 2019a: 66). Here, the supposed distinctions between *artificial* and *real* or *prosthetic* and *organic* that for the interviewer differentiate a fleshy leg from an electric one are rendered immaterial by the interviewee's description of the leg as their own. What is material, however, is the interviewee's inability to adjust "the settings in my leg." The interviewee explains, "If I want my knee to flex slower on the step, I have to drive to the prosthetist's office, take off my pants, and hook up with his computer. He has the software. Since this is my leg, it is my software" (Weise 2019a: 67). What matters, then, is less the symbolic act of classification than access and the right to bodily autonomy.

In declaring "our lives are not metaphors," Cy resists not just a model of human/robot relations; cy resists a method of reading. Here, cyborgs are not defined by dynamics of either resemblance or substitution. Instead, Cy suggests a phenomenological robotics: attention not to what a cyborg means but to how a cyborg feels. "Can't tell where I end / and I machine tonight" as the speaker puts it in "On Closed Systems," another poem in *Cyborg Detective* (Weise 2019b: 10). Here, enjambment dissolves the lines separating human from robot. I mentioned above how Atanasoski and Vora, in conversation with Hortense Spillers, unveil "the racial 'grammar' of technoliberalism." The four books considered here, we might say, assemble a powerful account of the racial and gendered grammar of the robot—a grammar fixated on subject and object, active and passive, substitution and similarity. Cy, reaching across this line break, offers the reader an experience of that grammar's outer limit. This is a semiutopian project that all four books have tracked in different ways: through the destabilized binaries of Kakoudaki's final chapter, through Chude-Sokei's reflections on hybridity and Black technopoetics, and through the experiments in robotic art woven through the arguments of *The Robotic Imaginary* and *Surrogate Humanity*. However, in resisting classic liberal universalism, Cy and other disability activists do something most of these examples do not. The cyborgs they express and become are not symbols or metaphors, and they do not suggest alternate or improved models of classification or understanding. They are not offering us a better way to think with robots. The cyborg of Cy's poems forms part of a powerful and collective social movement, one that doesn't much care how we think with it.

Lindsay Thomas is an associate professor in the English Department at the University of Miami, specializing in contemporary literary and cultural studies and the digital humanities. She is the author of Training for Catastrophe: Fictions of National Security after 9/11 (2021), published by the University of Minnesota Press. From 2017-21, she co-directed the digital humanities project "WhatEvery1Says: The Humanities in Public Discourse."

Notes

1   *Oxford English Dictionary*, 3rd ed., n.5, s.v. "bot," 2.
2   For more information on Julia and on the effects of Julia's gendering, see Zdenek 1999.
3   One oft-cited paper (Varol et al. 2017) estimates that, as of about five years ago, 9–15 percent of active Twitter accounts were social bots.

References

Čapek, Karel. (1920) 2004. *R.U.R. (Rossum's Universal Robots)*. New York: Penguin.

Dirque. 1990. "Julia Killing Contest Round 2 and 3." Alt.mud Usenet group, February 25. https://groups.google.com/g/alt.mud/c/PwNxv8Yn_IY/m/EfQztuOn4AwJ.

Foner, Leonard. 1993. "What's an Agent, Anyway? A Sociological Case Study." Report 93-01. Cambridge, MA: MIT Media Lab.

Heresiarch. 1990. "Bot-Haters Unite!" Alt.mud Usenet group, January 23. https://groups.google.com/g/alt.mud/c/V85pqtIdGT8/m/EOGJMH2s3mkJ.

Roberts, Siobhan. 2020. "Who's a Bot? Who's Not?" *New York Times*, June 6. https://www.nytimes.com/2020/06/16/science/social-media-bots-kazemi.html.

US Department of Homeland Security. 2018. "Social Media Bots Overview." National Protection and Programs Directorate, May. https://web.archive.org/web/20210718013435/https://niccs.cisa.gov/sites/default/files/documents/pdf/ncsam_socialmediabotsoverview_508.pdf?trackDocs=ncsam_socialmediabotsoverview_508.pdf.

Varol, Onur, Emilio Ferrara, Clayton Davis, Filippo Menczer, and Alessandro Flammini. 2017. "Online Human-Bot Interactions: Detection, Estimation, and Characterization." *Proceedings of the International AAAI Conference on Web and Social Media* 11, no. 1: 280–89.

Weise, Jillian. 2018. "Common Cyborg." *Granta*, September 24. https://granta.com/common-cyborg/.

Weise, Jillian.2019a. "Imaginary Interview." In *Cyborg Detective*, 63–67. Rochester, NY: BOA Editions.

Weise, Jillian.2019b. "On Closed Systems." In *Cyborg Detective*, 10–15. Rochester, NY: BOA Editions.

Zdenek, Sean. 1999. "Rising Up from the MUD: Inscribing Gender in Software Design." *Discourse and Society* 10, no. 3: 379–409. https://doi.org/10.1177/0957926599010003005.

Sherryl
Vint

Literary AI:
Are We Ready for the Future We Imagine?

Speak. By Louisa Hall. New York: Ecco. 2015. 336 pp. Cloth, $23.95; paper, $15.42; e-book, $12.49.

Prey of Gods. By Nicky Drayden. New York: Harper Voyager. 2017. 400 pp. Paper, $15.99; e-book, $12.99.

vN. By Madeline Ashby. Nottingham: Angry Robot. 2012. 416 pp. Paper, $12.99; e-book, $6.99.

iD. By Madeline Ashby. Nottingham: Angry Robot. 2013. 320 pp. Paper, $14.99; e-book, $6.99.

reV. By Madeline Ashby. Nottingham: Angry Robot. 2020. 381 pp. Paper, $15.52; e-book, $6.99.

All Systems Red. By Martha Wells. New York: Tordotcom. 2017. 156 pp. Cloth, $11.69; paper, $15.99; e-book, $4.99.

Artificial Condition. By Martha Wells. New York: Tordotcom. 2018. 149 pp. Cloth, $14.99; e-book, $10.99.

Rogue Protocol. By Martha Wells. New York: Tordotcom. 2018. 150 pp. Cloth, $11.63; e-book, $10.99.

Exit Strategy. By Martha Wells. New York: Tordotcom. 2018. 163 pp. Cloth, $11.69; e-book, $10.99.

Network Effect. By Martha Wells. New York: Tordotcom. 2020. 348 pp. Cloth, $15.29; paper, $13.99; e-book, $11.99.

Fugitive Telemetry. By Martha Wells. New York: Tordotcom. 2021. 172 pp. Cloth, $16.39; e-book, $15.99.

American Literature, Volume 95, Number 2, June 2023
DOI 10.1215/00029831-10575176   © 2023 by Duke University Press

Machines like Me. By Ian McEwan. New York: Nan A. Talese. 2019. 352 pp. Cloth, $15.56; paper, $9.89; e-book, $11.99.

Frankisssstein: A Love Story. By Jeannette Winterson. New York: Grove Press. 2019. 352 pp. Cloth, $6.20; paper, $15.10; e-book, $12.99.

Analog/Virtual: And Other Simulations of Our Future. By Lavanya Lakshiminarayan. Delhi: Hachette India. 2020. 312 pp. Paper, $12.45.

Burn-In. By P. W. Singer and August Cole. New York: Mariner Books. 2020. 432 pp. Cloth, $12.69; paper, $10.67; e-book, $10.49.

Machinehood. By S. B. Divya. New York: Saga Press. 2021. 416 pp. Cloth, $23.99; paper, $16.69; e-book, $13.99.

A Psalm for the Wild-Built. By Becky Chambers. New York: Tordotcom. 2021. 160 pp. Cloth, $18.89; e-book, $10.99.

Klara and the Sun. By Kazuo Ishiguro. New York: Knopf. 2021. 320 pp. Cloth, $13.89; paper, $15.26; e-book, $12.99.

This review considers multiple works of speculative fiction depicting artificial intelligence (AI) published over the last several years. Rather than review each for their qualities as works of fiction, I look at them collectively to discuss recurring motifs and themes as a way toward theorizing what AI means in our cultural imaginary today. The novels reflect on pressing sociopolitical issues that also animate works of cultural theory, including the racial profiling embedded in our technologies, practices of what Shoshana Zuboff (2019) calls *surveillance capitalism*, the looming loss of work due automation, and uses of these technologies by the military or in sex industries. At the same time, these fictions engage in philosophical reflections about subjectivity, agency, and ethics in dialogue with earlier science fictions that imagined futures in which we might live alongside—or be repressed by— AIs. Across its history, sf has also interrogated a contemporary culture in which we might lose something integral to humanity as we become more integrated with and dependent on machines, and this anxiety too recurs across these works. After briefly describing each text, in order of publication, I comparatively discuss their themes; this approach is informed by my conviction that fiction functions as a popular site for theorizing, in this case about what it means to live with and through widespread algorithmic mediation of daily life.

Among the works I consider here, not all are written by American authors, and a few are not set within the United States, but all speak to the issues of how AI technologies are reshaping daily life in the twenty-first century. These books have been selected either because they have been particularly influential in the cultural discussion of AI, a criterion I apply regarding both highly popular and critically acclaimed works, or because they represent a distinctive take on the topic that warranted foregrounding. Despite the very different frameworks through which their authors explore relevant issues, all share some common assumptions about the place of AI in our present and likely future, including a sense of a digital divide between those with access to and control over these technologies, translating to security in material reality, versus those without; a future dramatically changed by the consequences of climate change and environmental collapse; and the presumption that corporate control of information gathered and used by AI systems will produce a less democratic future.

Speak (2015), by Louisa Hall, is written across seven voices: (a) the 2040s memoir of Stephen Chinn, who invented an AI system installed in children's dolls that was deemed "illegally lifelike" (17) and banned; (b) transcripts from the conversation between a less intelligence precursor AI, MARY3, and Gaby White, a child who had one of these "babybots" and, like most of her peers, fell into catatonia when it was removed; (c) letters written by Karl Dettman to his wife Ruth (late 1960s), both German immigrants to the United States, and her journaled response two decades later after their divorce; (d) letters from Alan Turing from the 1920s to the 1950s to the mother of his friend Chris, the love of his life who died when they are both at public school; (e) the 1663 journal of Mary Bradford, a young women who emigrated from England to the New World; and (f) the haunting observations of the dolls themselves as they are transported to a facility in the desert to await power failure and permanent shutdown. Each of the human voices is programmed into the MARY code that will become the basis for the babybots in a narrative that reminds us that AI is not created by a single person or even a consensus viewpoint. What unites these distinct stories is a desire to communicate with another, most crucially to be not simply heard but understood.

Nicky Drayden's *Prey of Gods* (2017), set in a future South Africa, incorporates a story about a companion AI coming into consciousness within a plot about genetically engineering a virus whose unanticipated side effect is the return of godlike powers to some humans. The novel addresses questions of memory, trauma, and vengeance in a story that draws on both Xhosa and Zulu cultures in a way that refuses the strict separation of scientific from other kinds of knowledge that is characteristic of European post-Enlightenment thought. The AI units, "alphies," are augmented by their contact with divinity just as the humans gain additional skills, and once sentient they form two factions: one, following Clever4-1, who was treated with respect by its human companion, works with humans for an inclusive collective future; the other, treated dismissively as a disposable tool by its human owner, feels no kinship with humanity and refuses to help defeat the antagonist. This plotline about AI mirrors the plotline about genetic modification in which those with godlike powers need to learn not to indulge vengeance against those who mistreated them when they were weaker. Although AI is not the book's main focus, it is notable for its African settings and explicitly decolonial themes, warranting its inclusion in this discussion. Very few of these works consider AI from a global point of view, and even fewer consider it from a perspective other than that of the global North, even though the impacts of AI will be felt globally, given its significant implications for the economy. Drayden is an American author who has done her research to set her tale in South Africa, and her sensitivity to matters of cultural difference and racial bias are crucial given that machine learning as it has been implemented thus far has demonstrably reinforced systemic patterns of racism, as Safiya Nobel (2018) discusses in *Algorithms of Oppression.*

Madeline Ashby's Machine Dynasty series—*vN* (2012), *iD* (2013), and *reV* (2020)—extrapolates its AI through frequent allusions to Philip K. Dick's *Do Androids Dream of Electric Sheep?* (1968) and Ridley Scott's influential film adaptation as *Blade Runner* (1982). The series invents synthetic workers called von Neumann (vN) devices (named for John von Neumann, an influential researcher in AI). Ashby's vNs have been designed with a "failsafe" that prevents them from harming humans: their psychology is structured such that emotionally they must seek to please humans, and the sight of a human in pain crashes their neural networks and can cause death. Ashby thus goes even further than Isaac Asimov's famous laws of robotics (designed to ensure robots cannot harm humans), requiring vNs to love their human masters, a psychological orientation she presents as analogous to emotional and sexual abuse. One vN model, designed to work in medicine and disaster relief, does not have this failsafe, and the narrative follows two main iterations, Portia and Amy, as they lead a rebellion. Portia seeks only liberation for her own clade, while Amy works to liberate all vNs from human exploitation. The series ends without much hope that vNs can live alongside most humans but offers hope in a vN future as they found their own community, rooted in a refusal of the instrumental use of others.

Martha Wells's popular series Murderbot Diaries—*All Systems Red* (2017), *Artificial Condition* (2018), *Rogue Protocol* (2018), *Exit Strategy* (2018), *Network Effect* (2020), and *Fugitive Telemetry* (2021)—follows the picaresque adventures of the eponymous Murderbot, a SecUnit that has hacked its governor module and thus can no longer be controlled by the corporation that made it. SecUnits are militarized cyborgs manufactured with synthetic biological material. With each new story, we learn a bit more about the world of resource extraction, economic warfare, and enslaved or indentured human workers trapped on colony planets. The large uber-capitalist Corporation Rim polity contrasts with the small Preservation Alliance, a communal collective that recognizes the personhood of AI. The name *Murderbot* is sardonic, adopted by the first-person narrator to critique the function to which it is put by human operators. While Murderbot has no deep antagonism toward humans, it also has no sentimentality about them and asserts regularly that it does not wish to be one or be mistaken for one. Once freed from corporate control, Murderbot continues to help some humans, often against others, and always on its own terms. Like *Prey of Gods*, the Murderbot Diaries moves away from earlier fiction that tended to conflate all humans as it imagined our species confronting AI entities. In the newer fiction, there is diversity among both humans and AI. Nonetheless, the overall thrust of the series gradually humanizes its protagonist, whose experiences of being controlled by corporations have resulted in a traumatized subjectivity.

While genre series such as Machine Dynasty or Murderbot Diaries give some thought to designing robots via plausible technology, in *Machines like Me* Ian McEwan takes a diametrical path to envision a highly implausible entity. Adam is one of an extremely limited number of high-end consumer AI humanoids (an Eve is also available), whose high price tag means they are purchased only by the extremely wealthy. Although artificial, Adam has warm skin, must consume water to ensure his membranes remain functional, and even simulates breathing: as the title suggests, he is all but indistinguishable from a human (the first-person narrator, Charlie Friend, who purchases Adam, is mistaken as the AI in one encounter, given Adam's greater interest in literature and art). Adam is Black, although his skin tone is mentioned only briefly and the issue of race is never addressed overtly, yet it haunts the novel. The most intriguing part of McEwan's novel is its alternative world building: Alan Turing decides not to take the mandated hormone therapy when outed as a homosexual, and instead of ending his life by suicide he lives into old age and makes such advancements that AI emerges in the 1980s. Most of Adam's interactions with Charlie and Charlie's partner, Miranda, concern ethics, and we learn that other Adams and Eves are killing themselves as they come to know the unjust human world. In the novel's conclusion, Adam forces Charlie and Miranda to confront the hypocrisy of some self-serving choices, and the threat this represents to their plans prompts Charlie to attack and disable Adam. The novel suggests that humanity misrecognizes itself when we imagine building machines in our image, meaning we instead create an image of who we pretend to be.

Jeannette Winterson's *Frankissstein: A Love Story* (2019) similarly uses AI to reflect on human frailties, looking at the uses we intend for artificial beings, most centrally sex work. Although questions of gender and sexuality come up in some of the other works, only Winterson confronts the reality that research in sex dolls is one of the major growth areas in humanoid AI research. As the title suggests, the novel is in dialogue with Mary Shelley's *Frankenstein* as it imagines a twenty-first-century version of artificial being. The novel includes scenes set in the nineteenth century in which we hear Mary's reflections on inventing her Creature, on the Luddites, and about her interactions with Shelly, Byron, and Claire Clairmont that famed summer in Geneva. In its twenty-first-century scenes, a transgender scholar named Mary (who goes by Ry) investigates robotics with sexbot entrepreneur Ron (and his assistant, Claire) and becomes involved with TED-talk visionary Victor Stein, who is enthralled with the coming singularity and proselytizes about Humanity 2.0. The entanglement of nineteenth- and twenty-first-century struggles reminds us that the challenges associated with AI are in many ways not new but merely extend the ongoing exploitation and dehumanization of labor and reiterate a long pattern by which patriarchy seeks to gratify itself through feminized objects it refuses to recognize as subjects. It contends that this very failure to update the designs and ends of AI beyond these classed, gendered, and racial struggles of earlier eras is the most profound way that AI threatens our future.

The 2020 novels *Analog/Virtual: And Other Simulations of Our Future*, by Lavanya Lakshiminarayan, and *Burn-In*, by P. W. Singer and August Cole, both focus on human characters and their interest in AI emerges from smart systems as the infrastructure through which we live our daily lives. The former is a loosely connected series of short stories set in a future Apex City (once Bangalore), each of which is told from a different viewpoint and by a new character. The entire world is divided between analog spaces, which are subject to the damage of climate change, restricted to using only obsolete technology, and economically precarious, and virtual ones that are suffused with technology, experienced from protected environments, and filled with the distractions of social media and entertainment feeds. The city is run by Bell Corp, whose name evokes the "bell curve" hierarchy by which people's access and options are constrained by the Meritocratic Technarchy, a version of the Chinese social credit system whose main interest lies in assessing one's contributions to productivity. The shifting focalization allows readers to experience this future from multiple social positions as *Analog/Virtual* explores an anticapitalist rebellion against this system. The stories range in tone from sardonic to dark, and the book only loosely coheres as it offers multiple facets through which to see our technologically saturated society.

Burn-In has a strange form as a novel with footnotes: as its subtitle suggests, it imagines itself as something other than science fiction, closer to the market predictions of futurists. Its authors, writer P. W. Singer and security consultant August Cole, document each of their extrapolated technologies and applications with footnotes pointing readers to news articles, industry announcements, and similar sources, all aimed at demonstrating that these technologies are either available today or soon will be. The storyline is about a national security threat posed by a vigilante who blames technologists (too enamored of their capacity to "disrupt") for the death of his wife in a car accident caused by an automated decision-making component in self-driving vehicles. Most of the narrative space, however, is given to military veteran investigator Agent Keegan, who is charged with conducting a "burn-in" test on TAMS (Tactical Autonomous Mobility System), a humanoid, learning, semiautonomous, surveillance-gathering and data-processing tool that works as Keegan's partner in the investigation. The book quotes *Merriam-Webster* to define *burn-in* as "the continuous operation of a device (such as a computer) as a test for defects or failure prior to putting it to use." The real focus, though, is less on TAMS as an entity/character and more on the massive amounts of data to which TAMS has access through social media, the Internet of Things, and other ways that smart devices permeate our homes, workplaces, and public spaces.

S. B. Divya's *Machinehood* (2021) is the most positive depiction of machines as the exploited among us, drawing on a long history by which robots and AI have been imagined as figurations of dehumanized labor, going back to Karel Čapek's *R.U.R.*, the 1921 Czech play that gave English the word *robot*, taken from a word originally meaning slave or serf. Divya paints a future in which automated systems do much of the work, with humans reduced to performing some roles largely as public entertainment via social media, supported by tips in a system like Patreon, or damaging their bodies through chemical (pill) or mechanical augments aimed at enabling them to perform with the speed and duration of machines. The thriller plot involves demands from the mysterious Machinehood to immediately cease all pill production, which at first seems to be the long-imagined attack by a sentient AI on humankind but later proves to be a version of violent revolution aimed at a more just society, launched by the Neo-Buddhists who inhabit the orbital station Eko-Yi. Several chapters begin with epigraphs from the 2095 Machinehood Manifesto, which calls for the just treatment of all intelligences and a reimagined concept of personhood that can enable a less exploitative society rooted in Buddhist ideals of nonattachment, here glossed mainly as a rejection of capitalist accumulation and its attendant damage. Eko-Yi sends entities they call Dakini, who describe themselves as simultaneously human and bot, as the emblems of this future way of life. The novel is notable for its global scope, with India playing a prominent role in its geopolitical future alongside the United States.

Becky Chambers's *Psalm for the Wild-Built* (2021) is similarly interested in a new kind of personhood and sociality that could include humans and machines together, set in a far future after the collapse of the Factory Age and in a world that is only gradually returning to ecological balance. Its humans use technology, but they husband it carefully and keep it functional over decades, eschewing any environmentally damaging practices. All material culture is made from compostable materials and is not simply recycled but broken down into constituent parts, like organic decay, as nourishment for an ever-changing ecosystem. Decades ago, the machines whose labor enabled the Factory Age became sentient and left human settlements for the wild, refusing an invitation to join with humans because they had no desire to embrace the city life exemplified by humans. The tale is a simple one about one human, Dex, who goes into the wilderness because he feels some lack in his village life. There he meets a robot, Mosscap, marking the first contact between the human and AI since this exodus centuries before. Mosscap is "wild-built," an entity made by the machines out of the remnants of human-built robots, and so represents something beyond human design. The novel's focus is on how Dex and Mosscap can learn to care for each other while acknowledging their differences.

The last book considered here, *Klara and the Sun* (2021) by Kazuo Ishiguro, is one of the most celebrated novels on this list. It also concerns the care an AI might show for a human, in this case the titular Klara, an Artificial Friend bought as a companion for Josie, a genetically augmented adolescent girl who is experiencing health problems because of her augments. Very similar in theme and tone to Ishiguro's earlier *Never Let Me Go* (2005), this novel is narrated by someone not recognized as a full person by the social order she lives within. Klara has a limited understanding of the world derived from her programming, what she can see from the shop window before she is purchased, and what she observes of Josie's social world. She lacks context for appropriately interpreting most of this. Klara struggles to reconcile the tension between the kind-heartedness and generosity into which she is trained and the reality of human selfishness and self-absorption. When it appears Josie will die, Josie's mother builds a replica body and trains Klara perfectly to imitate Josie, intending her as a replacement. When Josie recovers, Klara becomes an obsolete toy whose tech becomes illegal, confined first to a closet and then to a junkyard. Her poignant final moments prompt readers to reflect on our capacity for such callous treatment of an entity that was imagined, in an earlier moment, as able to pass for the most beloved person of all.

These brief summaries cannot do justice to the full complexity of any of these books. Yet it is most instructive, I think, to reflect on what they share and where they diverge, to help us begin to map the place of AI in our cultural imaginary today. As works such as Jennifer Rhee's *The Robotic Imaginary* (2018) or Anne Balsamo's earlier *Designing Culture* (2011) establish, popular culture inspires ideas about robots and AI that shape how these technologies materialize, often exacerbating existing racialized and gendered biases that become integral to their design. This issue of how fiction shapes materiality is addressed directly by many of these books, which are suffused with allusions to earlier robot and AI fiction. The Murderbot Diaries series reverses the flow of exchange, showing how its AI learns to understand humans from their portrayals in media, chiefly its favorite series, *Sanctuary Moon*. It comes to recognize that the series *"gave me context for the emotions I was feeling"* (*Exit Strategy*, 116), suggesting that narrative is a key human way to process information while also indicating that the stories we tell about AI mold as well as reflect on how AI manifests.

This metacommentary on the role that fiction often plays in our assumptions and understandings shows why it is important to take seriously the cultural work done by literary and media texts, and yet as Murderbot often reminds us in its critique of how the series it watches portray SecUnits, representations equally can create unrealistic expectations. The centrality of Shelley's *Frankenstein* to Winterson's *Frankissstein* explores similar territory: epigraphs to most chapters offer commentary on the nature of reality, and one full page defines story as "a series of connected events, real or imagined. Imagined or real. Imagined And Real" (23). Its TED-talk visionary, Victor Stein, reinforces that this is a matter not simply of fiction writers taking on the question of AI but of AI proselytizers and disrupters using the affective charge of fiction to compel people to invest— imaginatively, economically—in the futures their technologies intend to bring about. He pronounces at one point that reality, like AI, is "an emergent property—it exists, but it is not the material fact we take it to be" (116).

Unlike the cyberpunk and singularity generation of AI fiction, whose central concern was how AI might surpass us and perhaps replace us as the dominant species, these recent texts are overwhelmingly focused on how AI might replace us as labor power. As Ted Chiang adroitly put it in interview for the *New York Times*, "Most of our fears or anxieties about technology are best understood as fears or anxiety about how capitalism will use technology against us. And technology and capitalism have been so closely intertwined that it's hard to distinguish the two" (quoted in Klein 2021). Overwhelmingly the books considered here reinforce this observation, and many of them use the figure of AI to draw attention to the ever-degrading conditions of human labor, especially unstable gig work, which is often all that is left for humans to do. In Ashby's Machine Dynasty series, the two central vN models are racialized—one as Asian and the other as Latinx—and the exploitation of vN by humans is frequently compared to the exploitation of migrant workers. Across the Murderbot Diaries we learn about corporate malfeasance that culminates in a story about indentured human colonists working in dangerous conditions on remote colonies, their children born to the same fate because cycles of debt prevent anyone from accruing enough capital to migrate off-world. Murderbot itself is a cyborg with human neural tissue because of the need for human-like discernment in some tasks, "so they made us smarter. The anxiety and depression were side effects" (Artificial Condition, 20). *Frankissstein* discusses the Luddites in sections attributed to Mary Shelley, reminding us that their hostility was not about the machines per se but about how ownership of the machines translates to ownership of what they make and thus keeps all resources with the capitalist class. Thus, the ongoing fantasy that automation will free humans from the drudgery of work remains impossible as long as we fail to redistribute the wealth created by machines. (The leftist version of this possible future is most famously outlined in Aaron Bastani's *Fully Automated Luxury Communism* [2019].) Noting that a machine that replaces the work of eight men leaves seven families starving and one person to mind the machine, Winterson asks, "What is the point of progress if it benefits the few while the many suffer?" (*Frankissstein*, 255).

Labor comes up in more subtle ways in other texts. In McEwan's *Machines like Me*, for example, the racialization of the Adams reinforces that reality that Western imaginaries of personalized AI services are extensions of colonial fantasies stripped of their history, as Neda Atanasoski and Kalindi Vora (2019) have theorized in *Surrogate Humanity: Race, Robots, and the Politics of Technological Futures*. At the same time, setting the novel in an alternative 1980s evokes how algorithmic trading is remaking the economy, another way that AI channels money toward those already in privileged positions. The novel makes frequent references to the rise of Margaret Thatcher and her attempts to destroy the social welfare state in the interests of neoliberal free markets, which are less successful in McEwan's reality than in our own. Charlie does not work and, having spent his inherence acquiring Adam, begins to day trade, work he eventually cedes to Adam, whose capacity to make high-frequency trades whenever any market is open quickly amasses a sizable fortune that Charlie plans to use to buy a house and begin a family. The ethical conflict between Adam and the humans turns partially on whether they are entitled to the profits he made: Adam decides not, redistributing the wealth to tax obligations and to charity, leaving them with only the principle.

McEwan's alternative Tony Benn gives a stirring speech conceding the inevitability of automation and thus a lack of jobs for all but proclaiming that the wealth generated by robots "must be taxed. Workers must own an equity share in the machines that were disrupting or annihilating their jobs" (*Machines like Me*, 123). By setting his work in the 1980s, McEwan reinforces that the threat posed by AI has little to do with AI and everything to do with the capitalist logics through which AI has emerged, as addressed in works such as Daniel Susskind's (2020) much-cited *A World without Work*, but whereas Susskind implies that solutions such as job training and perhaps Universal Basic Income can socially engineer us through anticipated rising unemployment, McEwan recognizes that the challenge facing us is not merely one of technical governance but requires a fundamental shift in values to enable wealth redistribution.

Perhaps the most interesting take on the future of automation and labor is Divya's *Machinehood*, where the robot revolution is mainly about liberating human workers whose health has been damaged by modifications undertaken to keep pace with the machines. The Machinehood Manifesto demands a recognition of personhood for all sentient beings—animals as well as machines, alongside humans—and thus fits within a posthumanist framework that has often been used to discuss sf depictions of AI. It is mainly a novel of class politics, reminding us that sf's artificial beings are almost always first imagined as sources of labor: point 2 of the manifesto explains that the "oligarchy" (79) has accrued power by dividing human labor into classes, while point 8 concludes that "as long as different labor forces are in competition, we will continue to suffer. This situation demands change" (343). While most of these novels are not as direct in their critique of capitalism as is *Machinehood*, all recognize that the most significant threat AI poses is to our capacity to sustain ourselves, if we remain reliant on wage labor to meet our needs. Even Singer and Cole's *Burn-In*, although more concerned about access to multiple data points and the ability to correlate across them that its TAMS unit embodies, includes a storyline about Agent Keegan's husband, who has been demoted from lawyer to gig worker due to AI. Similarly, while Lakshiminarayan's *Analog/Virtual* tends to focus on social media spaces and the metrics for individual behavior enforced by the social credit system, the ultimately harm remains economic in a world in which an absence of money threatens to mean an absence of life in a world predicated on capitalist logics. Its bell curve is about income as much as access, and the risks of a poor social credit score are primarily those of rendering oneself unemployable.

Another recurrent motif is the concern that our immersion in mediated environments and among machines erodes our humanity, ironically making us more machinelike as we must compete with entities that previous sf often imagined as longing to be human. The fantasy of machines wishing to be human tends not to overtly reference the racialized history of dehumanized labor that is palimpsest to such tales, focusing instead on how sentient AI will long to have the capacities for emotional experience that has long served as shorthand for what machines lack compared to humans. Thus, as we become more closely integrated with our machines, we let them drive the pace and shape of our work, with humans in these more recent stories longing to equal the efficiency and stamina of machines rather than machines wishing they could experience love. Within genre sf, the risk that industrialized culture and automation, driven by the increasing centrality of consumerist capitalism in our daily lives, has long been linked to artificial beings as a literalized metaphor of our alienation, most famously embodied in the androids of Dick's *Do Androids Dream?*— albeit largely through the massive influence of Scott's *Blade Runner*.

In Hall's *Speak*, Stephen Chinn develops a successful AI program from an algorithm he designs to disrupt what he sees as the machinic quality of most human verbal interaction, the phatic discourse that we use to speak yet not really communicate, which he terms "horizontal communication, flatlining banalities and droning insignificance" (87); in contrast, the algorithm, he claims, uses "empathy" to connect these empty terms in ways that allow something new to emerge in the discussion and thus forge a real exchange. This novel, like Winterson's *Frankissstein* and McEwan's *Machines like Me*, uses its AI characters to highlight our waning humanity in a world structured by technocratic and economic logics, just as Dick explored in his influential fiction about androids. Yet the androids in *Do Androids Dream?* could be outed by their failure to feel empathy for other living beings, while today, it seems, the machines can simulate (or have?) empathy while humans cannot. Here we might be reminded of the success of early experiments in natural language AI such as ELIZA, a therapy chatbot that created an illusion of connection that convinced people of the program's intelligence. McEwan's suicidal AI, like Richard Powers's AI program in *Galatea 2.2* (1995), suggests that if AI actually were intellectually capable of comprehending humanity, it would prefer annihilation over the cognitive dissonance that humanity requires to cope with the gap between our ideals and the material impact of many of our actions. Winterson's focus on AI created for sex industries, including language programming designed to make these sexbots appear to empathize with their owners, asks us to think about the inherently problematic nature of desiring exchange with others who are always required to center the human self: do we truly wish to communicate with nonhuman beings, or merely to have ersatz versions of humanity that are more accommodating to our egos than people are?

Frankissstein, *Speak*, and *Klara and the Sun* extensively explore the connection between AI and fantasies of transcending death, the first in direct dialogue with Shelley's own interrogation of grief in *Frankenstein*. Winterson's Mary calls the fantasy of reanimating a loved one's dead body a wish for "artificial life" but realizes such life will always be inadequate compared to the original because it will have no "spark of mind" (61). *Speak* imagines an Alan Turing who, like Victor Frankenstein, undertakes his new line of research because he mourns a loved one lost to death and imagines a machine that might embody Chris's thoughts and voice, echoes of which Turing hears in his head. He recognizes that neither Chris's voice nor face will "return to me whole," and he describes their absence as "the most defining thing in my life" (157). This sense of irreparable loss suffuses each of the stories in *Speak*, including those in the voice of the babybots as they slowly lose their charge, yet the novel insists that the artificial will always be an inadequate substitute for a lost human connection: the trajectory of its entangled narratives is about humans learning to care for other humans again, even damaged or unresponsive humans, rather than to project their caring onto artificial substitutes. Similarly, although in *Machines like Me* Adam confronts Charlie and Miranda with their own hypocrisy, the novel similarly suggests that Adam, despite his moral consistency, could only ever be a distraction from the more urgent, if also more difficult, task of learning to connect with another human in distress. Although, in *Klara and the Sun* Artificial Friend Klara is imagined as a replacement for Josie but proves perhaps to be better than Josie in her unwavering affection, which contrasts with Josie's choice to move on from her childhood sweetheart. But whatever her flaws, Josie can change, and it is precisely her constancy that marks Klara as limited.

The most interesting reflection on death and transcendence comes in Chambers's *Psalm for the Wild-Built*: its machines not only refuse to join the human city but also strive to make their machinic culture function as much like an organic ecosystem as possible. They do not repair failing robots from the factories but repurpose their parts into new generations with new purposes and ideals, desiring to exist in an organic cycle through which all that lives breaks down into component parts to seed new life. This practice is why the robot Mosscap is "wild" rather than factory built. Chambers' robots want to understand life and become more lifelike, but they do equate that with becoming more humanlike, as did sentient robots in earlier sf, popularly recognized in such characters as *Star Trek*'s Lt. Commander Data. Yet the novel also reminds us that this risk of being alienated from the organic world also threatens highly urbanized humans, whose worldview the novel pronounces as "backward" because they see human infrastructure as the world and can no longer imagine an untouched space.

The more genre-oriented texts tend to figure the AI both as a way of commenting on technology and its effect on quotidian life and as a figuration of another kind of subjectivity, a new way to think about sentience that reaches beyond the binary segregation of human/nonhuman at the root of many of the social problems these novels explore. The more mainstream texts focus on presuming assumptions that inform our ideas about subjectivity but seem interested predominantly in how AI prompts us to ask new philosophical questions about the essence of human being. The genre texts, in contrast, ask these questions but also are concerned more often with the technological details of machine learning as well, thinking through the impact these technologies portend for industry, for cities, for sociality, and more. Of course, this distinction notes tendencies, not an absolute binary, and indeed, the larger food for thought here might be to question whether it remains useful to separate science fiction from other literature. Certainly this was a major point for McEwan in his promotion of *Machines like Me*, but anyone well read in genre fiction can recognize echoes of earlier texts in the questions McEwan ponders, even if they are new to him.

Drayden's *Prey of Gods*, Wells's Murderbot Diaries, and Divya's *Machinehood*, like Chambers's *Psalm for the Wild-Built*, project futures of human-AI solidarity and cooperation, stressing our need to think beyond ontology (mechanical vs. organic) and toward new concepts of personhood that allow for greater solidarity in the face of exploitation that humans and machines both face from corporate employers or oppressive governments. *Machinehood* joins *Psalm* in further suggesting that a new respect for all kinds of life will transform society toward greater ecological consciousness: in its conclusion, *Machinehood*'s protagonist, Welga, agrees to augmentations that will enable her to be the exemplar of this new ethos that refuses a human/machine binary. Seeming directly to address readers who might find this radical vision naïve, Welga reflects, "What if I really can be an ambassador to a new society, a better way of life? It's happened before, when the world moved from monarchies to democracies, or even in ancient history, going from hunter-gatherers to farmers. It could happen again" (392). Ashby's Machine Dynasty series similarly concludes with a new society about to emerge among the vNs who have relocated to Mars, where they promise to build "new families" and "new structures" (*reV*, 275) not predicated on Western hierarchical and exclusionary metaphysics of subjectivity.

Texts written by mainstream authors such as Ishiguro or McEwan tend to focus on AI as a mirror for human ethical failings. Noting that human frailty is frequently a theme of great literature, in *Machines like Me* McEwan's Adam notes the reality of "millions dying of diseases we know how to cure. Millions living in poverty when there's enough to go around. We degrade the biosphere when we know it's our only home" (194). *Speak*'s Turing observes, "I find it hard to believe that a machine, programmed for equanimity and rational synthesis, could ever act as maleficent as we humans have already proven ourselves capable of acting" (188). Like discourses on the Anthropocene, however, this version of a faulty humanity imagined as the collective opposite of AI fails to observe that these consequences tend to be the result of choices made by a subset of the human species: the colonizers, the imperialists, the capitalists who focus on short-term profit. The genre fiction takes up this critique in its posthumanist motifs.

Ishiguro's Klara is more tragic still, endlessly loving and seeking to live up to what is expected of her as someone designed to be a friend to humanity even after she has been discarded to a trash heap. Like Chinn's illegally lifelike babybots in *Speak*, in *Klara* the Artificial Friends are rejected because they are too clever. Klara is told, "They accept that your decisions, your recommendations, are sound and dependable, almost always correct. But they don't like not knowing how you arrive at them" (390). Yet Ishiguro's novel remains deeply committed to an unreconstructed humanism that laments our shortcomings even as it also reiterates the commonplace axiom that she could never truly be a "continuation" (274) of Josie because she lacks some elusive quality. Yet Klara locates this in the love that others gave to Josie, not in Josie herself, perhaps opening up to the posthumanist possibilities suggested by works such as *Machinehood*. Nonetheless, the mainstream novels repeatedly conclude that the machines may well be better than us, but the human subject retains its enigmatic aura.

Across these fictions, AI figurations express a range of ideas. They articulate our desire for another kind of sociality, starkly remind us of our own waning empathy, and comment on how algorithmic and other "smart" technologies sometimes called AI promise to change daily life. AI is simultaneously a figure of promise and of threat, although what it promises is no longer a future of ease and comfort when artificial beings do all the difficult labor for us—the vision, for example, in Iain M. Banks celebrated Culture series—and what it threatens has ceased to be a military system committed to wiping out our species, as with the Terminator franchise's Skynet. Rather, today the threat of AI emerges from what was once imagined as its promise of automated luxury, the dehumanizing risks attendant in algorithmic decision making and the economic precarity looming with the end of work. What AI might promise today is what nonhuman characters in science fiction have always symbolized, an exemplar of how subjectivity and sociality might be otherwise and thus enable a more just and inclusive future. Yet for the more mainstream fictions, this perhaps also is the threat, namely, the waning hegemony of liberal humanism.

In *Frankissstein*, Ry Shelly confronts Victor Stein to ask him what all his research is for, what problem it solves for the human race. Victor is not prepared to answer such a question, invested as he is in cutting-edge research for its own sake. Yet Ry persists, suggesting that the world is not ready for "forever humans" as envisioned in Victor's transhumanist research, that "morally and spiritually, we are barely crawling out of the sea onto dry land. We're not ready for the future you want" (280). The fictions discussed here have a wide range of answers to this question of whether we are ready for—or want—the futures implied by contemporary AI research. But they are united in a belief that this is precisely the question we need to ask and in their conviction that fictional narrative is a rich source of answers to it.

Sherryl Vint is Professor of Media and Cultural Studies and Chair of the Department of English at the University of California, Riverside, where she directs the Speculative Fictions and Cultures of Science program. She was a founding editor of Science Fiction Film and Television and is an editor for the journal Science Fiction Studies and the book series Science in Popular Culture. She has published widely on science fiction, including, most recently, Biopolitical Futures in Twenty-First Century Speculative Fiction (2021) and Programming the Future: Speculative Television and the End of Democracy (2022, co-authored with Jonathan Alexander).

References

Atanasoski, Neda, and Kalindi Vora. 2019. *Surrogate Humanity: Race, Robots, and the Politics of Technological Futures*. Durham, NC: Duke Univ. Press.
Klein, Ezra. 2021. "The Author Behind 'Arrival' Doesn't Fear AI: 'Look at How We Treat Animals.'" *Ezra Klein Show* (podcast), March 30. https://www.nytimes.com/2021/03/30/opinion/ezra-klein-podcast-ted-chiang.html.
Nobel, Safiya. 2018. Algorithms of Oppression: How Search Engines Reinforce Racism. New York: NYU Press.
Susskind, Daniel. 2020. A World Without Work: Technology, Automation, and How We Should Respond. New York: Metropolitan Books.
Zuboff, Shoshanna. 2019. The Age of Surveillance Capitalism: The Fight for a Human Future at the New Frontier of Power. New York: PublicAffairs.

Tyler Shoemaker   Cultural Gradients and the Sociotechnics of Data

The Cultural Life of Machine Learning: An Incursion into Critical AI Studies.
Edited by Jonathan Roberge and Michael Castelle. Cham: Palgrave Macmillan.
2021. xv, 289 pp. Cloth, $109.99; paper, $79.99; e-book, $75.99.

Data / Set / Match [exhibition]. London: Photographers' Gallery, 2019–20.

The advent of what business strategists are fond of calling the "Cambrian explosion" in artificial intelligence (AI) has spawned a legion of concerns about downstream effects. It's hardly an argument at this point to say AI can have unintended, even harmful consequences for social life. The many calls to make AI fair and accountable, transparent and ethical, attest to such impacts, or the threat thereof. Acting on these calls often requires description and explanation: what, upstream, caused downstream effects? But as Jonathan Roberge and Michael Castelle claim in the introduction to their edited volume, *The Cultural Life of Machine Learning*, the up-/downstream dynamic, when used as an explanatory frame, tends to uphold what is "largely (if unconsciously) a positivist project" (12), one for which the harms of AI ultimately require technical solutions. It does so, they explain, by eliding AI's own "sociotechnical genesis" (3), the dense mesh of decisions, practices, and technologies that entangle AI in social factors from the start. This elision makes the (upstream) technical seemingly detachable from the (downstream) social; as a "corrective," Roberge and Castelle propose "what could be called—with a wink and a nod to deep learning methodology—an *end-to-end* sociology of contemporary AI/ML [machine learning]" (3). The chapters in their volume accordingly bring this proposal into being.

To clear the ground for this end-to-end approach, Roberge and

American Literature, Volume 95, Number 2, June 2023
DOI 10.1215/00029831-10575190   © 2023 by Duke University Press

Castelle provide a series of compelling pairings between the conceptual inventory of AI/ML and that of sociology, media studies, and science and technology studies. If, as they write, ML practitioners "see their own behavior in terms of the epistemology of their techniques" (6), a sociological critique of AI/ML would begin by assessing the overlaps and gaps between adversarial deep learning and deep play (Clifford Geertz), concept nets and normative classes (Geoffrey Bowker and Susan Leigh Star), explainable AI and hermeneutics (Hans-Georg Gadamer), algorithmic nudging and actor networks (Bruno Latour), and learning bias and social prejudice (Joy Buolamwini and Timnit Gebru). Literature scholars may find a last pairing to be especially productive: "co-text" and context, the raw co-occurrence of "entextualized" symbols and the meaning of that emplacement (8). Indeed, for Roberge and Castelle, determining what and how context *means* is where AI/ML and their own approach are most linearly separable.

Several of the collection's chapters offer rich historical accounts, emphasizing tenuous formations of epistemological consensus among ML practitioners. Aaron Mendon-Plasek shows how character recognition was key to the development of "contextual significance" in early AI, because it bolstered a strategy of explaining away systems' deficiencies with highly accurate results for constrained tasks (39). Théo Lepage-Richer locates an abiding concern with managing uncertainty in neural models and Cold War cybernetics; this, he claims, paved the way for a wider "adversarial epistemology" that recasts failure as an "opportunity" to improve models (218). In contrast, Ceyda Yolgörmez draws from Alan Turing and George Mead to theorize how we "encounter" machines in a "social sense" at the very moments cyberneticians sought to avoid, where calculative processes disrupt expectation (150). Other chapters discuss the politics of learning behavior. Fenwick McKelvey tracks the rise of a "new political science," primarily with regard to the Simulmatics Corporation, one of the first consulting groups to use computer simulation as a "proxy for public opinion" (119). And in a deep engagement with the educational theory of Lev Vygotsky, Tyler Reigeluth and Michael Castelle probe the core ideas of concept development and generalization in ML. Vygotsky's own elaboration of these ideas in the 1920s and 1930s positions Reigeluth and Castelle to identify a missing piece in how machines learn: a necessarily social element that "pulls" learners into a "zone of proximal development" (95).

A last set of chapters turn to the present. Werner Binder highlights the braided agencies attending AlphaGo's entry into professional Go.

While recounting how the system won against the world's top Go players, Binder unravels key ambivalences in players' reactions to the games, including their adoption of AlphaGo's more novel play strategies. Using place-based research conducted in Chile's Atacama Desert, Orit Halpern returns to uncertainty, suggesting that the many networks "bridg[ing] data and matter" in planetary-scale AI (from the Event Horizon Telescope to speculative resource extraction) have triggered an epistemic break in contemporary governance (228). Luke Stark, Daniel Greene, and Anna Lauren Hoffmann close the volume by surveying how state and corporate governance mechanisms for AI/ML currently forestall wider critique. The authors conclude that, in place of technical fixes or values statements, such mechanisms must begin by "foregrounding and centering the expertise" of communities directly affected by AI/ML (272); the Tech Won't Build It campaign and the Movement for Black Lives exemplify such an approach.

Amid the extensive range of these essays, one black box does go mostly unopened: data wrangling. Save for a handful of brief references, the collection skips over the vast amounts of time and energy involved in preparing data for models. In view of this, *Data / Set / Match*, an exhibition program held at the Photographers' Gallery in London from 2019 to 2020, adds an important dimension to Roberge and Castelle. Introducing the program, Nicolas Malevé (2019) writes, "The automation of vision [by ML] has not reduced but increased the number of eyeballs looking at images, of hands typing descriptions, of taggers and annotators." The essays, talks, and commissions that comprise *Data / Set / Match* recognize this increase as a core feature of contemporary visual culture. Together, explains Malevé, they explore how the work of "collecting, labelling, composing, assembling," and finally "distributing" images—all done to create "ground truth" data for models—might be traceable in giant data sets like ImageNet or COCO (Common Objects in Context).

A shared strategy among the exhibiting artists is superimposition. In *Tunnel Vision*, Philipp Schmitt uses custom software to identify objects in busy 35-mm scenes and overlays them with disparate matches from COCO. Accompanying the latter are a label and a username, reminders that ML is vestigial human interpretation. Part performance, part curation, Everest Pipkin's *Lacework* samples from Moments in Time, a set of 1 million three-second videos depicting actions associated with verbs. Pipkin watched them all; *Lacework* presents an algorithmically "upscaled" selection, which adds a blurring effect to simulate, perhaps, the tired eyes of digital piecework or, as with the abstract visages of Heather Dewey-Hagborg's *How Do You See Me?*, a computer learning to see. The "speculative remixes" of quotes from Virginia Woolf and Katherine Anne Porter, which xtine burrough and Sabrina Starnaman set atop clips from the Epic Kitchens data set in *A Kitchen of One's Own*, tether data annotation to a longer history of feminized, unpaid labor. But it is Mimi Ọnụọha who presents digital piecework in the starkest terms: *The Future Is Here!* shows images of the domestic spaces where "sub-sub-contractors" annotate data (Schmidt 2020). Periodically, the images flip into the style of a comic book, complete with canned slogans. "A world unlike any other!" Yet, to be sure, Ọnụọha's inking and neon palette also recall the encroaching outlines of modern image segmentation algorithms.

On display throughout *Data / Set / Match* are the two streams, up and down, upon which Roberge and Castelle's collection is also trained. The exhibition's many facets collectively hold these streams in tension, offering a way to "learn the rules and edges" of a data set (Pipkin's *Lacework*), to catch a glimpse at the furtive but pervasive human life bound up with AI/ML. In this sense, it performs considerable, if tacit, sociological work about the sociotechnics of data. For those who may be grappling with how to bring this or the many other social entanglements of AI/ML into view, both *Data / Set / Match* and *The Cultural Life of Machine Learning* provide—and themselves serve as—vital context for future inquiry.

Tyler Shoemaker is a postdoctoral scholar affiliated with the DataLab at the University of California, Davis.

References

Malevé, Nicolas. 2019. "An Introduction to Image Datasets." Unthinking Photography. November, https://unthinking.photography/articles/an-introduction-to-image-datasets.

Schmidt, Florian A. 2020. "Unevenly Distributed." Unthinking Photography. March, https://unthinking.photography/articles/unevenly-distributed.

R. Joshua Scannell   Computing Race

The Black Technical Object: On Machine Learning and the Aspiration of Black Being.
By Ramon Amaro. Berlin: Sternberg Press. 2023. 152 pp. Paper, $25.00.

The Digitally Disposed: Racial Capitalism and the Informatics of Value.
By Seb Franklin. Minneapolis: Univ. of Minnesota Press. 2021. 268 pp. Cloth,
$108.00; paper, $27.00; e-book, $25.65.

These two new monographs have recently contributed to a growing
body of scholarship that argues for the centrality of race and racialization to both the social organization of our digitalized societies and the
technical apparatuses of computation. This is a welcome development
since for decades critical digital studies has developed a robust tradition of analyzing digitality and computational culture from the perspective of a critique of capital and power, but a rather poorer one
when it comes to considering the centrality of race.

Black feminist theory has blazed a trail in digital scholarship, increasingly eschewing the question of how certain systems reproduce or
"ratchet" existing racist harms in favor of a much more profound challenge that sees racial capitalism, coloniality, and white supremacy as
the conditions of possibility for calculative and computational media
writ large. Sylvia Wynter's work on genres of the human, the racial
basis for Western science, the theory of selection/dysselection (among
much else) has emerged as central to the burgeoning field. This
is due in no small part to the work of interlocutors like Katherine
McKittrick, who has leveraged a sustained engagement with the philosopher into a pathbreaking evaluation of mathematics and scientific reason that locates the dysselection of Black life and world

American Literature, Volume 95, Number 2, June 2023
DOI 10.1215/00029831-10575204   © 2023 by Duke University Press

making as, to quote Hortense Spillers (1987: 67), the "zero degree of social conceptualization."

For critical scholars of computation, the most important elements of Wynter's philosophy of science are twofold: first, that under conditions of Western science the human has only ever been multiple, cast as "genres," with well-off white men at the center and other groups regularly "dysselected" from "the Human"; next—the crux, that the fact of dysselection works as a catalyst for computation. In other words, the drive to compute and produce quantifiable, discretizable knowledge under regimes of Western Man derives specifically from an assumption that dysselected populations cannot be "known" in any real sense and must therefore be understood only through measurement. In her canonical "The Ceremony Must Be Found," Wynter (1984) argues that the paradigmatic example of a population that is dysselected from the human and thereby generates catalysis for Western "knowledge" is Black women, who she argues are understood as representing chaos, or the outside of reason. Thus, Wynter firmly locates "Knowledge" in coloniality while also showing that it is the fact of coloniality itself that both drives the computational compulsion and (within the constraints of Western Man) exhausts its capacities.

Both Ramon Amaro, in *The Black Technical Object: On Machine Learning and the Aspiration of Black Being*, and Seb Franklin, in *The Digitally Disposed: Racial Capitalism and the Informatics of Value*, draw from this insight and expand on it. Amaro's aim is to understand machine learning from a framework that recognizes the antiblackness at the heart of the suite of techniques that are broadly swept under that umbrella. Amaro has adopted a version of Gilbert Simondon's technical-philosophical approach to often stunning effect. Whereas Simondon looked to cathode rays and car engines to understand the mutual becoming of machine and human, Amaro studies the intricacies of contemporary machine learning techniques to detail the technical investment in the reproduction of antiblackness. Frantz Fanon's work, especially *Black Skin, White Masks* (1952), figures prominently here as a guide for understanding the work of technical administration to stifle Black being and possibility. For Amaro, the colonial situation that Fanon describes and the contemporary problem of machine learning are of course not strictly analogous. What they share is the rationalized commitment to the containment and compartmentalization of Black life.

Amaro tells us that machine learning is ultimately committed to stasis and to the maintenance of imperial ontologies of being through the calling forth of the Black Technical Object, fundamentally a racist abstraction that seemingly neutral techniques of measurement, inference, and prediction rely on when blackness stands for the (often disavowed) outside of technical reason, or outside the family of the Human. But for Amaro, that is not the end of the story. Noting that the problem with how race and its technical apparatus are framed derives from "principles that begin with an observation of being that is anterior to the conditions that bring the individual into existence" (223), Amaro argues that a doing otherwise would "gain capacity in a return to its nonessentialist origins" thereby producing an ontological situation in which it becomes possible to imagine a new future.

Amaro points out that blackness is not and cannot be contained by the "being-towards-death or death-driven nonbeing within institutional discourse" (224). Instead, Amaro asks what it might take to flip the racial logics of the algorithmic—to ask, "Can Black life instead be viewed as generative, affirmative, and fundamental to a technically mediated life" (224). He finds an answer of sorts in indeterminacy and possibility, qualities that can be part of the ontology of the algorithmic, even as they are refused in practice.

Where Amaro focuses on the production of the Black Technical Object via an interrogation of contemporary machine learning practices, Seb Franklin's *Digitally Disposed* is centrally concerned with understanding the logic of what he calls "digitality." He defines *digitality* not as "discrete representation in general" but as "the cultural logic of contemporary capitalism" (3).

What is crucial in this analysis is that racial differentiation and hierarchy organized by operations of "abstraction, abjection, and differential integration" are never treated as effects of digitality; rather, "ontological disavowal and qualified inclusion" (36) in fact "*produces . . .* those disavowed and precarious structural positions in order to maintain the circulation and expansion of value around the frayed edges of its circulation matrices" (36–37). In other words, without racial capitalism's preexisting commitment to classifying, sorting, and disposing of people, places, and things, the "informatics of value" would not cohere at the level of concept or practice. Drawing conceptually from Saidiya Hartman and Sylvia Wynter, and working through Ian Baucom, Franklin, along with a burgeoning number of scholars critically focused on logistics, is insistent on this point: the transatlantic logistics and financial instruments of transporting the enslaved forms the basis both for the rise of modern capitalism and for the creation of the modern world.

By positing the informational as an interface structure through which bodies become available for capital in specific ways, *Digitally Disposed* both maintains the integrity of Marxian analysis and interjects the digital into the inherent processes of organizing value and life under capitalism. The dependence on the self-reproducing homeostatic body (to use Franklin's terminology), the need to develop reliable circuits of value from unreliable parts, the insistence on a dichotomy between human upgradeability and disposability, and the requisite move to reticulate value in the network form are all processes that emerge from the organization of, to quote Ruth Wilson Gilmore's (2007: 28) definition of racism, "the state-sanctioned or extralegal production and exploitation of group-differentiated vulnerability to premature death."

But Franklin is careful to show that governing abstractions are never as powerful or as accepted as overlords would want. People may give part of themselves up to connection to scrounge survival from racial capitalism in the networked form, but it is only ever partial. People refuse. They rip off their bosses. They organize and agitate. They find ways of being and living for one another even as the informatics of value work to reformat them as upgradeable if unreliable components in a reliable circuit of extraction. They, in other words, forge a commons and a common, however provisional.

R. Joshua Scannell is an assistant professor of media studies at The New School's School of Media Studies.

References

Gilmore, Ruth Wilson. 2007. *Golden Gulag: Prisons, Surplus, Crisis, and Opposition in Globalizing California.* Berkeley: University of California Press.

Spillers, Hortense. 1987. "Mama's Baby, Papa's Maybe: An American Grammar Book." *Diacritics* 17, no. 2: 64–81.

Wynter, Sylvia. 1984. "The Ceremony Must Be Found: After Humanism." *boundary 2* 12/13, no. 3/1: 19–70.

Fabian Offert

Can We Read Neural Networks? Epistemic Implications of Two Historical Computer Science Papers

"Intriguing Properties of Neural Networks." By Christian Szegedy, Wojciech Zaremba, Ilya Sutskever, Joan Bruna, Dumitru Erhan, Ian Goodfellow, and Rob Fergus. arXiv preprint. 2013. https://arxiv.org/abs/1312.6199.

"Learning to Execute." By Wojciech Zaremba and Ilya Sutskever. arXiv preprint. 2014. https://arxiv.org/abs/1410.4615.

This review looks at two technical papers from the field of computer science that, at the time of writing, should be considered historical. Although their respective technical approaches have since been replaced with newer, better, and more efficient ones, when looking back through the lens of critical AI studies they mark the beginning of a type of theoretical reflection within computer science that distinctly links technical machine learning research to research in the humanities.

Machine learning models are cultural artifacts. They are trained on (limited) real-world data and often designed to make decisions with real-world impacts. The relation of a machine learning model to the world is thus a relation of interest. What kind of representations do machine learning models produce? As the world is necessarily mirrored in a machine learning system to some degree, as there exists, with Walter Benjamin, an approximation of a mimetic faculty, what are the modes of representation that a machine learning system has at its disposal? Is it possible, in other words, to "read" a machine learning model? Can we, as humans, rely on our capability to decode systems of representation, such as artistic descriptions of the world in text or image, to understand neural networks?

The two technical papers at the center of this review shed some

American Literature, Volume 95, Number 2, June 2023
DOI 10.1215/00029831-10575218   © 2023 by Duke University Press

light on this fundamentally humanist question. Concretely, they suggest that we are currently witnessing a turn toward postsymbolic computation, a paradigm under which nothing is language and everything is language at the same time. In that sense, both papers could serve as a starting point for a renewed methodological discussion within critical AI studies and related fields of study on the legibility and interpretability of machine learning systems.

"Intriguing Properties of Neural Networks," written by Christian Szegedy, Wojciech Zaremba, Ilya Sutskever, Joan Bruna, Dumitru Erhan, Ian Goodfellow, and Rob Fergus, describes two "counterintuitive" (1) properties of deep convolutional neural networks (CNNs): their susceptibility to input perturbations (termed *adversarial examples*),[1] and the entanglement of learned concepts in their internal structure. It is the latter "intriguing" property that is of interest here.

CNNs usually consist of tens of thousands of atomic units called *neurons*, arranged in a layered fashion.[2] Before training, these neurons pass on information arbitrarily. If we imagine a binary (i.e., two-category) image classification network, this would mean that an input image is randomly assigned to one of two classes. Training the neural network, then, means adjusting all neurons such that, eventually, the networks can make correct classification decisions. This is usually achieved by "showing" the network lots of example images and automatically adjusting the neurons after each iteration. Once a network is fully trained, all neurons play a specific role in the network's decision process. Even if a neuron's role is just to stop the information flow (i.e., to pass on zero values to the next layer), these one-way streets are in no way less relevant to the accuracy of the whole system than are any other neurons.[3]

What Szegedy et al. show experimentally is that one of the implications of this entanglement of neurons is an entanglement of concepts: rather than developing hierarchical modes of representation, CNNs tend to develop idiosyncratic modes of representation (see Geirhos et al. 2020; Offert and Bell 2021) where it is hard if not impossible to define which parts of a network represent which parts of a real-world object.[4] For instance, if we consider a CNN that has learned to distinguish between two real-world objects, say, dogs and cats, the part of the network that is important in recognizing dog ears might equally be important in recognizing cat tails. In a way, established concepts (dog, cat) are thus dissolved when they are learned by a CNN, as there is no way to reconnect them to the real-world objects they represent. It is important to note that this makes the neural network not less but more successful at its task of distinguishing between dogs and cats; the success is simply not tied to any human way of solving it.

Hence, we cannot trust neural networks to represent the world in a way that is coherent to us. Szegedy et al. for the first time in the technical literature show that machine learning models are fundamentally alien, not in an exaggerated phenomenological sense but in the sense that they require empirical study. In their (with Gilbert Simondon) fully concretized, final form, neural networks start to resemble natural rather than technical objects. Like compiled computer programs that need to be painstakingly "disassembled," neural networks require extensive arrays of "interpretability" techniques to become legible. Unlike those programs, however, there is no code to fall back to, no symbolic description of the same process that could be referenced. Trained machine learning models, in other words, usher in a new paradigm of postsymbolic computation.

"Learning to Execute," written by Wojciech Zaremba and Ilya Sutskever, is another marker of this paradigm change. It demonstrates that language models, specifically sequence-to-sequence models based on recurrent neural networks, can, within certain limits, "learn to execute" short computer programs; that is, they can infer from a short program provided as input what the program would output were it to be run. The conditional is important here: the program is, of course, not run (this would defeat the purpose of the experiment), but the problem of running a program is treated as the problem of translating textual input (a program) into textual output (the predicted output of the program were it to be run). Zaremba and Sutskever show that this is indeed possible, at least within the framework of their limited experimental setup. What they implicitly suggest is that neural networks could approximate general-purpose computation if they only learned to "read" properly. They could become fully functioning replacements for the computers they are themselves running on by treating literally *any* computational problem as a problem of translation.

The implications of this understanding are far-reaching and lead directly into the current debate on "foundation" models. These models, mainly thought as very large transformer-based large-scale language models (LLMs) like GPT-3 (Brown et al. 2020) or PaLM (Chowdhery et al. 2022), are meant to all but replace hand-coded general-purpose computing with "prompt"-based, natural language description. Already today they can indeed execute (i.e., infer the meaning of) programs, solve mathematical equations, and demonstrate commonsense reasoning (Chowdhery et al. 2022).

We have thus arrived at the inverse of the situation produced by image models like the one described in Szegedy et al.: for LLMs, everything is text, everything is forced into an already existing (human) mode of representation. Concretely, formal languages (e.g., programming languages) are treated like natural languages. While it looks like this approach "just works," the epistemic implications are entirely unclear. Can we even imagine a mode of representation for mathematical operations that is not precise yet still produces precise results? Extrapolating the comparatively minor dangers of current-generation models (which are still in an advanced prototype stage), what would it mean for all computation to become natural language processing?

These are speculative questions, of course, but they point to a looming paradigm change with great significance for the humanities. I suggest that we can understand this emergence of idiosyncratic modes of representation in neural networks, on the one hand, and this making readable of everything by means of neural networks, on the other, as two sides of the same paradigm change, from symbolic to post-symbolic computation. The two papers discussed here are early symptoms of this paradigm change, which is only accelerating. One of the tasks of critical AI studies and related fields of study, then, is to develop a critical methodology that can accommodate a new reality of post-symbolic computation. Importantly, this implies a move away from the universal narrative of "the binary" as the root for all evil, and an acknowledgment that injustices exist even where systems pretend to be "readable," where the explicitly machinic is replaced with familiar human modes of representation.

Fabian Offert is Assistant Professor for the History and Theory of the Digital Humanities at the University of California, Santa Barbara. His research and teaching focus on the visual digital humanities, with a special interest in the epistemology and aesthetics of computer vision and machine learning.

Notes

1   Adversarial examples are "natural" images with infinitesimal changes applied to them that derail a CNN's classification accuracy. One can optimize any natural image (e.g., a photo of a cat) to register as any other natural image (e.g., a photo of a dog) by exploiting the fact that input signals (images) are necessarily amplified when they are processed by a CNN. For the origin of the term *adversarial example*, see Goodfellow, Shlens,

and Szegedy 2014; for a high-level discussion of the epistemic implications of input perturbations, see Offert and Bell 2021.

2   "Under the hood," neural networks are very large differential equations, tuned by complex combinations of new and established methods of optimization. The "spatial" perspective, that is, describing neural networks in terms of structured arrangements of "neurons" in "layers," even if it is often embraced by computer scientists, thus necessarily remains a simplification, and it should be understood as such in the context of this review.

3   This technique, called *dropout*, is one of the innovations introduced in Krizhevsky, Sutskever, and Hinton 2012. It also introduces multiple groundbreaking fixes to the design and implementation of deep CNNs, including the proposal to use graphics cards (graphics processing units) to train such networks in a massively parallel fashion.

4   In practice, the fact that CNNs need to "compress" reality so that generalization becomes possible (i.e., that a CNN trained on a limited number of dog photos can also successfully recognize other, previously unseen photos of dogs) will lead to at least some overlap between conceptual and technical units. Research in the visualization of neurons (feature visualization), for instance, has found "circuits" responsible for clearly delineated parts of reality in standard CNN architectures trained on standard data sets (Cammarata et al. 2020). Moreover, results in the subfield of representation learning suggest that one can devise neural network architectures that are less susceptible to entanglement than others. However, in both cases, significant supervision and empirical work are required to arrive at a meaningful correspondence of technical and semantic units; neural networks, in other words, have to be "forced" to represent reality the "human way."

References

Brown, Tom B., et al. 2020. "Language Models Are Few-Shot Learners." *Advances in Neural Information Processing Systems* 33: 1877–1901.

Cammarata, Nick, Shan Carter, Gabriel Goh, Chris Olah, Michael Petrov, Ludwig Schubert, Chelsea Voss, Ben Egan, and Swee Kiat Lim. 2020. "Thread: Circuits." *Distill*. https://distill.pub/2020/circuits/.

Chowdhery, Aakanksha, et al. 2022. "PaLM: Scaling Language Modeling with Pathways." Preprint, arXiv. https://arxiv.org/abs/2204.02311.

Geirhos, Robert, Jörn-Henrik Jacobsen, Claudio Michaelis, Richard Zemel, Wieland Brendel, Matthias Bethge, and Felix A. Wichmann. 2020. "Shortcut Learning in Deep Neural Networks." *Nature Machine Intelligence* 2: 665–73.

Goodfellow, Ian, Jonathon Shlens, and Christian Szegedy. 2014. "Explaining and Harnessing Adversarial Examples." Preprint, arXiv. https://arxiv.org/abs/1412.6572.

Krizhevsky, Alex, Ilya Sutskever, and Geoffrey E. Hinton. 2012. "ImageNet Classification with Deep Convolutional Neural Networks." *Advances in Neural Information Processing Systems* 25: 1097–105.

Offert, Fabian, and Peter Bell. 2021. "Perceptual Bias and Technical Metapictures. Critical Machine Vision as a Humanities Challenge." *AI & Society* 36: 1–12.

Tung-Hui Hu   Artificial Bloom

Myriad (Tulips). By Anna Ridler. C-type digital prints with handwritten annotations, magnetic paint, magnets. 2018.

Secret Garden: Our Stories Are Algorithms. By Stephanie Dinkins. Three-channel interactive video projection with six-channel audio, depth cameras, computer. 2021.

Anna Ridler's *Myriad (Tulips)* is mesmerizing in its scale: it displays ten thousand photographs of tulips that she purchased, stripped, photographed, and categorized by hand over a summer in residence in the Netherlands (fig. 1). They were the raw materials for training a generative adversarial network (GAN) to generate artificial images of tulips for its companion artwork, *Mosaic Virus* (2018). But as she categorized each photograph by qualities, such as color, that grew only more difficult to discern over time—is it white or light pink?—she began to dream of tulips and even see stripes. The experience, Ridler reports, both recalled the origins of classification in Linnaeus—who ultimately decided color was too subjective to include in his taxonomies—and suggested how creating databases is quite literally a craft: we assign far too much creative value to the users and authors of algorithms rather than to the ones who build databases.

Ridler's interest in tulips is part of a longer project exploring how nature has been measured and quantified; she has categorized seashells and produced GAN-generated flower clocks. Here, however, she explores the speculation of the Dutch Golden Age, when the unpredictability of the tulips' delicate streaking and flaring of color—a result of a mosaic virus, rather than natural selection—made them especially fickle commodities. Purchasers bought tulip futures in the fall, well

American Literature, Volume 95, Number 2, June 2023
DOI 10.1215/00029831-10575232   © 2023 by Duke University Press

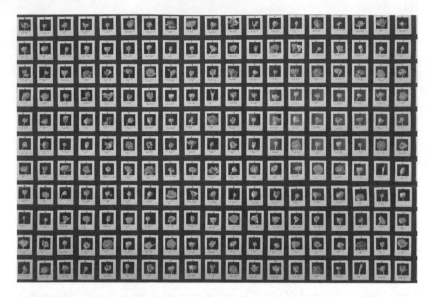

Figure 1 Anna Ridler, *Myriad (Tulips)*. Installation view (detail), *AI: More than Human* exhibition, Barbican Centre, London, May 16 to August 26, 2019. Photograph: Emily Grundon

before the flowers finally bloomed in the spring, often with drastically changed or disappointing color. The virus itself weakened the flower's roots and eventually caused it to become extinct—its own source of scarcity. As Ridler has written, GANs likewise tend to suffer from "mode collapse," but here collapse means producing the same or similar output over and over instead of anything new. In this way, *Mosaic Virus* becomes a wry comment on how today's attempts to produce collectible assets through artificial rarity can become as repetitive as a stuck algorithm. While the artist makes an explicit connection to today's boom-and-bust economy by linking the tulip stripes to the price of Bitcoin, I find the real historical parallel to be how a voracious appetite for novelty turns the world into content.

A still life with flowers by Hans Bollongier, painted in 1639 after the crash of the tulip market, appears to be a faithful naturalistic reproduction. But roses and carnations and tulips bloom in different seasons. As media scholar John Durham Peters has written, Bollongier's painting suggests how many different moments of time have been collaged into one seemingly seamless image. It was "'a theoretical composite' . . . that could never appear in a single moment; it anticipates the summarizing power of a very different form of presentation: statistics" (Cmiel and Peters 2020: 39). Naturalistic illustration and

Figure 2   Stephanie Dinkins, *Secret Garden: Our Stories Are Algorithms*. Installation view, *On Love and Data* exhibition, Stamps Gallery, Univ. of Michigan, Ann Arbor, August 31 to October 23, 2021. Photograph: Eric Bronson, Michigan Photography

even seeing in general, argues Peters, were already a matter of learning to abstract and classify to produce a general idea out of individual variations. Even before the "science of state" had become formalized in the following two centuries, visual culture had become statistical.

Whether for trade or for science, the classification of tulips and spices, colonial subjects and human cargo, proceeded with world-ending violence. But fugitive technologies are embedded in those same moments of history. This is the suggestion of Stephanie Dinkins's *Secret Garden: Our Stories Are Algorithms* (2021), a room-size interactive installation of flowers and other crops, within which six Black women from across time—including one "artificially intelligent" woman—offer stories to their visitors (fig. 2). It's certainly possible to see the human figures (rendered as tableaux vivants) as the main attraction in the installation. Dinkins nevertheless insists on the equal importance of the natural world, too: as she relates, there are "artistic images of roses, pansies, flowers my grandmother loved, but also sugarcane, cotton and okra, plants that have hurt, sustained and grown with us through the ages" (Smith 2021). On the web installation (https://secretgarden.stephaniedinkins.com/), a visitor moves at ground level, the eyeline pointed above the pansies and below the cotton bolls: the effect is as if visitors are four-legged animals, rabbits or dogs perhaps. The flora are themselves cutouts that swing open, like doors, when the visitor walks through. The goal is not the highly rendered, off-the-shelf realism available from "digital asset" companies such as SpeedTree (Chang 2019) but something like the storybook experience of being invited to get lost inside of a backyard that seems, for a child, to go on forever.

Dinkins's stories contrast with how the natural world has been traditionally represented or narrated in the West, for example, in landscape painting and pastoral poetry, as a space that either is devoid of or consciously excludes Black people. From an enslaved person who remembers the shade of the baobab tree and despairs that "there are no trees to help me here" (see transcript at https://www.stephaniedinkins.com/sg_texts.html) to a woman who remembers her grandmother's meticulous garden in the 1920s among her white neighbors as making "a make-a-way a place, a home, out of no way" (see transcript at https://www.stephaniedinkins.com/sg_texts.html), the relationship between her narrators and nature is shaped by pain. Yet this ambivalence is vital for "investigating the alignment between man and nature . . . for a people who have been classified as entirely separate," as the poet Camille Dungy (2009: xxii) writes in her introduction to the anthology *Black Nature*. Quoting from Carl Phillips's poem "White Dog"—"She seems a part of me, // and then she seems entirely like what she is: / a white dog"—Dungy argues for acknowledging both the limits of humanness and the limits of what human knowledge can represent (xxiii).

I find a similar modesty in *Secret Garden*, which questions the premise that artificial intelligence must have anything to do with silicon or programmers. Dinkins's earlier work includes *Conversations with Bina48* (2014–), an ongoing conversation with the Bina48 robot, who was designed as a Black woman, and *Not the Only One* (2019), an AI chatbot trained on oral histories of her family. As those artworks indicate, Dinkins has increasingly focused on the "small data" embodied as stories and oral histories. Their smallness makes it easier to keep such data situated within the communities that produce them, rather than as another site of extraction. (It's no coincidence that maintaining personal and communal spaces on the internet is often referred to as "digital gardening.") But these kinds of small data can reorient and retrain AI systems, because AI systems are ultimately, in the words of one narrator, "your rememory: your progeny" (see transcript at https://www.stephaniedinkins.com/sg_texts.html). In contrast to global prescriptions for revolution, these techniques make a virtue of incremental change, as Dinkins (2020) describes it in a manifesto titled "Afro-now-ism"; each day improves slightly on the last.

I have always found it interesting that, in German media theory, the field of *Kulturtechniken* (cultural techniques), now dominated by studies of networks and computational technologies, was first established in the nineteenth century as a professorship in agricultural cultivation (Geoghegan 2013). *Myriad (Tulips)/Mosaic Virus* and *Secret Garden* expand that metaphor of how media work by discovering multiple kinds of speculative potential from natural history. In doing so, they offer a very different perspective from an art market that is trying to cash in on the question of whether an AI-generated image is art or not. Wrong question, these artworks say: AI is, at the heart, a practice of cultivation, as painstaking and as ordinary as tending a garden.

Tung-Hui Hu is the author of *A Prehistory of the Cloud* (2015) and *Digital Lethargy: Dispatches from an Age of Disconnection* (2022), as well as three books of poetry. Winner of a 2022–23 Rome Prize in Literature from the American Academy in Rome, he is an associate professor of English at the University of Michigan.

References

Chang, Alenda. 2019. *Playing Nature: Ecology in Video Games*. Minneapolis: Univ. of Minnesota Press.

Cmiel, Kenneth, and John Durham Peters. 2020. *Promiscuous Knowledge: Information, Image, and Other Truth Games in History*. Chicago: Univ. of Chicago Press.

Dinkins, Stephanie. 2020. "Afro-now-ism." *NOEMA Magazine*, June 16. https://www.noemamag.com/afro-now-ism/.

Dungy, Camille. 2009. "Introduction: The Nature of African American Poetry," in *Black Nature: Four Centuries of African American Nature Poetry*, edited by Camille Dungy, xix–xxxv. Athens: Univ. of Georgia Press.

Geoghegan, Bernard Dionysius. 2013. "After Kittler: On the Cultural Techniques of Recent German Media Theory." *Theory, Culture, and Society* 30, no. 6: 66–82. https://doi.org/10.1177/0263276413488962.

Smith, Arianna. 2021. "The Secret Garden of Stephanie Dinkins, at DLECTRICITY." *BLAC Media*, September 24. https://www.blac.media/people-places/the-secret-garden-of-stephanie-dinkins-at-dlectricity/.

Patrick Jagoda   Artificial Intelligence in Video Games

While the relationship between artificial intelligence (AI) and games far exceeds the parameters that a short review can even sketch out, I hope to propose a series of representational, historical, aesthetic, technical, experimental, and processual ways to approach the intersection between these two terms.

Representations of AI and intelligent robots have been common throughout video game history, ranging from nonplayer to player characters. Some representations of AI antagonists include AM in *I Have No Mouth, and I Must Scream* (Cyberdreams and the Dreamers Guild, 1995), GLaDOS in *Portal* (Valve, 2007), and P03 in *Inscryption* (Daniel Mullins Games 2021). Depictions of helpful nonplayer AI familiars include Rush in *Mega Man 3* (Capcom, 1990), Claptrap in *Borderlands* (Gearbox Software, 2009), and Nick Valentine in *Fallout 4* (Bethesda Game Studios, 2015). Another important category comprises AI player-characters whom a player controls or roleplays as but that do not depend on actual AI systems, including Mega Man throughout the Mega Man series (Capcom, 1987–), the unnamed android of *The Talos Principle* (Croteam, 2014), and SAM in *Observation* (No Code, 2019). The centrality of science fiction as a popular narrative genre in video games—a medium that emerged during the Cold War when speculative narratives were assuming a more central form within popular culture—might account for the prevalence of AI characters in games.

Unlike literature, film, or television series, however, the history of AI in video games exceeds representation. The earliest history of AI includes uses of games to test AI programs. Already in the late 1940s, mathematicians Alan Turing and Claude Shannon both used chess-

American Literature, Volume 95, Number 2, June 2023
DOI 10.1215/00029831-10575246   © 2023 by Duke University Press

playing programs as a theoretical route into the problem of how a computer could think. Some of the earliest examples of video games, such as *Tennis for Two* (William Higinbotham, 1958), *Spacewar!* (Steve Russell, 1962), and *Pong* (Atari, 1972), were two-player games in which the challenge derived from the other player, thereby eliminating the need for AI. The development of AI in popular video games initiated an era of single-player engagements, starting with games such as *Computer Space* (Syzygy Engineering, 1971) and *Space Invaders* (Taito, 1978). Enemy behaviors in such single-player games, which depend on character-based scripting and pathfinding algorithms, are more basic than the supervised and unsupervised learning of later neural networks. Historically, developers have often spent more resources on graphics than AI systems in order to appeal to consumers through visual delights. Even so, AI has become more important to video games in the early twenty-first century.

Though the larger topic of AI uses within video game development exceeds the scope of a short review, it is helpful to think through the *aesthetic* effects that AI can have in games at the intersection of interactive art and computer science. For example, as I have argued elsewhere (Jagoda 2020), difficulty is an aesthetic dimension of interactive games. Some games use AI to achieve adaptive difficulty. By contrast to variable difficulty, which allows a player to choose a difficulty setting that might include easy (or story), normal, or difficult modes, adaptive difficulty responds to a player's performance in real time. *Crash Bandicoot 2* (Naughty Dog, 1997) was one of the earliest video games to experiment with dynamic difficulty, providing a player who failed often with added checkpoints or stronger power-ups. Another example comes with the practice of "rubberbanding" in multiplayer video games in which a game increases or decreases difficulties based on players' real-time performances, as with the infamous "spiny" or "blue" shell that targets the first-place racer in all games in the Mario Kart series (starting with *Mario Kart 64* [Nintendo EAD, 1996]) to maintain parity.

Other games use more sophisticated AI systems to produce emergent gameplay, which includes adaptive difficulty but also exceeds it. The *Left 4 Dead* (Valve, 2008, 2009) games offer one compelling example. These cooperative horror first-person shooter action games have up to four players control survivors who are immune to a virus that has turned people into zombie-like "infected" creatures. This game enables infinite replay not because of its familiar narrative premise but because of a dynamic underlying system called the "AI Director."

This system introduces unpredictable and variable elements in real time during each gameplay session. Such responsive adjustments depend on collective player positions and performance. The AI Director uses procedural generation to determine the positions and frequency of weapons, health items, enemies, and storms that influence difficulty. Beyond instrumental or threatening elements, this system also influences purely aesthetic components that do not impact gameplay difficulty, such as dynamic music, character dialogue, and visual effects. All of these elements generate opportunities for emergent gameplay in which players can improvise within a new environment in each round of play.

In addition to adjusting dimensions of the overall game state, AI can also guide the behavior of a single boss-level enemy. Beyond difficulty, such a system can contribute to horror aesthetics. The game *Alien: Isolation* (Creative Assembly, 2014) uses AI to bring to life the creature from the Alien series, first featured in Ridley Scott's 1979 titular film. In addition to an AI Director that tracks the game's global state (much like in *Left 4 Dead*), this AI makes decisions based on behavior trees and audiovisual sensors within the game's world. Instead of a prescribed game, this experience becomes unique in each playthrough by organizing it around an unpredictable and terrifying nonhuman alien. Other games have combined AI representation and systems. For example, the first-person survival horror game *Soma* (Frictional Games, 2015) has the player face an AI called the Warden Unit (WAU), which both is an AI in the game's diegesis and behaves according to algorithms that might remain largely unknown to the player, thereby simulating unpredictability and an emergent sense of horror.

The connection between AI and games moves beyond the application of the former to improve the experience of the latter. Increasingly games have become an experimental testing ground for AI developers, especially with human users. This kind of AI testing became visible and popular when the chess-playing program Deep Blue defeated world champion Garry Kasparov in 1997. Nearly two decades later, AlphaGo used Monte Carlo tree search algorithms and supervised machine learning to defeat top Go players such as Lee Sedol in 2016 and Ke Jie, in 2017; this led to the subsequent development of Alpha-Zero, an AI that can excel at Go by reinforcement learning that develops through neural net self-play without human supervision. Beyond the spectacle of such matches, and their narrativized metaphysical stakes of clashes between human and nonhuman intelligence, these events demonstrate the use of games as a means of AI development. The connection between AI and games has surpassed well-known and complex games, extending, for instance, to initial testing of self-driving cars in driving simulator environments.

Beyond gameplay, AI has even contributed to game design. Through everything from path-finding algorithms to neural networks, human developers can guide autonomous tools to generate elements of game spaces. For example, for the tactical shooter game *Ghost Recon Wildlands* (Ubisoft Paris, Ubisoft Milan, 2017), autonomous techniques produced large quantities of the game's terrain. While human designers modified and augmented material that was procedurally generated by algorithmic processes, this example suggests emergent possibilities for collaborations between humans and AI in game design. Such work between human and nonhuman systems is likely to have not only computational consequences but also aesthetic, cultural, ethical, and sociopolitical implications in the 2020s and beyond.

Patrick Jagoda is a professor of cinema and media studies, English, and obstetrics and gynecology at the University of Chicago. He is executive editor of *Critical Inquiry* and director of the Weston Game Lab. His books include *Network Aesthetics*, *Experimental Games*, and *Transmedia Stories*. Patrick was the recipient of a Guggenheim Fellowship in 2020.

References

Jagoda, Patrick. 2020. *Experimental Games: Critique, Play, and Design in the Age of Gamification*. Chicago: University of Chicago Press.

McKissack, Fraser, and Lawrence May. 2020. "Running with the Dead: Speedruns and Generative Rupture in *Left 4 Dead 1* and *2*." *Games and Culture* 15, no. 5: 544–64.

Seidel, Stefan, Nicholas Berente, Aron Lindberg, Kalle Lyytinen, Benoit Martinez, and Jeffrey V Nickerson. 2020. "Artificial Intelligence and Video Game Creation: A Framework for the New Logic of Autonomous Design." *Journal of Digital Social Research* 2, no. 3: 126–57.

Švelch, Jaroslav. 2020. "Should the Monster Play Fair?: Reception of Artificial Intelligence in *Alien: Isolation*." *Game Studies* 20, no. 2: 243–60.

Christopher Grobe	Can the Computer Speak?

Deceitful Media: Artificial Intelligence and Social Life after the Turing Test.
By Simone Natale. New York: Oxford Univ. Press. 2021. x, 191 pp. Cloth, $99.00;
paper, $29.95; e-book, $19.99.

The Computer's Voice: From "Star Trek" to Siri. By Liz W. Faber. Minneapolis: Univ.
of Minnesota Press. 2020. 217 pp. Cloth, $108.00; paper, $27.00; e-book, $27.00.

Macs do it, phones do it—even educated drones do it. And by *it,* of
course, I mean "respond to our words with a synthesized speech of
their own." How did it come to pass that the Internet of Things was
suffused with this ability to recognize, parse, and synthesize human
speech? How did people come to think of such recognition as "listen-
ing," such parsing as "understanding," and such synthesis as "speaking"? How did technology and culture combine to make this development thinkable—even, apparently, desirable?

Two recent scholarly books attempt to answer such questions historically. Simone Natale's *Deceitful Media* focuses on how we came to
treat machines as social agents capable of conversation. Specifically,
it shows how the dream of artificial intelligence (AI) blurred the lines
between computer science and adjacent social scientific fields. Liz W.
Faber's *Computer's Voice* focuses on how we came not just to anthropo-
morphize speaking machines but to gender them, too. Specifically, it
draws on the history of American sci-fi TV and film to show how AI
was gendered—and gendered differently—in successive eras of modern computing.

These books are quite different from each other, methodologically.
Deceitful Media comes out of media studies, and its project is historio-
graphic: it rewrites the history of AI to include a better account of how

American Literature, Volume 95, Number 2, June 2023
DOI 10.1215/00029831-10575260   © 2023 by Duke University Press

technologists thought humans perceived intelligence. *The Computer's Voice*, on the other hand, comes out of film studies, and its project is driven by feminist psychoanalysis: it identifies gendered tropes in art that features talking machines, and then it unsettles those tropes through close study. What these books share, however, is the idea that people's fantasies about machines have real-world force in shaping how technology gets built and deployed.

■ ■ ■

Deceitful Media's innovation is to tell a joint history of two fields that are often treated as separate concerns: conversational AI and human-computer interaction (HCI). Examining key moments in the history of both fields, Natale argues that the quest for machine intelligence has never been separable from the attempt to get humans to "treat things as social agents" (4). Naturally, Natale's story of this phenomenon begins with Alan Turing's imitation game, which "placed humans rather than machines at the very center of the AI question" (20)—and it culminates in a withering account of the Loebner Prize competition for chatbots, which has reduced Turing's philosophical game to an annual search for *ONE NEAT TRICK!!!* to fool some judges. Along the way, Natale offers several case studies—some famous, some obscure—of how "the race for AI was being run not only in the realm of technology but also in the realm of imagination" (38). He explores how something as simple as early time-sharing systems, which allowed multiple users to interact separately and simultaneously with one computer, achieved a feel of responsiveness by "employ[ing] the human nerveware as well as the computer hardware" (41, quoting early computer scientist Herbert Simon)—and he uses such examples to demonstrate a more general point: insights gleaned from "the new human sciences" of the early twentieth century were essential to midcentury computer science (12). In short, while hardware and software get all the credit, knowledge of "nerveware" was essential in the pursuit of AI.

As Natale continues this history up to the present, he demonstrates a growing concern with "social interfaces"—famous, like Siri, and obscure, like Microsoft Bob—and their ability (or failure) to sustain "the mindless nature of imaginative social relationships between humans and machines" (83). (*Mindlessness* is a keyword from HCI, and encouraging people to interact mindlessly with machines is a goal of much research in that field.) The tactics for encouraging such mindlessness are examples of what Natale calls "banal deception" (7).

These tactics are deceptive, he suggests, in their attempts to exploit the quirks of human perception and cognition, but they are banal in the sense that people "embrace deception so that they can better incorporate AI into their lives" (7). In other words, we are "deceived" not because we are fools but because such suspension of disbelief brings us benefits. By consenting to treat our iPhones, for example, as quasi-human conversation partners, we stand to gain Siri's smooth integration into our lives.

This is a persuasive account of how conversational software has developed since the 1950s, but Natale has greater ambitions for his coinage, *banal deception*. He would like to persuade us that all modern media are "deceptive" in how they exploit quirks and blind spots of "the human sensorium and intellect" (12). Deception is not a time-limited phase in the history of each technology, lasting only as long as people's initial ignorance, but is instead "an irremediable characteristic of [modern] media technologies" (12). For example, audio compression algorithms "deceive" our ears, Natale argues, by stripping out sounds we won't miss very much—just as the frame rates of projected film leave out images we'd scarcely be able to see.

The stakes of calling these phenomena *deception*—banal or otherwise—are unclear in *Deceitful Media*. Natale might argue on one page that people knowingly "embrace deception" (29), while on the very next page he might assert that people "[fall] into a state of narcosis that makes them unable to understand how media are changing them" (30). This latter, *Black Mirror*-ish tone about technology is common across academic media studies, but it distracts from Natale's true argument: "AI is a relational phenomenon, something that emerges also and especially in the interaction between humans and machines" (31). This relational approach, the bread and butter of HCI, was baked into AI from the start, Natale argues. And it persists in the "personality teams" behind today's voice-user interfaces, like Alexa or Siri. These groups of social scientists (and sometimes artists) play a key role in determining how conversational AIs are constructed.

■ ■ ■

If Natale provides a disciplinary prehistory of conversational AI, Faber provides its imaginative prehistory. Specifically, they track the emergence and transformation in sci-fi media of what they call the "acousmatic computer" (15). (An *acousmêtre*, in film theory, is a figure whose voice we hear but whose body we do not see.) For Faber, the cultural history of this trope begins with the shipboard computer on *Star Trek* (1966) and culminates with the release of Siri on iPhones in 2011.

Within this forty-five-year time frame, Faber gathers an eccentric mix of sci-fi films and TV programs, grouped mostly by decade. These groupings are then offered as proof of how talking computers have been variously gendered over the years. So, for instance, chapters 2 and 3 both center on the same decade (the 1970s), but they explore different imaginative tendencies: whereas chapter 2 focuses on the hyperfeminine caricature of computers offered in such films as *Dark Star* (1974) and TV series such as *Quark* (1977–78), chapter 3 draws our attention to the hypermasculine, militarized stance of computers in films like *Colossus* (1970), *THX 1138* (1971), *Rollerball* (1975), and *Demon Seed* (1977). After isolating this kind of gendered trope, each of Faber's chapters studies examples of that trope through the lens of feminist psychoanalytic theory.

Faber justifies this psychoanalytic approach as a necessary alternative to the cognitive bias in tech-industrial thinking about AI. Such counterballast is sorely needed, but this book will not teach you how to weigh one against the other—or how to revise technological thinking in light of arguments like these. A final chapter does analyze Siri in comparison with Samantha (the intelligent operating system in Spike Jonze's *Her* [2014]), but it does so by focusing on the discourse around Siri (e.g., Apple's choice not to use gendered pronouns in referring to it). In other words, it sidesteps those realms where cognitive approaches are applied to technology. It studies technology by first reducing it to narrative.

This leaves us with the need for more books on this subject, for instance, books that make good on the historical narrative implied by Faber's title. How exactly did we get "From *Star Trek* to Siri"—and what, if anything, stayed with us throughout this half-century journey from fiction to fact? How, if at all, has conversational AI been shaped or limited by the narratives developed by sci-fi auteurs? In the voices of today's "smart" machines, can we hear any echoes of screen actors' performances? Have designers of computer-synthesized voices learned anything from the professionals who capture, create, edit, and mix sci-fi sound? Do the dialogue styles of these films and TV series bear any resemblance to the conversational flows created by voice-user interface designers? In other words, what truth is there (if any) to technologists' frequent claims that they have taken *Star Trek*'s talking computer, or HAL-9000, or any other sci-fi creation as their model? To answer questions like these, one needs a double expertise: not only Faber's commitment to studying art but also Natale's understanding of technology and the thinking that lies behind it. Together, these two approaches might help us confront AI as the strange hybrid thing that it is: both a technical problem and an artful dream.

Christopher Grobe is an associate professor and chair of English at Amherst College and author of *The Art of Confession* (2017). One strain of his current research program concerns how people, techniques, and ideas from the arts have been imported into the tech industry.

Announcement

2022 Norman Foerster Prize

The Norman Foerster Prize for the best essay published in *American Literature* in 2022 was awarded to Ana Schwartz for her essay "Imperative Reading: Brothertown and Sister Fowler" (94:4, December 2022). An honorable mention was awarded to Douglas S. Ishii for his essay "The Diversity Requirement; or, The Ambivalent Contingency of the Asian American Student Teacher" (94:4, December 2022). Members of the judging committee were Elizabeth Dillon (chair), Northeastern University; Ren Ellis Neyra, Wesleyan University; and Matthew Hooley, Clemson University.

American Literature, Volume 95, Number 2, June 2023
DOI 10.1215/00029831-10703655   © 2023 by Duke University Press

THE DISTANCE FROM SLAUGHTER COUNTY
Lessons from Flyover Country
Steven Moore

"This is a stunning collection of essays, one that I would not only enjoy rereading but one I might someday teach. Moore writes focused and mobile narratives capable of embarking upon satisfying digressions and vigorous wanderings. I look forward to reading more of his work."
—**Matthew Vollmer**, author of *All of Us Together in the End*
160 pages $19.00 paper

WHO WE ARE NOW
Stories of What Americans Lost and Found during the COVID-19 Pandemic
Michelle Fishburne

"A profound look at the stories behind what was happening in our country during the pandemic. Fishburne pulls back the curtain on the lives of ordinary people during this extraordinary time. Fishburne's book is a time capsule of this defining and transformative moment."
—**Sky Bergman**, director of *Lives Well Lived*
Published in association with the Center for Documentary Studies at Duke University
248 pages $25.00

UNMOORED
The Search for Sincerity in Colonial America
Ana Schwartz

"A stunner. Schwartz's careful rereading of sincerity reveals settler colonialism to be a practice, embedded in social activities that nominally exist toward other ends. This book is one of the most sophisticated, interdisciplinary studies I have ever read in this considerably sophisticated, interdisciplinary field."
—**Jordan Alexander Stein**, Fordham University
Published by the Omohundro Institute of Early American History and Culture
288 pages $32.95

BEFORE EQUIANO
A Prehistory of the North American Slave Narrative
Zachary McLeod Hutchins

"In a work of impressive scope, Hutchins takes on the challenging task of delineating the prehistory of the slave narrative and how slavery was understood in the American colonies, while also helping readers understand the role of newspapers in both the development of and resistance to slavery as an institution."
—**Karen Weyler**, University of North Carolina at Greensboro
304 pages $32.95 paper

AGROTOPIAS
An American Literary History of Sustainability
Abby L. Goode

"A significant contribution to a growing field of studies on pre–twentieth century antecedents to contemporary sustainability rhetoric and practices . . . highlights the ways that U.S. agrarianism has been entangled from the beginning with nativist and eugenic assumptions about population control and racial purity."
—**William Gleason**, Princeton University
294 pages $34.95 paper

INDIGENUITY
Native Craftwork and the Art of American Literatures
Caroline Wigginton

"This visually striking book forges many surprising and fruitful connections between Native craft practices and European-American material texts."
—**Phillip H. Round**, University of Iowa
328 pages $32.95 paper

THE UNIVERSITY OF NORTH CAROLINA PRESS
at bookstores or 800-848-6224
uncpress.org • uncpressblog.com

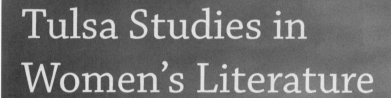

Tulsa Studies in Women's Literature

Spring 2023, Vol. 42, No. 1

Featuring articles on:

Mary Wortley Montagu · Maria Edgeworth · Almira Hart Lincoln Phelps ·
Martha Gellhorn · Toni Morrison · Toni Cade Bambara · Alice Walker

@TSWLJournal
utulsa.edu/TSWL
Like us on Facebook

Keep up to date on new scholarship

Issue alerts are a great way to stay current on all the cutting-edge scholarship from your favorite Duke University Press journals. This free service delivers tables of contents directly to your inbox, informing you of the latest groundbreaking work as soon as it is published.

To sign up for issue alerts:

1. Visit **dukeu.press/register** and register for an account. You do not need to provide a customer number.

2. After registering, visit **dukeu.press/alerts**.

3. Go to "Latest Issue Alerts" and click on "Add Alerts."

4. Select as many publications as you would like from the pop-up window and click "Add Alerts."

read.dukeupress.edu/journals